You Can
Live Forever
in Paradise
on Earth

It is the hope of this book's publishers
that you will be among those of
whom the Bible says: "The righteous
themselves will possess the earth,
and they will reside forever upon it."
—Psalm 37:29.

Contents

Chapter 1

Living Forever
Not Just a Dream

HAPPINESS on earth—it does not seem possible to enjoy it even for a short time. Sickness, aging, hunger, crime—to mention only a few problems—often make life miserable. So, you may say, to talk about living forever in paradise on earth is to close your eyes to the truth. You may feel that it is a waste of time to talk about it, that living forever is just a dream.

[2] No doubt most people would agree with you. So, then, why can we be so sure that *you can live forever in paradise on earth?* Why can we believe that everlasting life is not just a dream?

WHY WE CAN BELIEVE

[3] We can believe because a Supreme Power, Almighty God, prepared the earth with everything needed to satisfy what we want. He made the earth just perfect for us! And he created man and woman in the best way for them to enjoy life to the full in this earthly home—forever.—Psalm 115:16.

[4] Scientists have long known about the human body's power to renew itself. By wonderful means the body cells are either replaced or repaired, as the need may be. And it seems that this process of self-renewal should go on forever. But it does not, and this is something that scientists cannot explain. They still do not fully understand why people grow old. They say that, under right conditions, humans should be able to live forever. —Psalm 139:14.

1, 2. Why is it hard to believe that people can live forever in happiness on earth?
3. What shows that God wants humans to be happy on earth?
4. What have scientists learned about the human body that shows it was made to live forever?

⁵ Yet, is it really God's purpose that people live happily on earth forever? If it is, then everlasting life is not just a wish or a dream —it is sure to come! What does the Bible, the book that tells of God's purposes, say about the matter? It calls God "the Former of the earth and the Maker of it," and adds: "He the One who firmly established it, who did not create it simply for nothing, *who formed it even to be inhabited.*"—Isaiah 45:18.

⁶ Does it seem to you that the earth is now inhabited in the way that God meant it to be? True, people are living in practically all parts of the earth. But are they living together happily as a united family, in the good way their Creator meant for them? Today the world is divided. There is hatred. There is crime. There is war. Millions of people are hungry and sick. Others have daily worries about housing, work and expenses. And none of these things bring honor to God. Evidently, then, the earth is not being inhabited in the way Almighty God originally meant it to be.

⁷ After creating the first human couple, God placed them in an earthly paradise. He wanted them to enjoy life on earth forever. His purpose for them was to spread their paradise over all the earth. This is shown by his instructions to them: "Be fruitful and become many and fill the earth and subdue it." (Genesis 1:28) Yes, God's purpose was, in the course of time, to have the entire earth brought under the control of a righteous human family all living together in peace and happiness.

5. What does the Bible say about God's purpose for the earth?
6. (a) What are conditions like on earth today? (b) Is this the way God wants it to be?
7. What was God's purpose for the earth when he created the first human couple?

Did God intend the world to be like this?

[8] Although the first human couple disobeyed God, thus proving to be unfit to live forever, God's original purpose did not change. It must be fulfilled! (Isaiah 55:11) The Bible promises: "The righteous themselves will possess the earth, and *they will reside forever upon it.*" (Psalm 37:29) Often the Bible tells of God's arrangement to give humans who serve him everlasting life.—John 3:14-16, 36; Isaiah 25:8; Revelation 21:3, 4.

8. Although the first couple disobeyed God, why can we be sure that God's purpose for the earth did not change?

THE DESIRE TO LIVE—WHERE?

[9] We can truly be happy that it is God's purpose that we live forever. For think: If you had to decide, on what date would you choose to die? You cannot pick one, can you? You do not want to die, and neither does any other normal person who has a measure of health. God made us with the desire to live, not the desire to die. Regarding the way God made humans, the Bible says: "He has even put eternity into their minds." (Ecclesiastes 3:11, *Byington*) What does this mean? It means that ordinarily people desire to live on and on, without dying. Due to this desire for an endless future, men have long searched for a way of staying young forever.

[10] Where is it that humans normally want to live forever? It is where they have become used to living, here on earth. Man was made for the earth, and the earth for man. (Genesis 2:8, 9, 15) The Bible says: "He [God] has founded the earth upon its established places; it will not be made to totter to time indefinite, or forever." (Psalm 104:5) Since the earth was made to last forever, then man also should live forever. Surely a loving God would not create humans with a desire to live forever and then not make it possible for them to fulfill that desire!—1 John 4:8; Psalm 133:3.

THE KIND OF LIFE YOU DESIRE

[11] Look at the following pages. What kind of life are these people enjoying? Would you like to be one of them? Why, yes, you say! Look how healthy and youthful they appear! If you were told that these people had already lived thousands of years, would you believe it? The Bible tells us that the old will become young again, the sick will be made well and the lame, blind, deaf and speechless will have all their ailments healed. When he was on earth Jesus Christ performed many miracles by healing sick people. By doing this he was showing how, in this glorious

---

9. (a) What desire do people normally have? (b) What does the Bible mean when it says 'God has put eternity into their minds'?
10. (a) Where is it man's natural desire to live forever? (b) Why can we be confident that God will make it possible for us to live forever on earth?
11. What does the Bible say to show that people can live forever in perfect health?

time not far off, all who are living will be restored to perfect health.—Job 33:25; Isaiah 33:24; 35:5, 6; Matthew 15:30, 31.

[12] See what a lovely garden home this is! As Christ promised, it is truly a paradise, similar to the one lost by the disobedient first man and woman. (Luke 23:43) And note the peace and harmony that exist. People of all races—the black, the white, the yellow—are living as one family. Even the animals are peaceful. See the child playing with the lion. But there is

12. What conditions do we see in these pictures?

no cause for fear. In this regard the Creator declares: "With the kid the leopard itself will lie down, and the calf and the maned young lion and the well-fed animal all together; and a mere little boy will be leader over them. . . . And even the lion will eat straw just like the bull. And the sucking child will certainly play upon the hole of the cobra."—Isaiah 11:6-9.

13 In the paradise that God purposes for humans, there

13. What will be gone from the earth when God's purposes are carried out?

will be every reason to be happy. The earth will produce plenty of good things to eat. No one will ever go hungry again. (Psalm 72:16; 67:6) Wars, crime, violence, even hatred and selfishness, will be things of the past. Yes, they will be gone forever! (Psalm 46:8, 9; 37:9-11) Do you believe that all of this is possible?

[14] Well, consider: If you had the power, would you bring to an end all the things that cause human suffering? And would you bring about the conditions for which the human heart longs? Of course you would. Our loving heavenly Father will do just that. He will satisfy our needs and desires, for Psalm 145:16 says of God: "You are opening your hand and satisfying the desire of every living thing." But when will this occur?

GRAND BLESSINGS ARE NEAR

[15] To make possible these fine blessings on earth, God promises to bring to their end both wickedness and those who cause it. At the same time, he will protect those who serve him, for the Bible says: "The world is passing away and so is its desire, but he that does the will of God remains forever." (1 John 2:17) What a change that will be! The end of the world will not mean the end of our earth. Rather, as happened at the worldwide flood in Noah's day, it will mean the end only of bad people and their way of living. But those who are serving God will survive the end. Then, on an earth made clean, they will enjoy freedom from all who want to hurt and oppress them.—Matthew 24:3, 37-39; Proverbs 2:21, 22.

[16] But someone may say: 'Conditions are getting worse, not better. How can we be sure this grand change is near?' Jesus Christ foretold many things that his future followers should watch for so that they would know it was God's time to bring an end to the world. Jesus said that the last days of this system would be marked by such things as major wars, food shortages, great earthquakes, increasing lawlessness and a growing loss of

14. What makes you believe that God will bring an end to suffering?
15. (a) What will the end of the world mean for the earth? (b) What will it mean for bad people? (c) What will it mean for those who do God's will?
16. What events were foretold for the "last days"?

love. (Matthew 24:3-12) He said there would be "anguish of nations, not knowing the way out." (Luke 21:25) Also, the Bible further says: "In the last days critical times hard to deal with will be here." (2 Timothy 3:1-5) Are not these the very conditions that we are now experiencing?

¹⁷ Many persons who study world events say that a great change is in the making. For example, the editor of the Miami, U.S.A., *Herald,* wrote: "Anyone with half a logical mind can put together the cataclysmic events of the past few years and see that the world is at a historic threshold. . . . It will change forever the way men live." In a similar vein, the American writer Lewis Mumford said: "Civilization is going downhill. Very definitely. . . . In the past when civilizations went downhill, it was a relatively local phenomenon. . . . Now, with the world more closely knit and held together by modern communications, when civilization goes downhill, the whole planet goes down."

¹⁸ The very conditions in the world today show that we are now living at the time when the destruction of this entire system of things is due to happen. Yes, very soon now God will cleanse the earth of all who would ruin it. (Revelation 11:18) He will remove present-day governments to make way for his righteous government to rule all the earth. It is this Kingdom government for which Christ taught his followers to pray.—Daniel 2:44; Matthew 6:9, 10.

¹⁹ If you love life and want to live forever on earth under God's rule, then you must hurry to take in accurate knowledge of God, his purposes and his requirements. Jesus Christ said in prayer to God: "This means everlasting life, their taking in knowledge of you, the only true God, and of the one whom you sent forth, Jesus Christ." (John 17:3) What a joy it is to know that we can live forever—that it is not just a dream! But to enjoy this fine blessing from God we need to learn about an enemy who is trying to keep us from realizing this blessing.

17. What have thinking persons been saying about conditions today?
18. (a) What do world conditions show about the future? (b) What will replace present-day governments?
19. If we want to live forever, what must we do?

Chapter 2

An Enemy of Everlasting Life

HAPPINESS on earth—nearly everyone wants it. Then why are so many unhappy? What is wrong? Since almost everybody wants peace, why do nations go to war and why do people hate one another? Is there some guiding force that moves them to do these bad things? Could it be that a common invisible power controls the nations?

² Many have wondered about this when they have considered the terrible cruelty of mankind—the fearful gases used in warfare to choke and burn persons to death, as well as the napalm bombs and the atomic bombs. Also, consider the flamethrower, the concentration camps, the mass murder of millions of helpless people, such as in Cambodia in recent years. Do you think that all these evils simply happened by chance? While man is capable on his own of committing terrible deeds, when you consider the gross wickedness of his acts, does it not seem that he has been influenced by an evil, invisible power?

³ There is no need to guess at the matter. The Bible clearly shows that an intelligent unseen person has been controlling both men and nations. In the Bible, Jesus Christ calls this powerful one "the ruler of this world." (John 12:31; 14:30; 16:11) Who is he?

⁴ To help us to find out who he is, think about what happened at the beginning of Jesus' ministry here on earth. The Bible tells us that after Jesus was baptized he went into the wilderness where he was tempted by an unseen creature called Satan

1. Since happiness and peace are not often enjoyed, what questions arise?
2. What crimes in history cause many to wonder whether an evil, unseen power may be controlling humans?
3. What does the Bible say about the rulership of the world?
4. What did the Devil show Jesus, and what offer did he make to him?

the Devil. Part of that tempting is described this way: "Again the Devil took him along to an unusually high mountain, and showed him all the kingdoms of the world and their glory, and he said to him: 'All these things I will give you if you fall down and do an act of worship to me.'"—Matthew 4:8, 9.

⁵ Think about what the Devil offered Jesus Christ. It was "all the kingdoms of the world." Did all these worldly governments really belong to the Devil? Yes, for how else could he have offered them to Jesus? Jesus did not deny that they were Satan's, which he would have done if Satan did not own them. Satan is really the unseen ruler of all the nations of the world! The Bible plainly says: "The whole world is lying in the power of the

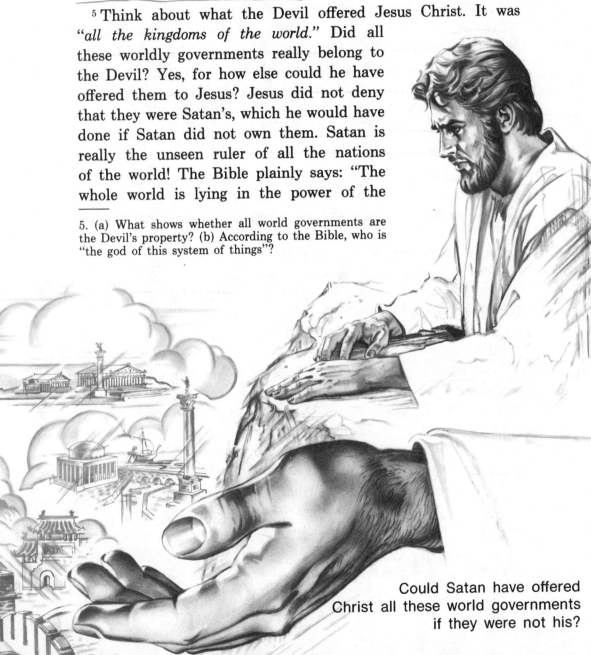

5. (a) What shows whether all world governments are the Devil's property? (b) According to the Bible, who is "the god of this system of things"?

Could Satan have offered Christ all these world governments if they were not his?

wicked one." (1 John 5:19) God's Word, in fact, calls Satan "the god of this system of things."—2 Corinthians 4:4.

⁶ This information helps us to understand why Jesus said: "My kingdom is no part of this world." (John 18:36) It also helps us to understand why nations hate and try to destroy one another when it is the desire of all normal persons to live at peace. Yes, "Satan . . . is misleading the entire inhabited earth." (Revelation 12:9) He would like to mislead us too. He does not want us to receive God's gift of everlasting life. So we have to fight to keep from being influenced by him to do what is bad. (Ephesians 6:12) We need to know about Satan and how he works in order to resist his efforts to mislead us.

WHO THE DEVIL IS

⁷ Satan the Devil is a real person. He is not merely the evil in all mankind, as some persons may believe. Of course, humans cannot see the Devil, for the same reason that they cannot see God. Both God and the Devil are spirit persons, forms of life higher than humans and unseen to our eyes.—John 4:24.

⁸ 'But if God is love,' someone may ask, 'why did he make the Devil?' (1 John 4:8) The fact is, God did not create the Devil. 'Yet if God created everyone,' a person may say, 'he *must* have created the Devil. Who else could have? Where did the Devil come from?'

⁹ The Bible explains that God created many, many spirit persons similar to himself. In the Bible, these spirits are called angels. Also, they are called "sons of God." (Job 38:7; Psalm 104:4; Hebrews 1:7, 13, 14) God created them all perfect. Not one of them was a devil, or a satan. The word "devil" means slanderer and the word "satan" means opposer.

¹⁰ The time came, however, when one of these spirit sons of

6. (a) What does this information about Satan's rulership help us to understand? (b) What would Satan like to do to us, so what must we do?
7. Why can we not see the Devil?
8. Why do many persons believe that God created the Devil?
9. (a) What kind of persons are the angels? (b) What do the words "devil" and "satan" mean?
10. (a) Who made Satan the Devil? (b) How might a good person make himself a criminal?

This thief was not born a thief,
just as the Devil was not created a "devil"

God made himself the *Devil*, that is, a hateful liar who speaks bad things about another. He also made himself *Satan*, that is, an opposer of God. He was not created that way, but later became that kind of person. To illustrate: A thief is not born a thief. He may have come from a good family, having honest parents and law-abiding brothers and sisters. But his own desire for what money can buy is what may have caused him to become a thief. How, then, did one of God's spirit sons make himself Satan the Devil?

¹¹ The angel that became the Devil was present when God created the earth and later the first human couple, Adam and Eve. (Job 38:4, 7) So he would have heard God tell them to have children. (Genesis 1:27, 28) He knew that after a while the whole earth would be filled with righteous people worshiping God. That was God's purpose. However, this angel thought a great deal of his own beauty and intelligence and wanted to receive for himself the worship that would be given to God. (Ezekiel 28:13-15; Matthew 4:10) Instead of putting this wrong desire out of his mind, he kept thinking about it. This led to his

11. (a) What purpose of God did a rebellious angel know about? (b) What desire did this angel have, and what did it lead him to do?

taking action to obtain the honor and importance he desired. What did he do?—James 1:14, 15.

¹² The rebellious angel used a lowly serpent to speak to the first woman, Eve. He did this much as a skilled person can make it seem as if a nearby animal or a dummy figure is talking. But it was really this rebellious angel, the one called in the Bible "the original serpent," who was speaking to Eve. (Revelation 12:9) He said that God was not telling her the truth, and was holding back from her knowledge that she should have. (Genesis 3:1-5) This was a hateful lie and it made him a devil. He thus became also an opposer of God, or a Satan. As you can see, it is wrong to think of the Devil as a creature with horns and a pitchfork who oversees some underground place of torment. He is really a very powerful, but wicked, angel.

SOURCE OF WORLD TROUBLES

¹³ The lie the Devil told Eve worked just as he planned. She believed it and so disobeyed God. And she was able to get her husband to break God's law also. (Genesis 3:6) The Devil's claim was that humans can get along without God. He argued that people can rule themselves successfully, without God's help. The Devil also claimed that he could turn away from God all those who would be the offspring of Adam and Eve.

¹⁴ Of course, God could have destroyed Satan right away. But that would not have answered the questions that Satan had raised, questions that could stay in the minds of the angels who were watching. So God allowed time for Satan to try to prove his claims. With what results?

¹⁵ The passage of time has proved that humans cannot rule themselves successfully without God's help. Their attempts have failed completely. The people have suffered terribly under the

12. (a) How did this angel speak to Eve, and what did he tell her? (b) How did this angel become Satan the Devil? (c) What is a wrong view regarding the appearance of the Devil?
13. (a) How did Eve respond to the Devil's lie? (b) What claims did the Devil make?
14. Why did God not destroy Satan right away?
15, 16. (a) What has the passing of time proved with regard to the Devil's claims? (b) What event is near at hand?

War in heaven ended with Satan and the demons being hurled down to earth. You are now feeling the effects

governments of men, which, as the Scriptures show, have been controlled from behind the scenes by the Devil. Also, God's allowing time has clearly shown that Satan has not been able to turn all persons away from worshiping God. There have always been some who have remained faithful to God's rulership. You can read in the Bible, for example, that Satan tried, without success, to stop Job from serving God.—Job 1:6-12.

16 Thus the claims of the Devil have been proved false. He most certainly deserves destruction for having started a wicked rebellion against God. Happily, we have now reached the time for God to bring Satan's rule to an end. Describing the first step in doing this, the Bible tells of an important battle in heaven, which, of course, was not seen or heard by people on earth. Read carefully the following Bible account:

17 "War broke out in heaven: Michael [who is the resurrected Jesus Christ] and his angels battled with the dragon, and the dragon and its angels battled but it did not prevail, neither was a place found for them any longer in heaven. So down the great dragon was hurled, the original serpent, the one called Devil and Satan, who is misleading the entire inhabited earth; he was hurled down to the earth, and his angels were hurled down with him. 'On this account be

17. (a) How does the Bible describe the war in heaven? (b) What was its result to those in heaven, and to those on earth?

glad, you heavens and you who reside in them! Woe for the earth and for the sea, because the Devil has come down to you, having great anger, knowing he has a short period of time.'" —Revelation 12:7-9, 12.

[18] When did this war in heaven take place? The evidence shows that it happened around the time of World War I, which began in 1914. As the Revelation points out, Satan was removed from the heavens at that time, which means we have been living in his "short period of time" since then. Thus, these are the "last days" of Satan's world. The increasing of lawlessness, the fear, the wars, the food shortages, the diseases and other distressing conditions we have been experiencing are proof of this fact. —Matthew 24:3-12; Luke 21:26; 2 Timothy 3:1-5.

[19] Since Satan knows his "short period of time" is about up, he is trying harder than ever before to keep persons from serving God. He wants to take as many persons as he can down into destruction with him. With good reason the Bible describes him as a roaring lion that is looking for someone to eat. (1 Peter 5:8, 9) If we do not want to be caught by him, we need to learn how he attacks and also the ways in which he misleads people. —2 Corinthians 2:11.

HOW SATAN MISLEADS PEOPLE

[20] Do not think that Satan's methods of getting people to follow him are always easy to see. He is a master at fooling people. His methods over the thousands of years have, in fact, been so clever that today many people do not even believe that he exists. To them wickedness and evil are simply normal conditions that will always be. Satan operates much like modern-day crime leaders who put on the front of being respectable, but who, behind the scenes, do very wicked things. The Bible explains: "Satan himself keeps transforming himself into an angel

18. (a) When did the war in heaven take place? (b) What has been occurring on earth since Satan was "hurled down"?
19. (a) What is Satan now trying hard to do? (b) What would it be wise for us to do?
20. (a) How successful has Satan's attack been? (b) Why could we expect that often his schemes would appear innocent, even beneficial?

of light." (2 Corinthians 11:14) Thus we can expect that his schemes for misleading people would often appear innocent, even beneficial.

²¹ Recall that Satan posed as a friend to Eve. Then he tricked her into doing what she thought would be for her own good. (Genesis 3:4-6) It is the same today. For example, through his human representatives Satan cunningly encourages people to put the interests of human governments even above their service to God. This has given birth to the spirit of nationalism, resulting in terrible wars. In recent times Satan has moved people to bring forth various schemes in their search for peace and security. One of these is the United Nations. But has this created a peaceful world? Far from it! Rather, it has proved to be a means of turning the people's attention away from God's arrangement for bringing peace to mankind, his incoming kingdom under Jesus Christ, the "Prince of Peace."—Isaiah 9:6; Matthew 6:9, 10.

²² If we are to receive everlasting life, we need accurate knowledge about God, his King-Son and his kingdom. (John 17:3) You can be sure that Satan the Devil does not want you to have this knowledge, and that he will do all in his power to stop you from getting it. How will he do this? One way is by seeing to it that you receive opposition, perhaps in the form of ridicule. The Bible tells us: "All those desiring to live with godly devotion in association with Christ Jesus will also be persecuted." —2 Timothy 3:12.

²³ It may be that even close friends or relatives will tell you that they do not like your examining the Scriptures. Jesus Christ himself even warned: "Indeed, a man's enemies will be persons of his own household. He that has greater affection for father or mother than for me is not worthy of me; and he that has greater affection for son or daughter than for me is not worthy of me." (Matthew 10:36, 37) Relatives may try to discourage you, doing so in all sincerity because they do not know the wonderful truths found in the Bible. But

21. What is one scheme that Satan has used?
22. What knowledge does Satan not want us to have?
23. (a) How might Satan even use friends and relatives to discourage us? (b) Why should you never give in to opposition?

There may be opposition to your continued study of the Bible

if you give up a study of God's Word when opposition comes, how will God view you? Also, if *you* give up, how will those friends and loved ones be helped by you to understand that accurate knowledge of the Bible is of life-or-death importance? Your staying with the things you learn from God's Word may in time influence them likewise to learn the truth.

24 On the other hand, Satan may be responsible for tempting you to share in some immoral activity, which is displeasing to God. (1 Corinthians 6:9-11) Or it may be that he will cause you to feel that you are too busy to study the Bible. But when you think about it, could there ever be anything more important than obtaining this kind of knowledge? Do not allow anything to stop you from gaining this knowledge that can lead to your receiving everlasting life in paradise on earth!

25 The Bible urges: "Oppose the Devil." If you do this, "he will flee from you." (James 4:7) Does this mean that if you resist Satan's attack he will give up and no longer cause you trouble? No, he will try over and over again to get you to do what he wants. But if you keep on opposing him, he will never be able to get you to take a course in opposition to God. So, be diligent to get the all-important knowledge of the Bible and practice what you learn. This is vital in order to prevent you from being deceived by another of Satan's means for misleading people, false religion.

24. (a) What other ways does the Devil use to keep people from taking in life-giving knowledge? (b) How important do you feel it is to study God's Word?
25. If we continue to oppose the Devil, what will he not be able to do to us?

Chapter 3

Your Religion Really Matters

'ALL RELIGIONS are good,' many people say. 'They are simply different roads leading to the same place.' If this were true, your religion would not really matter, for it would mean that all religions are acceptable to God. But are they?

[2] When Jesus Christ walked the earth, there was a religious group known as the Pharisees. They had built up a system of worship and believed it had God's approval. Yet, at the same time, the Pharisees were trying to kill Jesus! So Jesus told them: "You do the works of your father." In answer they said: "We have one Father, God."—John 8:41.

[3] Was God really their father? Did God accept their form of religion? Not at all! Even though the Pharisees had the

---

1. What do some persons believe about religion?
2. (a) How did the Pharisees treat Jesus? (b) Whom did the Pharisees claim as their father?
3. What did Jesus say about the father of the Pharisees?

Were the religious leaders who were trying to kill Jesus serving God?

Scriptures and thought they were following them, they had been misled by the Devil. And Jesus told them so, saying: "You are from your father the Devil, and you wish to do the desires of your father. That one was a manslayer when he began, and he did not stand fast in the truth, . . . he is a liar and the father of the lie."—John 8:44.

4 Clearly, the religion of the Pharisees was false. It served the interests of the Devil, not God. So rather than viewing their religion as good, Jesus condemned it. He said to those religious Pharisees: "You shut up the kingdom of the heavens before men; for you yourselves do not go in, neither do you permit those on their way in to go in." (Matthew 23:13) Because of their false worship, Jesus called those Pharisees hypocrites and poisonous snakes. Because of their bad course, he said that they were on the way to destruction.—Matthew 23:25-33.

5 So Jesus Christ did not teach that all religions are simply different roads leading to the same place of salvation. In his famous Sermon on the Mount, Jesus said: "Go in through the narrow gate; because broad and spacious is the road leading off into destruction, and many are the ones going in through it; whereas narrow is the gate and cramped the road leading off into life, and few are the ones finding it." (Matthew 7:13, 14) Because they fail to worship God in the right way, most persons are on

4. How did Jesus view the religion of the Pharisees?
5. How did Jesus show that the many religions are not simply different roads leading to the same place?

the road to destruction. Only a few are on the road leading to life.

⁶ A look at the way God dealt with the nation of Israel makes it clear how important it is to worship God in the way that he approves. God warned the Israelites to keep away from the false religion of the nations round about them. (Deuteronomy 7:25) Those people sacrificed their children to their gods, and

Most persons are on the broad road to destruction, Jesus said. Only a few are on the narrow road to life

they engaged in unclean sex practices, including homosexuality. (Leviticus 18:20-30) God commanded the Israelites to avoid these practices. When they disobeyed and worshiped other gods, he punished them. (Joshua 24:20; Isaiah 63:10) So their religion really did matter.

FALSE RELIGION TODAY?

⁷ What about the hundreds of religions today? Probably you agree that many things done in the name of religion are not approved by God. During the recent world wars, which millions of persons now living survived, the religions on both sides encouraged their people to kill. "Kill Germans—do kill them," said the bishop of London. And, on the other side, the archbishop of Cologne told Germans: "We command you in the name of

6. What can we learn from a look at the worship of the nation of Israel?
7, 8. (a) What position did religion take during the world wars? (b) How do you think God feels about what religion has done during wartime?

God, to fight to the last drop of your blood for the honor and glory of the country."

[8] So Catholics killed Catholics with the approval of their religious leaders, and Protestants did the same. Clergyman Harry Emerson Fosdick admitted: "Even in our churches we have put the battle flags . . . With one corner of our mouth we have praised the Prince of Peace and with the other we have glorified war." How do you think God feels about a religion that claims to do his will but glorifies war?

[9] Because of the crimes committed in the name of God by the members of many different religions throughout history, millions of persons today have turned away from God and Christ. They blame God for the terrible religious wars, such as those between Catholics and Muslims called the Crusades, the wars between Muslims and Hindus, and the wars between Catholics and Protestants. They point to the murder of Jews in the name of Christ, and the cruel Catholic inquisitions. Yet, even though the religious leaders responsible for such horrible crimes claimed God as their Father, were they not just as much children of the Devil as were the Pharisees whom Jesus condemned? Since Satan is the god of this world, should we not expect that he also controls the religions practiced by people of the world? —2 Corinthians 4:4; Revelation 12:9.

[10] No doubt there are many things done in the name of religion today that you do not think are right. Often you may hear about people who have very immoral ways of life, but who are respectable members of churches. You may even know about religious leaders who have a very bad way of life, but who are still accepted as good religious leaders in their churches. Some religious leaders have said that homosexuality and having sex relations without being married are not wrong. But you may know that the Bible does not say that. In fact, God had his people of Israel punished with death because they practiced such things. For the same reason he destroyed Sodom and Gomorrah.

9. (a) How have many people felt about the crimes committed by members of different religions? (b) When religion makes itself part of the world, what must we conclude?

10. What are some things done in the name of religion that you do not approve of?

"They publicly declare they know God, but they disown him by their works."
—Titus 1:16.

(Jude 7) Soon he will do the same to all modern-day false religion. In the Bible, such religion is represented as a prostitute because of its immoral relations with the "kings of the earth." —Revelation 17:1, 2, 16.

WORSHIP THAT GOD APPROVES

11 Since God does not approve of all religions, we need to ask: 'Am I worshiping God in the way that he approves?' How can we know if we are? It is not any man, but God, who is the judge of what is true worship. So if our worship is to be acceptable to God, it must be firmly rooted in God's Word of truth, the Bible. We should feel the same way as the Bible writer who said: "Let God be found true, though every man be found a liar."—Romans 3:3, 4.

12 The first-century Pharisees did not feel that way. They set up their own beliefs and traditions and followed these rather than God's Word. With what result? Jesus told them: "You have made the word of God invalid because of your tradition. You

11. What is required if our worship is to be acceptable to God?
12. Why did Jesus say that the worship of the Pharisees was not approved by God?

hypocrites, Isaiah aptly prophesied about you, when he said, 'This people honors me with their lips, yet their heart is far removed from me. It is in vain that they keep worshiping me, because they teach commands of men as doctrines.' " (Matthew 15:1-9; Isaiah 29:13) So if we want God's approval, it is necessary that we make sure that what we believe is in agreement with the teachings of the Bible.

[13] It is not enough for us to say we believe in Christ and then do what *we* think is right. It is absolutely necessary that we find out what *God's* will is on the matter. Jesus showed this in his Sermon on the Mount when he said: "Not everyone saying to me, 'Lord, Lord,' will enter into the kingdom of the heavens, but *the one doing the will of my Father who is in the heavens will.*"—Matthew 7:21.

[14] We could even be doing what we believe to be "good deeds," and be doing these in the name of Christ. Yet all of these would be of no value if we failed to do God's will. We would be in the position of the ones Christ next mentions: "Many will say to me in that day, 'Lord, Lord, did we not prophesy in your name,

13. What did Jesus say we must do to be approved by God?
14. Why might Jesus regard us as "workers of lawlessness" even though we were doing "good deeds"?

Because of difference of religion, Paul shared in the stoning of Christ's disciple Stephen

and expel demons in your name, and perform many powerful works in your name?' And yet then I will confess to them: I never knew you! Get away from me, you workers of lawlessness." (Matthew 7:22, 23) Yes, we can be doing things that *we think* are good—and for which other humans may thank us and even praise us—but if we fail to do what *God says* is right we will be regarded by Jesus Christ as "workers of lawlessness."

[15] Since many religions today are not doing God's will, we cannot simply assume that the teachings of the religious organization we are associated with are in agreement with God's Word. The mere fact that the Bible is used by a religion does not of itself prove that all the things it teaches and practices are in the Bible. It is important that we ourselves examine whether they are or not. Persons in the city of Beroea were commended because, after the Christian apostle Paul preached to them, they checked the Scriptures to make sure that the things he was telling them were true. (Acts 17:10, 11) The religion that is approved by God must agree in every way with the Bible; it will not accept certain parts of the Bible and reject other parts. —2 Timothy 3:16. All scripture is inspired of God, beneficial for teaching, setting thing straight ...

SINCERITY ALONE NOT ENOUGH

[16] But someone may ask: 'If a person is sincere in his beliefs, won't God approve of him even if his religion is wrong?' Well, Jesus said he would not approve of "workers of lawlessness" even though they believed they were doing what was right. (Matthew 7:22, 23) So sincerity alone would not be approved by God either. Once Jesus told his followers: "The hour is coming when everyone that kills you will imagine he has rendered a sacred service to God." (John 16:2) Such killers of Christians might sincerely believe that they were thereby serving God, but clearly they were not. God does not approve of what they did.

[17] Before he became a Christian, the apostle Paul helped in

15. Why is the course taken by people in ancient Beroea a wise one for us to follow?
16. What did Jesus say to show that sincerity alone is not enough for a person to be approved by God?
17. Even though Paul was sincere, what did he do before becoming a Christian?

the murder of Stephen. Later, he looked for ways to kill more Christians. (Acts 8:1; 9:1, 2) Paul explained: "To the point of excess I kept on persecuting the congregation of God and devastating it, and I was making greater progress in Judaism than many of my own age in my race, as I was far more zealous for the traditions of my fathers." (Galatians 1:13, 14) Yes, Paul was sincere, but that did not make his religion right.

[18] At the time, Paul was a member of the Jewish religious system, which had rejected Jesus Christ, and so it, in turn, was rejected by God. (Acts 2:36, 40; Proverbs 14:12) So to gain God's approval Paul needed to change his religion. He also wrote of others who had "a zeal for God"—who were sincere but were not approved by God because their religion was not based on accurate knowledge of God's purposes.—Romans 10:2, 3.

[19] The truth will not allow for all the different kinds of religious doctrine in the world. For example, either humans have a soul that survives the death of the body or they do not. Either the earth will last forever or it will not. Either God will bring wickedness to an end or he will not. These and many other beliefs are either right or wrong. There cannot be two sets of truth when one does not agree with the other. One or the other is true, but not both. Sincerely believing something, and practicing that belief, will not make it right if it really is wrong.

[20] How should you feel if proof is given that what you believe is wrong? For example, say that you were in a car, traveling for the first time to a certain place. You have a road map, but you have not taken time to check it carefully. Someone has told you the road to take. You trust him, sincerely believing that the way he has directed you is correct. But suppose it is not. What if someone points out the error? What if he, by referring to your own map, shows that you are on the wrong road? Would pride or stubbornness prevent you from admitting that you are on

---

18. (a) What was Paul's religion when he persecuted Christians? (b) Why did Paul and others in his day need to change their religion?
19. What shows that the truth will not allow for different kinds of religious doctrine?
20. With regard to religion, how may we follow the correct "road map"?

If you were on the wrong road, would pride or stubbornness prevent you from admitting it?

the wrong road? Well, then, if you learn from an examination of your Bible that you are traveling a wrong religious road, be willing to change. Avoid the broad road to destruction; get on the narrow road to life!

DOING GOD'S WILL NECESSARY

²¹ It is important to know the truths of the Bible. Yet this knowledge is worthless if you do not *worship* God in truth. (John 4:24) *Practicing the truth, doing* God's will, is what counts. "Faith without works is dead," the Bible says. (James 2:26) To please God, then, your religion must not only be in full agreement with the Bible but also be applied in every activity of life. Therefore, if you learn that you are doing what God says is wrong, will you be willing to change?

²² There are great blessings in store for you if you do God's will. Even now you will benefit. Practicing true religion will make you a better person—a better man, husband or father, a better woman, wife or mother, a better child. It will produce in you godly qualities that will cause you to stand out among others because you do what is right. But even more, it will mean that you will be in position to receive the blessings of everlasting life in happiness and perfect health on God's paradise new earth. (2 Peter 3:13) There is no question about it—your religion really does matter!

21. (a) In addition to knowing the truth, what is necessary? (b) What will you do if you learn that God does not approve of certain things you are doing?
22. What benefits may we enjoy now and in the future, if we practice true religion?

Chapter 4

God—Who Is He?

WORLDWIDE there are many gods worshiped. In the Shinto, the Buddhist, the Hindu and the tribal religions there are millions of gods. Gods such as Zeus and Hermes were worshiped in the days of Jesus' apostles. (Acts 14:11, 12) So the Bible agrees that "there are many 'gods,'" but it also says that "there is actually to us *one* God the Father, out of whom all things are." (1 Corinthians 8:5, 6) If you were asked, 'Who is this God?' what would you say?

1. (a) What gods have been worshiped by people? (b) What distinction does the Bible make between "gods" and "God"?

If a house has a maker, . . .

[2] 'He is the Lord,' many answer. Or they may say: 'He is a Spirit in heaven.' A dictionary calls God: "The Supreme Being." When asked: 'What is God's name?' some persons answer, 'Jesus.' Others do not think of God as a person, but as a powerful force that is present everywhere. And some even doubt whether there is a God. Can we be sure he exists?

GOD REALLY EXISTS

[3] When you look at a beautiful building, have you ever wondered who the builder was? If someone told you that no one had built the building, but that it had simply come into existence by itself, would you believe it? Of course not! As a Bible writer said: "Every house is constructed by someone." Everyone knows that. Well, then, can we not accept the logical conclusion of the Bible writer: "He that constructed all things is God"?—Hebrews 3:4.

[4] Consider the universe with its billions of billions of stars. Yet all of them move in the heavens according to laws that keep them in perfect relation to one another. "Who has created these things?" was a question asked long ago. The answer given

surely the more complex universe must have a Maker too

makes sense: "It is the One who is bringing (God) forth the army of them even by number, all of whom he calls even by name." (Isa-

2. What different views do people have of God?
3. How does a house come into existence?
4. How did the many billions of stars come into existence?

iah 40:26) Surely it would be foolish to think that the billions of stars just made themselves, and, without any direction, formed the great star systems that move with such marvelous order! —Psalm 14:1.

⁵ This highly organized universe could not have just come about by itself. An intelligent Creator with great power was needed. (Psalm 19:1, 2) A businessman who was asked why he believed in God explained that in his factory it takes two days for a girl to learn how to put the 17 parts of a meat chopper together. "I am merely a plain manufacturer of cutlery," he said. "But this I do know, that you can shake the 17 parts of a meat chopper around in a washtub for the next 17 billion years and you'll never have a meat chopper." This universe, including the many forms of life on earth, is so much more complicated than a meat chopper. If such a machine requires a skilled maker, we can be certain that an Almighty God was needed to create all things. Should not credit go to him for what he has done? —Revelation 4:11; Acts 14:15-17; 17:24-26.

GOD A REAL PERSON?

⁶ While most people say they believe in God, many do not think of him as a real person. Is he? Well, it can be seen that where there is intelligence there is a mind. For example, we may say, 'I cannot make up my mind.' And we know that where there is a mind there is a brain in a body of a definite shape. So, then, the great mind responsible for all creation belongs to the great Person, Almighty God. Although he does not have a material body, he has a spiritual one. A spirit person has a body? Yes, the Bible says: "If there is a physical body, there is also a spiritual one."—1 Corinthians 15:44; John 4:24.

⁷ Since God is a person with a spiritual body, he must have a place to live. The Bible tells us that the heavens are God's "established *place* of dwelling." (1 Kings 8:43) Also, we are told

5. (a) What chance is there that, by themselves, the pieces could come together to make a meat chopper? (b) What does this show about our universe?
6. Why can we be sure that God is a real person?
7. (a) What shows that God has a place where he lives? (b) What shows that he has a body?

that "Christ entered . . . into heaven itself, now to appear *before the person of God* for us." (Hebrews 9:24) Some humans will be rewarded with life in heaven with God, at which time they will receive spirit bodies. They will then see God, the Bible says, and also be like him. (1 John 3:2) This, too, shows that God is a person, and that he has a body.

8 But someone may ask: 'If God is a real person who lives at a certain place in heaven, how can he see everything that happens everywhere? And how can his power be felt in every part of the universe?' (2 Chronicles 16:9) The fact that God is a person in no way limits his power or greatness. Nor should it lessen our respect for Him. (1 Chronicles 29:11-13) To help us to understand this, consider the far-reaching effects of an electric power plant.

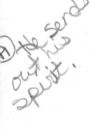

9 A power plant has a certain location in or near a city. But its electricity is distributed over all that area, providing light and power. It is similar with God. He is in the heavens. (Isaiah 57:15; Psalm 123:1) Yet his holy spirit, which is his invisible active force, can be felt everywhere, over all the universe. By means of his holy spirit God created the heavens, the earth and all living things. (Psalm 33:6; Genesis 1:2; Psalm 104:30) To create these things, God did not need to be present in body. He can send out his spirit, his active force, to do whatever he wants even though he is far away. What a marvelous God!—Jeremiah 10:12; Daniel 4:35.

THE KIND OF PERSON GOD IS

10 Is God the kind of person we would grow to love if we got to know him well? 'Perhaps so,' you may say, 'but since we cannot see God, how can we get to know about him?' (John 1:18) The Bible shows one way when it says: "For his invisible qualities are clearly seen from the world's creation onward, because they are perceived by the things made, even his eternal power and Godship." (Romans 1:20) So the things that God has created can

8, 9. (a) How can the example of an electric power plant show God's far-reaching power? (b) What is God's holy spirit, and what can it do?
10. What is one way in which we can get to know God?

help us to understand what God is like, if we really examine them and think about them.

¹¹ As we have seen, a look at the starry heavens surely tells us of God's greatness and tremendous power! (Psalm 8:3, 4; Isaiah 40:26) Then consider the earth. God placed it in the heavens so it gets just the right amount of heat and light from the sun. And consider the water cycle. The rain falls to water the earth. The water runs into the rivers, which flow into the seas. The sun lifts the water from the seas as vapor, which falls as rain to water the earth again. (Ecclesiastes 1:7) There are so many marvelous cycles that God put into operation to provide food, shelter and all things that man and animals need! And what do all these wonderful things tell us about the kind of person God is? That he is a God of great wisdom and that he is most generous and cares for his creations.—Proverbs 3:19, 20; Psalm 104:13-15, 24, 25.

¹² Consider your own body. It obviously was made to do more than just *live*. It was marvelously designed really to *enjoy life*. (Psalm 139:14) Our eyes can see not just in black and white but in color, and the world is filled with a wealth of colors to enjoy. We can smell and taste. So eating is not merely a necessary function; it can be delightful. Such senses are not absolutely necessary for life, but they are gifts from a loving, generous, thoughtful God.—Genesis 2:9; 1 John 4:8.

¹³ A look at God's dealings with humankind also shows what kind of God he is. He has a strong sense of justice. He does not show favoritism to certain races of people. (Acts 10:34, 35) He is also merciful and kind. The Bible says of his dealings with the nation of Israel, whom he delivered from slavery in Egypt: "He was merciful; . . . he kept remembering that they were flesh." Yet the Israelites often were disobedient, and that made God sad. As the Bible says: "They would make him *feel hurt* . . . and they *pained* even the Holy One of Israel." (Psalm 78:38-41; 103:8, 13, 14) On the other hand, when his servants are obedient

---

11. What can we learn about God from the things he has made?
12. What does your own body teach you about God?
13. What do you learn about God from his way of dealing with humans?

to his laws, God rejoices. (Proverbs 27:11) Also, God describes how he feels when his servants are made to suffer by enemies: "He that is touching you is touching my eyeball." (Zechariah 2:8) Are you not moved to love a God who has such affection for lowly, insignificant humans of all races and peoples?—Isaiah 40:22; John 3:16.

IS GOD JESUS OR A TRINITY?

[14] Who is this wonderful God? Some persons say his name is Jesus. Others say he is a Trinity, although the word "trinity" does not appear in the Bible. According to the teaching of the Trinity, there are three persons in one God, that is, there is "one God, Father, Son and Holy Spirit." Many religious organizations teach this, even though they admit it is "a mystery." Are such views of God correct?

[15] Well, did Jesus ever say that he was God? No, he never did. Rather, in the Bible he is called "God's Son." And he said: "The Father is greater than I am." (John 10:34-36; 14:28) Also, Jesus explained that there were some things that neither he nor the angels knew but that only God knew. (Mark 13:32) Further, on one occasion Jesus prayed to God, saying: "Let, not *my* will, but *yours* take place." (Luke 22:42) If Jesus were the Almighty God, he would not have prayed to himself, would he? In fact, following Jesus' death, the Scripture says: "This Jesus God resurrected." (Acts 2:32) Thus the Almighty God and Jesus are clearly two separate persons. Even after his

Since Jesus prayed to God, asking that God's will, not his, be done, the two could not be the same person

14. What is the Trinity teaching?
15. How does the Bible show that God and Jesus are two separate persons who are not equal?

death and resurrection and ascension to heaven, Jesus was still not equal to his Father.—1 Corinthians 11:3; 15:28.

[16] 'But isn't Jesus called a god in the Bible?' someone may ask. This is true. Yet Satan is also called a god. (2 Corinthians 4:4) At John 1:1, which refers to Jesus as "the Word," some Bible translations say: "In the beginning was the Word, and the Word was with God, and the Word was God." But notice, verse 2 says that the Word was "in the beginning *with* God." And while men have seen Jesus, verse 18 says that "no man hath seen God at any time." (*Authorized* or *King James Version*) So we find that some translations of verse 1 give the correct idea of the original language when they read: "The Word was with God, and the Word was divine," or was "a god," that is, the Word was a powerful godlike one. (*An American Translation*) Clearly, Jesus is not Almighty God. In fact, Jesus spoke of his Father as "my God" and as "the only true God."—John 20:17; 17:3.

[17] As for the "Holy Spirit," the so-called third Person of the Trinity, we have already seen that this is not a person but God's active force. John the Baptizer said that Jesus would baptize with holy spirit, even as John had been baptizing with water. Hence, in the same way that water is not a person, holy spirit is not a person. (Matthew 3:11) What John foretold was fulfilled when, following the death and resurrection of Jesus, holy spirit was poured out on his followers gathered in Jerusalem. The Bible says: "They all became filled with holy spirit." (Acts 2:4) Were they "filled" with a person? No, but they were filled with God's active force. Thus the facts make clear that the Trinity is not a Bible teaching. Actually, long before Jesus walked the earth

16. Even though Jesus is referred to as "God," what shows that he is not Almighty God?

17. How does the pouring out of holy spirit on Jesus' followers prove that it is not a person?

How could the holy spirit be a person, when it filled about 120 disciples at the same time?

gods were worshiped in groups of three, or trinities, in places such as ancient Egypt and Babylon.

GOD'S NAME

[18] No doubt everyone whom you know has a name. God also has a personal name to set him apart from all others. 'Is not "God" his name?' some may ask. No, for "God" is merely a title, just as "President," "King" and "Judge" are titles. We learn God's name from the Bible, where it appears about 7,000 times. For example, in the *King James Version*, Psalm 83:18

18. (a) Is "God" the personal name of Almighty God? (b) What is his personal name?

reads: "That men may know that thou, whose name alone is JEHOVAH, art the most high over all the earth." Also, God's name is found in most Bibles at Revelation 19:1-6 as part of the expression "Alleluia" or "Hallelujah." This means "praise Jah," a shortened form of Jehovah.

[19] Some persons are surprised to see God's name in their Bible. This often is because their Bible is one that seldom uses God's name. The *King James Version*, for example, uses the name "Jehovah" by itself only at Exodus 6:3, Psalm 83:18 and Isaiah 12:2 and 26:4. However, when this Bible translates God's name by the title "Lord" or "God," it always puts this title in capital letters, as "LORD" and "GOD," which sets it apart from the common words "Lord" and "God." Note this at Psalm 110:1.

[20] 'But why,' you may ask, 'is God's name not used in every place that it occurs in the original Bible text? Why are the titles LORD and GOD generally used in its place?' In its preface the *American Standard Version* explains why it uses God's name Jehovah, and why for a long time that name was not used: "The American Revisers, after a careful consideration, were brought to the unanimous conviction that a Jewish superstition, which regarded the Divine Name as too sacred to be uttered, ought no longer to dominate in the English or any other version . . . This personal name, with its wealth of sacred as-

19. (a) Why are some persons surprised to see God's name in their Bible? (b) Where does the name appear in the *King James Version*?
20. (a) Why has God's name often not been used? (b) Should it be?

2 And God spake unto Moses, and said unto him, I *am* the LORD:
3 And I appeared unto Abraham, unto Isaac, and unto Jacob, by *the name* of God Almighty, but by my name JEHOVAH was I not known to them.
4 And I have also established my covenant with them, to give them the land of Cā'-nă-ăn, the

Exodus 6:3

Psalm 83:18

with thy storm.
16 Fill their faces with shame; that they may seek thy name, O LORD.
17 Let them be confounded and troubled for ever; yea, let them be put to shame, and perish:
18 That *men* may know that thou, whose name alone *is* JEHOVAH, *art* the most high over all the earth.

The four places where God's name appears in the King James Version are seen here

AND in that day thou shalt say, O LORD, I will praise thee: though thou wast angry with me, thine anger is turned away, and thou comfortedst me.
2 Behold, God *is* my salvation; I will trust, and not be afraid: for the LORD JEHOVAH *is* my strength and *my* song; he also is become my salvation.
3 Therefore with joy shall ye

Isaiah 12:2

Isaiah 26:4

peace, *whose* mind *is* stayed *on thee:* because he trusteth in thee.
4 Trust ye in the LORD for ever: for in the LORD JEHOVAH *is* everlasting strength:
5 ¶ For he bringeth down them that dwell on high; the lofty city, he layeth it low; he layeth it low, *even* to the ground; he bringeth it *even* to the dust.

sociations, is now restored to the place in the sacred text to which it has an unquestionable claim." Yes, men who translated that Bible into English felt that the reasons why God's name had been left out were not good. So they put it back into the Bible in its rightful places.

[21] There are those, however, that argue that the word "Jehovah" should not be used because it is not really the name of God. For example, the Catholic *Douay Version*, which does not use God's name in its main text, says in its footnote to Exodus 6:3: "Some moderns have framed the name *Jehovah* . . . the true pronunciation of the name, which is in the Hebrew text, by long disuse, is now quite lost."

[22] Yes, as the Catholic Bible here says, God's name does appear in the Hebrew text, Hebrew being the language in which the first 39 books of the Bible were written. The name is represented there by four Hebrew letters, YHWH. In ancient times the Hebrew language was written without vowels, letters such as *a, e, i, o* and *u,* which help us to give the proper sound to words. Therefore, the problem today is that we have no way of knowing exactly which vowels the Hebrews used along with the consonants YHWH.

[23] To help us to understand the problem, consider the word "building." Suppose that it began always to be written "bldg," and that, in time, the word was never pronounced. How, then, would a person living 1,000 years from now know how to pronounce "bldg" when he saw it in writing? Since he had never heard it pronounced and did not know what the vowels were in the word, he would not know for sure. It is similar with God's name. It is not known exactly how it was pronounced, even though some scholars think "Yahweh" is correct. However, the form "Jehovah" has been in use for many centuries and is most widely known.

---

21. What does the Catholic *Douay Version* say about the name Jehovah?
22. (a) How is God's name represented in the Hebrew language? (b) Why is there a problem of knowing how God's name was originally pronounced?
23. How can the spelling "bldg" for "building" help us to understand the problem of pronouncing God's name?

[24] Yet, should we use God's name, even though we may not be saying it exactly the way it was originally pronounced? Well, we use the names of other persons in the Bible, even though we do not say them in the way the names were pronounced in the original Hebrew. For example, Jesus' name is pronounced "Yesh'ua" in Hebrew. Likewise, it is proper to use God's name, which is revealed in the Bible, whether we pronounce it "Yahweh," "Jehovah," or in some other way common in our language. What is wrong is to *fail* to use that name. Why? Because those who do not use it could not be identified with the ones whom God takes out to be "a people for his name." (Acts 15:14) We should not only know God's name but praise it before others, as Jesus did when on earth.—Matthew 6:9; John 17:6, 26.

A GOD OF PURPOSE

[25] Although it may be hard for our minds to understand, Jehovah never had a beginning and will never have an end. He is the "King of eternity." (Psalm 90:2; 1 Timothy 1:17) Before he began to create, Jehovah was all alone in universal space. Yet he could not have been lonesome, for he is complete in himself and lacks nothing. It was love that moved him to begin to create, to give life to others to enjoy. God's first creations were spirit persons like himself. He had a great organization of heavenly sons even before the earth was prepared for humans. Jehovah purposed for them to find great delight in life and in the service he gave them to do.—Job 38:4, 7.

[26] When the earth was prepared, Jehovah placed a couple, Adam and Eve, in a part of the earth already made into a paradise. It was his purpose that they have children who would obey and worship him, and who would extend that paradise all over the earth. (Genesis 1:27, 28) As we have learned, however, that grand purpose was interfered with. Adam and Eve chose to disobey God, and his purpose has not been fulfilled. But

24. (a) To be consistent, why is it proper that we use God's name? (b) In view of Acts 15:14, why is it important to use God's name?
25. (a) What things about God may it be hard for us to understand? (b) What moved Jehovah to begin creating?
26. Why can we be certain that God's purpose for the earth will be fulfilled?

it will be, for it would be admitting defeat for Jehovah not to accomplish what he purposes. And that he could never do! "Everything that is my delight I shall do," he declares. "I have even spoken it; I shall also bring it in."—Isaiah 46:10, 11.

²⁷ Do you see where you can fit into God's purpose? It is not simply by doing whatever you want without considering what God's will is. That is what Satan and Adam and Eve did. They knew what God's will was but they did not do it. And God held them accountable. Are we, too, accountable to God? Yes, because God is the Source of our life. Our life is dependent on him. (Psalm 36:9; Matthew 5:45) To what extent, then, do we live our lives in harmony with God's purpose for us? We should think seriously about this, because our opportunity for everlasting life depends on it.

HOW TO WORSHIP JEHOVAH

²⁸ How we worship Jehovah is important. We should worship in the way that he says, even though this may be different from the way that we have been taught. For example, it has been the custom for some persons to use images in their worship. They may say that they do not worship the image, but that seeing and touching it helps them to worship God. Yet does God want us to worship him with the aid of images?

27. (a) Why are we accountable to God? (b) So what question should we think about seriously?
28. What aids have some persons used to worship God?

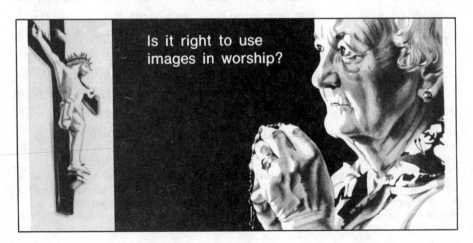

Is it right to use images in worship?

²⁹ No, he does not. And for this very reason Moses told the Israelites that God never appeared to them in any visible form. (Deuteronomy 4:15-19) In fact, one of the Ten Commandments says: "You shall not make yourself a carved image or any likeness of anything . . . you shall not bow down to them or serve them." (Exodus 20:4, 5, the Catholic *Jerusalem Bible*) Only Jehovah should be worshiped. Over and over again the Bible shows how wrong it is to make an image or to bow before it, or to worship anyone or anything except Jehovah.—Isaiah 44:14-20; 46:6, 7; Psalm 115:4-8.

³⁰ As we might have expected, then, Jesus never used images in worship. "God is a Spirit," he explained, "and those worshiping him must worship with spirit and truth." (John 4:24) Acting in harmony with this counsel, none of Jesus' early followers used images as aids in worship. In fact, his apostle Paul wrote: "We are walking by faith, not by sight." (2 Corinthians 5:7) And his apostle John warned: "Guard yourselves from idols." (1 John 5:21) Why not look around your home and ask yourself whether you are following this advice?—Deuteronomy 7:25.

³¹ Worshiping Jehovah, the Creator, in the way he directs is certain to bring us genuine happiness. (Jeremiah 14:22) The Bible shows that his requirements are for our good, with our eternal welfare in view. It is true that there may be times, because of our limited knowledge and experience, that we do not fully appreciate why a certain law given by God is so important, or how it really works for our good. Yet our firm belief that God knows far more than we do should move us to obey him with a willing heart. (Psalm 19:7-11) Let us, then, make every effort to learn all we can about Jehovah, accepting the invitation: "O come in, let us worship and bow down; let us kneel before Jehovah our Maker. For he is our God, and we are the people of his pasturage and the sheep of his hand."—Psalm 95:6, 7.

---

29. How does the Bible show that it is wrong to use images in worship?
30. (a) What did Jesus and his apostles say that shows that the use of images is wrong? (b) According to Deuteronomy 7:25, what should be done with images?
31. (a) Even if we may not understand the reason for a certain law of God, what will move us to obey it? (b) What should we try to do, and what invitation should we accept?

Chapter 5

Is the Bible Really from God?

HAS JEHOVAH GOD given us information about himself? Has he told us what he has done and what he yet purposes to do? A father who loves his children tells them many things. And from what we have seen, Jehovah is indeed a loving father.

2 How could Jehovah give information to humans living in many parts of the earth and in different periods of time? A fine way would be for him to have a book written and then see to it that it was made available to all. Is the Bible such a Book from God? How can we know if it is?

NO OTHER BOOK LIKE THE BIBLE

3 If the Bible really is from God, we should expect it to be the most outstanding book ever written. Is it? Yes, and for many reasons. First, it is very old; you would not expect God's Word to all mankind to have been written a short time ago, would you? The writing of it began some 3,500 years ago in the Hebrew language. Then, over 2,200 years ago, it began to be translated into other languages. Today almost everybody on earth can read the Bible in his own language.

4 Also, no other book comes close to the Bible in the number of copies that have been made. A book may be called a "best-seller" when only *thousands* of copies are produced. Yet every year many *millions* of Bibles are printed. And over the centuries *thousands of millions* have been made! There is hardly a place on earth, regardless of how isolated it may be, where

---

1. Why is it reasonable to believe that God would give us information about himself?
2. (a) What is a fine way for Jehovah to tell us about himself? (b) What questions does this raise?
3. What is one way in which the Bible is an outstanding book?
4. How does the number of Bibles produced compare with that of other books?

you cannot find a Bible. Is this not what you would expect of a book that really is from God?

[5] What makes this great distribution of the Bible even more outstanding is the fact that enemies have tried to destroy it. But should we not expect that a book from God would come under attack by agents of the Devil? This has happened. Bible burnings once were common, and those who were caught reading the Bible were often punished with death.

[6] You would expect a book from God to discuss important matters that all of us should want to know. 'Where did life come from?' 'Why are we here?' 'What will the future bring?' are some of the questions it answers. And it plainly says that the information it contains is from Jehovah God. One Bible writer said: "The spirit of Jehovah it was that spoke by me, and his word was upon my tongue." (2 Samuel 23:2) Another wrote: "All Scripture is inspired of God." (2 Timothy 3:16) Since the Bible so definitely states that it is the Word of God, would it not be wise to examine it to see if it is?

HOW THE BIBLE WAS WRITTEN

[7] 'Yet how could the Bible be from God when it was written by men?' you may ask. True, about 40 men shared in writing the Bible. These men did the actual writing of the Bible with the exception of the Ten Commandments, which were written personally by God on stone tablets by the direct action of his holy spirit. (Exodus 31:18) However, this does not make what they wrote any less the Word of God. The Bible explains: *"Men spoke from God as they were borne along by holy spirit."* (2 Peter 1:21) Yes, just as God used his powerful holy spirit to create the heavens, the earth and all living things, he also used it to direct the writing of the Bible.

[8] This means that the Bible has only one author, Jehovah God.

---

5. What efforts have been made to destroy the Bible?
6. (a) What important questions does the Bible answer? (b) From where do Bible writers claim they received their information?
7. (a) Who wrote the Bible? (b) How, then, can it be said that it is God's Word?
8, 9. What examples today can help us to understand how God had the Bible written?

God used men to write the Bible much as a businessman uses a secretary to write a letter

He used men to write the information down, much as a businessman uses a secretary to write a letter. The secretary writes the letter, but the letter contains the thoughts and ideas of the businessman. So it is *his* letter, not the secretary's, even as the Bible is *God's Book,* not the book of the men who were used to write it.

⁹ Since God created the mind, he surely did not find it hard to get in touch with the minds of his servants to provide them with the information to write. Even today a person can sit in his home and receive messages from a faraway place by means of a radio or a television set. The voices or pictures travel over long distances by the use of physical laws that God created. It is, therefore, easy to understand that Jehovah, from his place far away in the heavens, could direct men to write down the information that he wanted the human family to know.

¹⁰ The result has been a marvelous Book. Actually, the Bible is made up of 66 little books. The Greek word *biblia,* from which the word "Bible" comes, means "little books." These books, or letters, were written over a period of 1,600 years, from 1513 B.C.E. to 98 C.E. Yet, because of having just one Author, all these Bible books are in harmony with one another. The same theme runs throughout the whole, namely, that Jehovah God will bring back righteous conditions by his kingdom. The

10. (a) How many books make up the Bible, and over what period of time were they written? (b) What main theme runs throughout the Bible?

first book, Genesis, tells how a paradise home was lost because of rebellion against God, and the last book, Revelation, describes how the earth will be made a paradise again by God's rule. —Genesis 3:19, 23; Revelation 12:10; 21:3, 4.

¹¹ The first 39 books of the Bible were written mainly in the Hebrew language, with very small parts in Aramaic. The last 27 books were written in Greek, the common language of the people when Jesus and his Christian followers walked the earth. These two main sections of the Bible are properly called the "Hebrew Scriptures" and the "Greek Scriptures." Showing their agreement with each other, the Greek Scriptures quote from the Hebrew Scriptures more than 365 times, and make about 375 additional references to them.

MAKING THE BIBLE AVAILABLE TO ALL

¹² If only the original writings were available, how could everyone read God's Word? They could not. So Jehovah arranged that copies of the original Hebrew writings be made. (Deuteronomy 17:18) The man Ezra, for example, is called "a skilled copyist in the law of Moses, which Jehovah the God of Israel had

Some religious leaders fought to keep the Bible from the common people, even burning at the stake those who possessed it

11. (a) What were the languages used to write the Bible? (b) Into what two main sections is the Bible divided, but what shows their unity?
12. Why did Jehovah have copies made of the Bible?

given." (Ezra 7:6) Also, many thousands of copies of the Greek Scriptures were made.

[13] Do you read Hebrew or Greek? If not, you cannot read the early handwritten copies of the Bible, some of which are still in existence. Therefore, for you to read the Bible, someone had to put the words into a language you know. This *translating* from one language to another has made it possible for more persons to read God's Word. For example, about 300 years before Jesus lived on earth, Greek became the language most people began to speak. So the Hebrew Scriptures were put into Greek, beginning in 280 B.C.E. This early translation was called the "Septuagint."

[14] Later, Latin became the common language of many people, so the Bible was translated into Latin. But, as the centuries passed by, fewer and fewer people spoke Latin. Most people spoke other languages, such as Arabic, French, Spanish, Portuguese, Italian, German and English. For some time the Catholic religious leaders fought to keep the Bible from being put into the language of the common people. They even burned at the stake persons possessing the Bible. They did this because the Bible exposed their false teachings and bad practices. But, in time, these religious leaders lost the fight, and the Bible began to be put into many languages and distributed in large numbers. Today the Bible can be read, in its entirety or in part, in over 1,700 languages!

[15] As the years went by, many different translations of the Bible were produced in the same language. For example, in English alone there are dozens of Bible translations. Why? Would not just one be enough? Well, over the years a language will change a great deal. So if you were to compare older Bible translations with newer ones, you would note changes in the language. While they almost always give the same thought, you will notice that the translations printed in more recent years are

---

13. (a) What was needed so that most people could read the Bible? (b) When was the first translation of the Bible made?
14. (a) Why did some religious leaders fight to keep the Bible from being translated? (b) What shows that these lost the fight?
15. Why are newer Bible translations good to have?

generally easier to understand. So we can be thankful for new Bible translations, since they put God's Word into the common, easy-to-understand language of the day.

HAS THE BIBLE BEEN CHANGED?

[16] But you may ask: 'How can we be sure that our Bibles today have the same information that the Bible writers received from God?' With the copying and recopying of the Bible books over hundreds and even thousands of years, have not mistakes crept in? Yes, but these mistakes have been discovered and corrected in modern translations of the Bible. Today the information is the same as God provided to those who first wrote it down. What proof is there of this?

[17] Well, between 1947 and 1955 what are known as the Dead Sea Scrolls were found. These old scrolls include copies of books of the Hebrew Scriptures. They date from 100 to 200 years *before* Jesus was born. One of the scrolls is a copy of the book of Isaiah. Before this was found the oldest copy of the book of Isaiah available in Hebrew was one that had been made nearly 1,000 years *after* Jesus was born. When these two copies of Isaiah were compared there were only very small differences in them, most of which were small variations in spelling! This means that in more than 1,000 years of copying there had been no real change!

[18] There are more than 1,700 ancient copies of the various portions

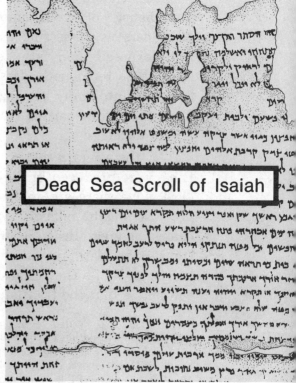

Dead Sea Scroll of Isaiah

---

16. Why do some people believe that the Bible has been changed?
17. What evidence is there that the Bible has not been changed?
18. (a) How have copyist mistakes been corrected? (b) What can be said about the accuracy of the Greek Scriptures?

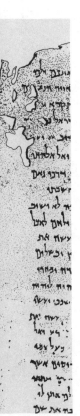

of the Hebrew Scriptures available. By carefully comparing these many very old copies, even the few mistakes copyists made can be found and corrected. Also, there are thousands of very old copies of the Greek Scriptures, some of which copies date back nearly to the time of Jesus and his apostles. Thus, as Sir Frederic Kenyon said: "The last foundation for any doubt that the Scriptures have come down to us substantially as they were written has now been removed."—*The Bible and Archaeology,* pages 288, 289.

[19] This does not mean that there have not been attempts to change God's Word. There have been. A notable example is 1 John 5:7. In the *Authorized Version* of 1611 it reads: "For there are three that bear record in heaven, the Father, the Word, and the Holy Ghost: and these three are one." Yet these words do not appear in any of the very early copies of the Bible. They were added by someone who was trying to support the Trinity teaching. Since it is clear that these words are not really part of God's Word, corrections have been made and the words do not appear in newer Bibles.

[20] So anyone who says that the Bible does not contain the same information as when it was originally written simply does not know the facts. Jehovah God has seen to it that his Word has been protected not only from mistakes copyists made but also from attempts of others to make additions to it. The Bible itself contains God's promise that his Word would be kept in a pure form for us today.—Psalm 12:6, 7; Daniel 12:4; 1 Peter 1:24, 25; Revelation 22:18, 19.

IS THE BIBLE REALLY TRUE?

[21] Jesus Christ said in prayer to God: "Your word is truth." (John 17:17) But do the facts support this? When the Bible is carefully examined, do we find that it really is the truth?

---

19. (a) What is an example of an attempt to add to the Bible? (b) How do we know that 1 John 5:7 does not belong in the Bible?
20. Why can we be sure that the Bible has been kept in a pure form?
21. How did Jesus view God's Word?

Students of history who have studied the Bible are often amazed at its accuracy. The Bible contains specific names and details that can be confirmed. Consider some examples.

Temple wall at Karnak, Egypt

22 Look at the pictures and writing on this temple wall at Karnak, Egypt. They tell of the victory, almost 3,000 years ago, of Pharaoh Shishak over the kingdom of Judah during the rule of Solomon's son Rehoboam. The Bible tells about the same event. —1 Kings 14:25, 26.

23 Look also at the Moabite Stone. The original can be seen in the Louvre Museum in Paris, France. The writing tells of the rebellion by King Mesha of Moab against Israel. This event is also reported in the Bible.—2 Kings 1:1; 3:4-27.

24 The Pool of Siloam and the entrance of a 1,749-foot-long (533-meter-long) water tunnel in Jerusalem are seen here at the far right. Many modern-day visitors to Jerusalem have waded through this tunnel. Its existence is further proof that the Bible is true. How so? Because the Bible explains that King Hezekiah had this tunnel built over 2,500 years ago to protect his water supply from an invading army.—2 Kings 20:20; 2 Chronicles 32:2-4, 30.

25 At the British Museum a visitor can see the Nabonidus Chronicle, a copy of which is seen to the right. It describes the fall of ancient Babylon, even as the Bible also does. (Daniel 5:30, 31) But the Bible says that Belshazzar was then king of Babylon. Yet the Nabonidus Chronicle does not even name Belshazzar. In fact, at one time all known ancient writings said that Nabonidus was Babylon's last king. So some who said the Bible is not true

22-25. What are a few examples that show that the Bible contains true history?

claimed that Belshazzar never existed and that the Bible was wrong. But in recent years ancient writings have been found that identified Belshazzar as a son of Nabonidus and coruler with his father in Babylon at the time! Yes, the Bible really is true, as so many, many examples prove.

[26] Yet the Bible does not contain only true history. *Everything* it says is true. Even when it touches on matters of science, it is marvelously accurate. To give just two examples: In ancient times it was commonly believed that the earth had some visible support,

Moabite Stone

26. What evidence is there that the Bible is scientifically accurate?

Nabonidus Chronicle

Entrance to Hezekiah's Tunnel and Pool of Siloam

that it rested on something, such as on a giant. Yet in perfect agreement with scientific evidence, the Bible reports that God is "hanging the earth upon nothing." (Job 26:7) And rather than saying that the earth is flat, as many believed in the past, the Bible says that God "is dwelling above the *circle* of the earth." —Isaiah 40:22.

[27] But the greatest proof that the Bible really is from God is its perfect record in foretelling the future. No book by men accurately reports history before it happens; yet the Bible does. It is filled with accurate prophecies, yes, of history actually written in advance. Some of the most remarkable of these are regarding the coming to earth of God's Son. The Hebrew Scriptures accurately foretold hundreds of years in advance that this Promised One would be born in Bethlehem, that he would be born of a virgin, that he would be betrayed for 30 pieces of silver, that he would be counted in with sinners, that not a bone of his body would be broken, that lots would be cast for his garments, and many, many more details.—Micah 5:2; Matthew 2:3-9; Isaiah 7:14; Matthew 1:22, 23; Zechariah 11:12, 13; Matthew 27:3-5; Isaiah 53:12; Luke 22:37, 52; 23:32, 33; Psalm 34:20; John 19:36; Psalm 22:18; Matthew 27:35.

[28] As was said in the first chapter of this book, the Bible also foretells that this old system of things will soon end and a righteous new one will replace it. (Matthew 24:3-14; 2 Peter 3:7, 13) Can we rely on such yet-to-be-fulfilled prophecies? Well, if someone told you the truth a hundred times, would you suddenly doubt him when he told you something new? If you had never found him wrong, would you now begin to doubt him? How unreasonable that would be! Likewise, there is no reason for us to doubt anything that God promises in the Bible. His Word can be trusted! (Titus 1:2) By continuing to study the Bible, you, too, will become ever more convinced by the facts that the Bible truly is from God.

---

27. (a) What is the strongest proof that the Bible is from God? (b) What things did the Hebrew Scriptures truthfully foretell about God's Son?
28. (a) Why can we be confident that even those Bible prophecies that have not yet been fulfilled will be? (b) Of what will a continued study of the Bible convince you?

Chapter 6

Jesus Christ – Sent by God?

NEARLY everyone today has heard of Jesus Christ. His influence on history has been greater than that of any other human. Indeed, the very calendar used in most parts of the world is based on the year he is thought to have been born! As *The World Book Encyclopedia* says: "Dates before that year are listed as B.C., or *before Christ*. Dates after that year are listed as A.D., or *anno Domini* (in the year of our Lord)."

[2] So Jesus was not an imaginary person. He really lived as a man on earth. "In ancient times even the opponents of Christianity never doubted the [actual existence] of Jesus," notes the *Encyclopædia Britannica*. So just who was Jesus? Was he really sent by God? Why is he so well known?

HE HAD LIVED BEFORE

[3] Unlike any other human, Jesus was born of a virgin. Her name was Mary. An angel said of her child: "This one will be great and will be called Son of the Most High." (Luke 1:28-33; Matthew 1:20-25) But how could a woman who had never had sexual relations with a man have a child? It was by means of God's holy spirit. Jehovah transferred the life of his mighty spirit Son from heaven to the womb of the virgin Mary. It was a miracle! Surely the One who made the first woman with the wonderful ability to produce children could cause a woman to have a child without a human father. The Bible explains: "When the full limit of the time arrived, God sent forth his Son, who came to be out of a woman."—Galatians 4:4.

1, 2. (a) What evidence is there that Jesus Christ was a real person? (b) What questions are raised about Jesus?
3. (a) According to the angel's words, Mary would give birth to whose son? (b) How was it possible for the virgin Mary to have Jesus?

⁴ So before being born on earth as a man Jesus had been in heaven as a mighty spirit person. He had a spirit body invisible to man, just as God has. (John 4:24) Jesus himself often spoke of the high position he had held in heaven. Once he prayed: "Father, glorify me alongside yourself with the glory that I had alongside you before the world was." (John 17:5) He also said to his listeners: "You are from the realms below; I am from the realms above." "What, therefore, if you should behold the Son of man ascending to where he was before?" "Before Abraham came into existence, I have been." —John 8:23; 6:62; 8:58; 3:13; 6:51.

⁵ Before coming to earth Jesus was called the *Word* of God. This title shows that he served in heaven as the one who spoke for God. He is also called God's "Firstborn," as well as his "only-begotten" Son. (John 1:14; 3:16; Hebrews 1:6) This means that he was created before all the other spirit sons of God, and that he is the only one who was directly created by God. The Bible explains that this "firstborn" Son shared with Jehovah in creating all other things. (Colossians 1:15, 16) Thus when God said, "Let *us* make man in our image," he was talking to this Son. Yes, the very one who later

Jesus left his carpentry work to be baptized and become the anointed of Jehovah

4. (a) What life did Jesus enjoy before he was born as a child? (b) What did Jesus say to show that he had lived before in heaven?

5. (a) Why had Jesus been called the "Word," "Firstborn" and "only-begotten"? (b) What work had Jesus shared in with God?

came to earth and was born from a woman had shared in the creation of all things! He had already lived in heaven with his Father for an unknown number of years!—Genesis 1:26; Proverbs 8:22, 30; John 1:3.

HIS LIFE ON EARTH

⁶ Mary had been promised in marriage to Joseph. But when he learned that she was pregnant he believed she had engaged in sexual relations with another man, and he was therefore not going to marry her. However, when Jehovah told him that it was by means of His holy spirit that the child had been conceived, Joseph took Mary as his wife. (Matthew 1:18-20, 24, 25) Later, while they were visiting the city of Bethlehem, Jesus was born. (Luke 2:1-7; Micah 5:2) When Jesus was still a baby, King Herod tried to kill him. But Jehovah warned Joseph so that he took his family and ran away to Egypt. After King Herod died, Joseph and Mary returned with Jesus to the city of Nazareth in Galilee. Here he grew up.—Matthew 2:13-15, 19-23.

⁷ When Jesus was 12 years old he traveled with his family to Jerusalem to attend the special celebration called the Passover. While there he spent three days in the temple listening to the teachers and asking them questions. All the people who listened to him were surprised at how much he knew. (Luke 2:41-52) As Jesus grew up in Nazareth, he learned to be a carpenter. He no doubt was trained to do this work by his foster father, Joseph, who also was a carpenter.—Mark 6:3; Matthew 13:55.

⁸ At 30 years of age a big change occurred in Jesus' life. He went to John the Baptizer and asked to be baptized, to be put completely under the waters of the Jordan River. The Bible reports: "After being baptized Jesus immediately came up from the water; and, look! the heavens were opened up, and he saw descending like a dove God's spirit coming upon him. Look! Also, there was a voice from the heavens that said: 'This is my

6. (a) What events happened shortly before and after Jesus' birth? (b) Where was Jesus born and where did he grow up?
7. (a) What happened when Jesus was 12 years old? (b) What work did Jesus learn to do as he was growing up?
8. What happened when Jesus was 30 years old?

Son, the beloved, whom I have approved.' " (Matthew 3:16, 17) There could be no doubt in the mind of John that Jesus had been sent by God.

⁹ By pouring out His holy spirit on Jesus, Jehovah was anointing him or appointing him to be the king of His coming kingdom. Being thus anointed with the spirit, Jesus became the "Messiah," or the "Christ," which words in the Hebrew and Greek languages mean "Anointed." Therefore, he became, in fact, Jesus *Christ,* or Jesus the *Anointed.* So his apostle Peter spoke of "Jesus who was from Nazareth, how God anointed him with holy spirit and power." (Acts 10:38) Also, by his baptism in water Jesus was presenting himself to God to carry out the work that God had sent him to earth to do. What was that important work?

WHY HE CAME TO EARTH

¹⁰ Explaining why he had come to earth, Jesus told the Roman governor Pontius Pilate: "For this I have been born, and for this [purpose] I have come into the world, that I should bear witness to the truth." (John 18:37) But what particular truths was Jesus sent to earth to make known? First, truths about his heavenly Father. He taught his followers to pray that his Father's name be "hallowed," or held holy. (Matthew 6:9, *King James Version*) And he prayed: "I have made your name manifest to the men you gave me." (John 17:6) Also, he said: "I must declare *the good news of the kingdom of God,* because for this I was sent forth."—Luke 4:43.

¹¹ How important to Jesus was this work of making known his Father's name and kingdom? He said to his disciples: "My food is for me to do the will of him that sent me and to finish his work." (John 4:34) Why did Jesus consider God's work to be as important as food? It was because the Kingdom is the means by

---

9. (a) When did Jesus, in fact, become *Christ,* and why then? (b) By his baptism, what was Jesus presenting himself to do?
10. What truths did Jesus come to earth to tell?
11. (a) Why did Jesus consider his work so important? (b) What did Jesus never hold back from doing? So what should we do?

which God will fulfill his wonderful purposes for humankind. It is this kingdom that will destroy all wickedness and will clear Jehovah's name of the reproach that has been brought upon it. (Daniel 2:44; Revelation 21:3, 4) So Jesus never held back from making known God's name and kingdom. (Matthew 4:17; Luke 8:1; John 17:26; Hebrews 2:12) He always spoke the truth, whether it was popular or not. He thus provided an example that we should follow if we want to please God.—1 Peter 2:21.

[12] Yet, to make it possible for us to gain everlasting life under the rule of God's kingdom, Jesus had to pour out his lifeblood in death. As two apostles of Jesus said: "We have been declared righteous now by his blood." "The blood of Jesus [God's] Son cleanses us from all sin." (Romans 5:9; 1 John 1:7) So an important reason why Jesus came to earth was to die for us. He said: "The Son of man came, not to be ministered to, but to minister and to *give his soul* [*or, life*] *a ransom in exchange for many.*" (Matthew 20:28) But what does it mean that Christ gave his life "a ransom"? Why was the pouring out of his lifeblood in death necessary for our salvation?

HE GAVE HIS LIFE A RANSOM

[13] The word "ransom" is often used when there is a kidnapping. After a kidnapper captures a person, he may say he will return the person if a certain amount of money is paid as a *ransom.* So a ransom is something that brings the deliverance of a person held captive. It is something that is paid so that he does not lose his life. Jesus' perfect human life was given to obtain mankind's release from bondage to sin and death. (1 Peter 1:18, 19; Ephesians 1:7) Why was such a release needed?

[14] This was because Adam, the forefather of all of us, had rebelled against God. His lawless act thus made him a sinner, since the Bible explains that "sin is lawlessness." (1 John 3:4; 5:17) As a result, he was not worthy of receiving God's gift of

12. For what other important reason did Jesus come to earth?
13. (a) What is a ransom? (b) What is the ransom price that Jesus paid to release us from sin and death?
14. Why was the ransom provided by Jesus needed?

everlasting life. (Romans 6:23) So Adam lost for himself perfect human life on a paradise earth. He also lost this wonderful prospect for all the children he would produce. 'But why,' you may ask, 'did all his children have to die, since it was Adam who sinned?'

15 This is because Adam, when he became a sinner, passed sin and death on to his children, including all humans now living. (Job 14:4; Romans 5:12) "All have sinned and fall short of the glory of God," the Bible says. (Romans 3:23; 1 Kings 8:46) Even godly David said: "With error I was brought forth with birth pains, and in sin my mother conceived me." (Psalm 51:5) People, therefore, have been dying because of the sin that was inherited from Adam. How was it possible, then, for the sacrifice of Jesus' life to free all people from bondage to sin and death?

16 A legal principle in God's law for the nation of Israel is involved. It states that 'life should be given for life.' (Exodus 21:23; Deuteronomy 19:21) By his disobedience the perfect man Adam lost *perfect life* on a paradise earth for himself and all his children. Jesus Christ gave his own *perfect life* to buy back what Adam lost. Yes, Jesus "gave himself a *corresponding ransom* for all." (1 Timothy 2:5, 6) Because he was a perfect man, even as Adam had been, Jesus is called "the last Adam." (1 Corinthians 15:45) No human other than Jesus could have provided the ransom. This is because Jesus is the only man who ever lived that was equal to Adam as a perfect human son of God.—Psalm 49:7; Luke 1:32; 3:38.

17 Jesus died at 33½ years of age. But on the third day after his death he was resurrected to life. Forty days later he returned to heaven. (Acts 1:3, 9-11) There, as a spirit person once more, he appeared "before the person of God for us," carrying the value of his ransom sacrifice. (Hebrews 9:12, 24) At that time the ransom was paid to God in heaven. Deliverance was now

---

15. Since it was Adam who sinned, why did his children have to suffer and die?
16. (a) In providing the ransom, how did God show regard for his law that 'life should be given for life'? (b) Why was Jesus the only human who could pay the ransom?
17. When was the ransom paid to God?

available for humankind. But when will its benefits be realized?

[18] Even now Jesus' ransom sacrifice can benefit us. How? By exercising faith in it we can enjoy a clean standing before God and come under his loving and tender care. (Revelation 7:9, 10, 13-15) Many of us may have committed terrible sins before we learned about God. And even now we make mistakes, sometimes very serious ones. But we can freely seek forgiveness from God on the basis of the ransom, with confidence that he will hear us. (1 John 2:1, 2; 1 Corinthians 6:9-11) Also, in the days ahead, the ransom will open up for us the way to receive God's gift of everlasting life in his righteous new order. (2 Peter 3:13) At that time all those exercising faith in the ransom will be released completely from bondage to sin and death. They may look forward to life forever in perfection!

[19] How do you feel on learning about the ransom? Does it not

18. (a) How can we benefit even now from the ransom? (b) What does the ransom make possible in the future?
19. (a) What effect does the provision of the ransom have upon you? (b) How did the apostle Paul say we should show our gratitude for the ransom?

Jesus was the equal of the perfect man Adam

Jesus was moved with pity
to help the sick and hungry

warm your heart toward Jehovah God to know that he cares for you so much that he gave his dear Son in your behalf? (John 3:16; 1 John 4:9, 10) But think, too, of Christ's love. *He willingly came to earth to die for us.* Should we not be grateful? The apostle Paul explained how we should show our gratitude when he said: "He died for all *that those who live might live no longer for themselves, but for him who died for them* and was raised up." (2 Corinthians 5:14, 15) Will you show your gratitude by using your life to serve God and his heavenly Son Jesus Christ?

WHY JESUS PERFORMED MIRACLES

[20] Jesus is well known for the miracles he performed. He had deep feeling for people who were in trouble, and he was eager to use his God-given powers to help them. For example, a person with the terrible disease leprosy came to him and said: "If you just want to, you can make me clean." Jesus "was *moved with pity,* and he stretched out his hand and touched him, and said to him: '*I want to.* Be made clean.'" And the sick man was healed!—Mark 1:40-42.

[21] Consider another Bible scene, and imagine Jesus' tender feeling for the people described: "Then great crowds approached him, having along with them people that were lame, maimed, blind, dumb, and many otherwise, and they fairly threw them at his feet, and he cured them; so that the crowd felt amazement as they saw the dumb speaking and the lame walking and the blind seeing, and they glorified the God of Israel."—Matthew 15:30, 31.

[22] That Jesus really cared about these suffering persons and truly *wanted* to help them can be seen by what he next told his disciples. He said: "*I feel pity for the crowd,* because it is already three days that they have stayed with me and they have nothing to eat; and I do not want to send them away fasting. They may possibly give out on the road." So Jesus, with just seven loaves

---

20. What do we learn about Jesus from his healing of the leper?
21. How did Jesus help the crowds?
22. What shows that Jesus really cared about the people whom he helped?

and a few little fish, miraculously fed the "four thousand men, besides women and young children."—Matthew 15:32-38.

23 On another occasion Jesus met a funeral procession that was coming out of the city of Nain. The Bible describes it, saying: "There was a dead man being carried out, the only-begotten son of his mother. Besides, she was a widow. . . . And when the Lord caught sight of her, *he was moved with pity for her.*" He deeply felt her sorrow. So, addressing the dead body, Jesus commanded: "Young man, I say to you, Get up!" And wonder of wonders! "The dead man sat up and started to speak, and he gave him to his mother." Think how that mother must have felt! How would you feel? News about this remarkable event spread far and wide. No wonder Jesus is so well known.—Luke 7:11-17.

24 Yet the miracles Jesus performed were of only temporary benefit. People that he healed developed physical problems again. And those he resurrected died again. But Jesus' miracles proved that he was sent forth by God, that he was really God's Son. And they proved that, with God's power, all human problems can be solved. Yes, they showed on a small scale what will take place on earth under the kingdom of God. At that time the hungry will be fed, the sick will be cured, and even the dead will be raised! And never again will sickness, death or any other troubles cause unhappiness. What a blessing that will be! —Revelation 21:3, 4; Matthew 11:4, 5.

RULER OF GOD'S KINGDOM

25 There are three parts to the life of God's Son. First, there are the unknown number of years he spent with his Father in heaven before he became a human. Next, the 33½ years he spent on earth after his birth. And now there is his life back in heaven as a spirit person. What position has he had in heaven since his resurrection?

26 Clearly, Jesus was to become a king. Even the angel an-

---

23. What moved Jesus to resurrect a widow's dead son?
24. What did Jesus' miracles show regarding the future?
25. Into what three parts can Jesus' life be divided?
26. By his faithfulness on earth, Jesus proved worthy of being what?

By raising the dead, Jesus showed what he would do on a much larger scale when God's kingdom rules

nounced to Mary: "He will rule as king . . . forever, and there will be no end of his kingdom." (Luke 1:33) During his earthly ministry he spoke all the time about the kingdom of God. He taught his followers to pray: "Let your kingdom come. Let your will take place, as in heaven, also upon earth." And he urged them to "keep on, then, seeking first the kingdom." (Matthew 6:10, 33) By his faithfulness on earth, Jesus proved that he was worthy to be king of God's kingdom. Did he begin ruling as king as soon as he returned to heaven?

²⁷ No, he did not. The apostle Paul refers to Psalm 110:1, explaining: "This man [Jesus] offered one sacrifice for sins perpetually and sat down at the right hand of God, from then on awaiting until his enemies should be placed as a stool for his feet." (Hebrews 10:12, 13) Jesus was awaiting Jehovah's command: "Go subduing in the midst of your enemies." (Psalm 110:2) When that time came, he began cleansing the heavens of Satan and his angels. The result of that war in heaven is stated in these words: "Now have come to pass the salvation and the power and the *kingdom of our God and the authority of his Christ,* because the accuser of our brothers has been hurled down, who accuses them day and night before our God!" (Revelation 12:10) As seen in an earlier chapter of this book, the facts show that this war in heaven has already taken place, and Jesus Christ is ruling right now in the midst of his enemies.

²⁸ Very soon Christ and his heavenly angels will take action to rid the earth of all present worldly governments. (Daniel 2:44; Revelation 17:14) The Bible says that he has "a sharp long sword, that he may strike the nations with it, and he will shepherd them with a rod of iron." (Revelation 19:11-16) To prove worthy of protection during this coming destruction, we must exercise faith in Jesus Christ. (John 3:36) We must become his disciples and submit ourselves to him as our heavenly King. Will you do that?

---

27. (a) What did Jesus do after his return to heaven? (b) What was Jesus' first act as king of God's kingdom?
28. (a) What will Christ soon do? (b) What must we do to enjoy his protection?

Chapter 7

Why We Are Here

PEOPLE have long wondered about the meaning of life on earth. They have looked at the huge star-filled sky. They have admired a colorful sunset and the beauty of the countryside. Thinking persons have reasoned that there must be some grand purpose to all these things. But often they have wondered where they fit in.—Psalm 8:3, 4.

[2] At some time in life most people ask: Are we just to live a short time, get what we can out of life, and then die? Where are we really going? Is there more that we can expect

1. What conclusion have thinking persons reached?
2. What questions have people asked?

Many wonder about the meaning of life

Did these things evolve, or were they made?

than the brief cycle of birth, life and death? (Job 14:1, 2) What will help us to understand this matter is the answer to the question: *How did we get here?*

EVOLUTION OR CREATION?

[3] In some places it is commonly taught that everything we see just happened by itself, that it came about by chance or accident. Over many millions of years, it is said, life evolved, or developed, from lower forms until finally humans came into existence. In many parts of the earth this theory of evolution is taught as a fact. But is it true that we came from an apelike beast that lived millions of years ago? Did this great universe just come about by accident?

[4] The Bible says: "In the beginning God created the heavens and the earth." (Genesis 1:1) And the facts of science agree that the heavens, with their billions of stars, and our earth had a beginning. They were created. The movements of the stars and the planets are so regular that even years in advance their position can be determined with perfect accuracy. The stars and the planets move in the universe according to the laws and

3. What is the teaching of evolution?
4. Why can we believe that "God created the heavens and the earth"?

principles of mathematics. A professor of mathematics from the University of Cambridge, P. Dirac, said, in the magazine *Scientific American:* "One could perhaps describe the situation by saying that God is a mathematician of a very high order, and He used very advanced mathematics in constructing the universe."

⁵ The Bible states: "Know that Jehovah is God. It is he that has made us, and not we ourselves." (Psalm 100:3) Our human body shows such wonderful design that one Bible writer was moved to say to God: "I shall laud you because in a fear-inspiring way I am wonderfully made. . . . My bones were not hidden from you when I was made in secret . . . Your eyes saw even the embryo of me, and in your book all its parts were down in writing." (Psalm 139:14-16) A baby develops inside its mother in a wonderful way. *Newsweek* magazine said of this: "It is, quite simply, a miracle." Then it added: "No technique can pinpoint the momentous time of conception. No scientist can tell what wondrous forces then take over to develop the organs and myriad nerve networks of a human embryo."

⁶ Think about our great universe, as well as our own body with its wonderful construction and design. Sound reasoning should tell us that these things did not simply evolve or come by themselves. They had to have a Designer, a Creator. Consider other things that we see around us. When you are in your house, ask yourself: Did my desk, lamp, bed, chair, table, walls, or even the house itself, evolve? Or did they need a maker? Of course intelligent persons had to make them! In what way, then, can it be claimed that our much more complex universe and we ourselves did not require a maker? And if God put us here, he surely had a reason for doing so.

⁷ Jesus Christ himself said of the first man and woman: "He who created them from the beginning made them male and female and said, 'For this reason a man will leave his father and

---

5. How does our physical body show that we were created rather than being a product of evolution?
6. Why does it make sense for us to believe in creation rather than in evolution?
7. (a) How did Jesus show that he believed in creation? (b) What further evidence is there that Adam was a real person?

his mother and will stick to his wife, and the two will be one flesh.' " (Matthew 19:4, 5) Here Jesus quoted from Genesis 1:27 and 2:24 regarding the creation of Adam and Eve. He was thus pointing to this Bible account as being the truth. (John 17:17) Also, the Bible calls Enoch "the *seventh one* in line from Adam." (Jude 14) If Adam had not been a real person, the Bible would not have identified him in this specific way.—Luke 3:37, 38.

[8] Some persons say that God used the process of evolution to create man. They claim that God allowed man to evolve, and when he reached a certain point He put a soul into him. But nowhere in the Bible does this idea appear. Rather, the Bible says that plants and animals were created "according to their kinds." (Genesis 1:11, 21, 24) And the facts show that one kind of plant or animal does not, in time, develop into another kind. More information to prove that we are not the product of evolution can be found in the book *Did Man Get Here by Evolution or by Creation?*

HOW GOD CREATED MAN

[9] God created man from the earth to live on the earth, as the Bible says: "Jehovah God proceeded to form the man out of dust from the ground and to blow into his nostrils the breath of life, and the man came to be a living soul." (Genesis 2:7) From this we can see that man was a direct creation of God. In a special act of creation, God made man a complete, whole person. When God blew into man's nostrils the "breath of life," man's lungs were filled with air. *But more than that was accomplished.* God thereby gave *life* to the man's body. This *life-force* is sustained, or kept going, by breathing.

[10] Notice, however, that the Bible does not say that God *gave* man a soul. Rather, it says that after God started man breathing *"the man came to be a living soul."* So the man *was* a soul, just as a man who becomes a doctor *is* a doctor. (1 Corinthians 15:45)

---

8. What view of man's beginning does the Bible not teach?
9. (a) How does the Bible describe man's creation? (b) What happened when God blew into man's nostrils the "breath of life"?
10. What is the human soul, and how was it created?

The "dust from the ground," from which the physical body is formed, is not the soul. Nor does the Bible say that the "breath of life" is the soul. Rather, the Bible shows that the putting together of these two things is what resulted in *'man's becoming a living soul.'*

[11] Since the human soul is man himself, then it cannot be some shadowy thing that lives inside the body or that can leave the body. Simply put, the Bible teaches that your soul is *you.* For example, the Bible speaks of the soul's wanting to eat physical food, saying: "Your soul craves to eat meat." (Deuteronomy 12:20) It also says that souls have blood traveling through their veins, for it speaks of "the blood marks of the souls of the innocent poor ones."—Jeremiah 2:34.

WHY GOD PUT MAN HERE

[12] It was not God's purpose for Adam and Eve to die after a while and live somewhere else. They were to stay here to take care of the earth and all its living things. As the Bible says: "God *blessed them* and God said to them: 'Be fruitful and become many and fill the earth and subdue it, and have in subjection the fish of the sea and the flying creatures of the heavens and every living creature that is moving upon the earth.' " (Genesis 1:28; 2:15) Adam and Eve, as well as all the children they would have, could have been happy on earth forever, doing the things that God wanted them to do.

[13] Notice that "God *blessed them.*" He really cared about his earthly children. So as a loving Father he gave them instructions that were for their good. They would have found happiness in obeying them. Jesus knew this and so later said: "Happy are those hearing the word of God and keeping it!" (Luke 11:28) Jesus kept God's word. "I always do the things pleasing to him," he said. (John 8:29) This is the key to the very reason we are here. *It is to have full, happy lives by living in harmony with*

---

11. What Bible facts about the human soul show that it could not be a shadowy thing that can exist apart from a person?
12. What was God's purpose for humans on the earth?
13. (a) How can we be happy? (b) What will give real meaning to our lives?

God's will. It will give real meaning to our lives now to serve Jehovah. And by doing so we will be putting ourselves in line to live forever in Paradise on earth.—Psalm 37:11, 29.

WHY WE GROW OLD AND DIE

[14] But now we all grow old and die. Why? As noted in the previous chapter, it is because of the rebellion of Adam and Eve. Jehovah had placed upon them a test that showed the need of their being obedient to God. He said to Adam: "From every tree of the garden you may eat to satisfaction. But as for the tree of the knowledge of good and bad you must not eat from it, for in the day you eat from it you will positively die." (Genesis 2:16, 17) By eating from this tree, Adam and Eve turned their backs on their heavenly Father and rejected his guidance. They disobeyed and took what did not belong to them. They could have lived happily in a paradise forever without poverty or sufferings, but now they brought upon themselves the penalty of sin. This penalty is imperfection and death.—Romans 6:23.

[15] Do you know how we got our sin from Adam? After Adam became imperfect, he passed on to all his children that imperfection and death. (Job 14:4; Romans 5:12) As a help in your understanding the situation, think of what happens when a baker bakes bread in a pan that has a dent in it. A mark will show on all the bread that is baked in that pan. Adam became like that pan, and we are like the bread. He became imperfect when he broke God's law. It was as if he received a dent or a bad mark. So when he had children all of them received this same mark of sin or imperfection.

[16] We get sick and grow old now because of the sin that all of us have received from Adam. One of the miracles Jesus performed shows this. While Jesus was teaching in the home where he was staying, a large crowd gathered so that nobody else could squeeze into the room. When four men brought a paralyzed man

---

14. By disobeying God's command, what did Adam and Eve do?
15. How did we get our sin from Adam?
16, 17. How does one of Jesus' miracles show that sickness has come upon the human family because of sin?

The Bible account of Jesus' healing of the paralytic shows that people get sick because of Adam's sin

lying on a cot, they saw they could not get inside. So they went up to the roof, made a hole in it, and lowered the cot with the paralyzed man on it right down next to Jesus.

17 When Jesus saw how much faith they had, he said to the paralyzed man: "Your sins are forgiven." But some of the people present did not think that Jesus could forgive sins. So Jesus said: " 'In order for you men to know that the Son of man has authority to forgive sins upon the earth,'—he said to the paralytic: 'I say to you, Get up, pick up your cot, and go to your home.' At that he did get up, and immediately picked up his cot and walked out in front of them all."—Mark 2:1-12.

18 Just think of what this power of Jesus can mean for us! Under the rule of God's kingdom, Christ will be able to forgive the sins of all persons who love and serve God. This means that all aches and pains and sicknesses will be removed. No one will ever have to grow old and die! What a wonderful hope this is for the future! Yes, there is truly much more that we can expect than being born, living a short time and then dying. By continuing to learn about God and by serving him, we really can live forever in Paradise on earth.

18. To what kind of future can servants of God look forward?

Chapter 8

What Happens at Death?

PERHAPS you know the empty feeling that comes with losing a loved one in death. How very sad and helpless you can feel! It is only natural to ask: What happens to a person when he dies? Is he still alive somewhere? Will the living ever again be able to enjoy on earth the company of those now dead?

[2] To answer such questions, it will be a help for us to know what happened to Adam at his death. When he sinned, God told him: "You [will] return to the ground, for out of it you were taken. For dust you are and to dust you will return." (Genesis 3:19) Think of what that means. Before God created him from the dust, there was no Adam. He did not exist. So, after he died, Adam returned to that same state of nonexistence.

[3] Simply stated, death is the opposite of life. The Bible shows this at Ecclesiastes 9:5, 10. According to the *Authorized* or *King James Version,* these verses say: "For the living know that they shall die; *but the dead know not any thing,* neither have they any more a reward; for the memory of them is for-

ADAM—

made from dust . . .

returned to dust

---

1. What questions do people often ask about the dead?

2. What happened to the first man, Adam, at his death?

3. (a) What is death? (b) What does Ecclesiastes 9:5, 10 say about the condition of the dead?

gotten. Whatsoever thy hand findeth to do, do it with thy might; for there is no work, nor device, nor knowledge, nor wisdom, in the grave, whither thou goest."

[4] This means that the dead cannot do anything and cannot feel anything. They no longer have any thoughts, as the Bible states: "Do not put your trust in nobles, nor in the son of earthling man, to whom no salvation belongs. His spirit goes out, he goes back to his ground; *in that day his thoughts do perish.*" (Psalm 146:3, 4) At death man's spirit, his life-force, which is sustained by breathing, "goes out." It no longer exists. So man's senses of hearing, sight, touch, smell and taste, which depend upon his being able to think, all stop working. According to the Bible, the dead enter a state of complete unconsciousness.

[5] When they are dead, both humans and animals are in this same state of complete unconsciousness. Note how the Bible makes this point: "As the one dies, so the other dies; and they all have but one spirit, so that there is no superiority of the man over the beast, for everything is vanity. All are going to one place. They have all come to be from the dust, and they are all returning to the dust." (Ecclesiastes 3:19, 20) The "spirit" that makes animals live is the same as that which makes humans live. When this "spirit," or invisible life-force, goes out, both man and beast return to the dust from which they are made.

THE SOUL DIES

[6] Some persons have said that what makes man different from the animals is that man has a soul but the animals do not. However, Genesis 1:20 and 30 says that God created *"living souls"* to live in the waters, and that the animals have *"life as a soul."* In these verses some Bibles use the words "creature" and "life" instead of "soul," but their marginal readings agree that the word "soul" is what appears in the original language. Among

---

4. (a) What happens to a person's thinking abilities at death? (b) Why do a person's senses all stop working at death?
5. (a) How does the Bible show that the condition of dead humans and dead animals is the same? (b) What is the "spirit" that makes both humans and animals live?
6. How does the Bible show that animals are souls?

What was Lazarus' condition
before Jesus raised him?

the Bible references to animals as souls is Numbers 31:28. There it speaks of "one soul out of five hundred, of humankind and of the herd and of the asses and of the flock."

[7] Since animals are souls, when they die their souls die. As the Bible says: "Every living soul died, yes, the things in the sea." (Revelation 16:3) What about human souls? As we learned in the previous chapter, God did not create man *with* a soul. Man *is* a soul. So, as we would expect, when man dies, his soul dies. Over and over again the Bible says that this is true. Never does the Bible say the soul is deathless or that it cannot die. "All

7. What does the Bible say to prove that both animal souls and human souls die?

those going down to the dust will bend down, and no one will ever preserve his own soul alive," Psalm 22:29 says. "The soul that is sinning—it itself will die," explains Ezekiel 18:4 and 20. And if you turn to Joshua 10:28-39, you will find seven places where the soul is spoken of as being killed or destroyed.

8 In a prophecy about Jesus Christ, the Bible says: "He poured out his soul to the very death . . . and he himself carried the very sin of many people." (Isaiah 53:12) The teaching of the ransom proves it was a soul (Adam) that sinned, and that in order to ransom humans there had to be a corresponding soul (a man) sacrificed. Christ, by 'pouring out his soul unto death,' provided the ransom price. Jesus, the human soul, died.

9 As we have seen, the "spirit" is something different from our soul. The spirit is our life-force. This life-force is in each of the body cells of both humans and animals. It is sustained, or kept alive, by breathing. What does it mean, then, when the Bible says that at death "the dust returns to the earth . . . and the spirit itself returns to the true God who gave it"? (Ecclesiastes 12:7) At death the life-force in time leaves all the body cells and the body begins to decay. But this does not mean that our life-force literally leaves the earth and travels through space to God. Rather, the spirit returns to God in the sense that now our hope for future life rests entirely with God. Only by his power can the spirit, or life-force, be given back so that we live again.—Psalm 104:29, 30.

LAZARUS—A MAN DEAD FOR FOUR DAYS

10 What happened to Lazarus, who was dead for four days, helps us to understand the condition of the dead. Jesus had told his disciples: "Lazarus our friend has gone to rest, but I am journeying there to awaken him from sleep." However, the disciples replied: "Lord, if he has gone to rest, he will get well." At that, Jesus told them plainly: "Lazarus has died."

---

8. How do we know that the human soul, Jesus Christ, died?
9. What is meant by the words, 'the spirit itself returns to God who gave it'?
10. Even though Lazarus had died, what did Jesus say about his condition?

Why did Jesus say Lazarus was sleeping when really he had died? Let us see.

[11] When Jesus got near the village where Lazarus had lived, he was met by Martha, the sister of Lazarus. Soon they, along with many others, went to the tomb where Lazarus had been put. It was a cave, and a stone was lying against it. Jesus said: "Take the stone away." Since Lazarus had been dead for four days, Martha protested: "Lord, by now he must smell." But the stone was removed, and Jesus called out: "Lazarus, come on out!" And he did! He came out alive, still wrapped in graveclothes. "Loose him and let him go," Jesus said.—John 11:11-44.

[12] Now think about this: What was Lazarus' condition during those four days he was dead? Had he been in heaven? He was a good man. Yet Lazarus did not say anything about being in heaven, which surely he would have done if he had been there. No, Lazarus was really dead, even as Jesus said he was. Then why did Jesus at first tell his disciples that Lazarus was only sleeping?

[13] Well, Jesus knew that the dead Lazarus was unconscious, as the Bible says: "The dead . . . are conscious of nothing at all." (Ecclesiastes 9:5) But a living person can be awakened from a deep sleep. So Jesus was going to show that, by means of God's power given to him, his friend Lazarus could be awakened from death.

[14] When a person is in a very deep sleep, he remembers nothing. It is similar with the dead. They have no feelings at all. They no longer exist. But, in God's due time, the dead who are ransomed by God will be raised to life. (John 5:28) Surely this knowledge should move us to want to win God's favor. If we do, even if we should die, we will be remembered by God and be brought back to life.—1 Thessalonians 4:13, 14.

---

11. What did Jesus do for the dead Lazarus?

12, 13. (a) Why can we be sure that Lazarus was unconscious when he was dead? (b) Why did Jesus say that Lazarus was asleep when, really, he was dead?

14. Knowledge of Christ's power to raise the dead should move us to do what?

Chapter 9

What Kind of Place Is Hell?

MILLIONS of persons have been taught by their religions that hell is a place where people are tormented. According to the *Encyclopædia Britannica*, "The Roman Catholic Church teaches that hell . . . will last forever; its suffering will have no end." This Catholic teaching, the encyclopedia goes on to say, "is still held by many conservative Protestant groups." Hindus, Buddhists and Muhammadans also teach that hell is a place of torment. No wonder that people who have been taught this often say that if hell is such a bad place they do not want to talk about it.

² This raises the question: Did Almighty God create such a place of torment? Well, what was God's view when the Israelites, following the example of peoples who lived nearby, began to burn their children in fire? He explains in his Word: "They have built the high places of Topheth, which is in the valley of the son of Hinnom, in order to burn their sons and their daughters in the fire, *a thing that I had not commanded and that had not come up into my heart.*"—Jeremiah 7:31.

³ Think about this. If the idea of roasting people in fire had never come into God's heart, does it seem reasonable that he created a fiery hell for those who do not serve him? The Bible says, "God is love." (1 John 4:8) Would a loving God really torment people forever? Would *you* do so? Knowing of God's love should move us to turn to his Word to find out just what hell is. Who go there, and for how long?

1. What have religions taught about hell?
2. What did God think of the burning of children in fire?
3. Why is it unreasonable, as well as unscriptural, to think that God would torment people?

SHEOL AND HADES

[4] *Webster's Dictionary* says that the English word "hell" is equal to the Hebrew word *Sheol* and the Greek word *Hades*. In German Bibles *Hoelle* is the word used instead of "hell"; in Portuguese the word used is *inferno,* in Spanish *infierno,* and in French *Enfer.* The English translators of the *Authorized Version,* or *King James Version,* translated *Sheol* 31 times as "hell," 31 times as "grave," and 3 times as "pit." The Catholic *Douay Version* translated Sheol 64 times as "hell." In the Christian Greek Scriptures (commonly called the "New Testament"), the *King James Version* translated Hades as "hell" each of the 10 times it occurs.—Matthew 11:23; 16:18; Luke 10:15; 16:23; Acts 2:27, 31; Revelation 1:18; 6:8; 20:13, 14.

[5] The question is: What kind of place is Sheol, or Hades? The fact that the *King James Version* translates the one Hebrew word *Sheol* three different ways shows that *hell, grave* and *pit* mean one and the same thing. And if hell means the common grave of mankind, it could not at the same time mean a place of fiery torture. Well, then, do Sheol and Hades mean the grave, or do they mean a place of torture?

[6] Before answering this question, let us make clear that the Hebrew word *Sheol* and the Greek word *Hades* mean the same thing. This is shown by looking at Psalm 16:10 in the Hebrew Scriptures and Acts 2:31 in the Christian Greek Scriptures, which verses you can see on the next page. Notice that in quoting from Psalm 16:10 where Sheol occurs, Acts 2:31 uses Hades. Notice, too, that Jesus Christ was in Hades, or hell. Are we to believe that God tormented Christ in a hell of fire? Of course not! Jesus was simply in his grave.

[7] When Jacob was mourning for his beloved son Joseph, whom he thought had been killed, he said: "I shall go down mourning

---

4. (a) What Hebrew and Greek words are translated "hell"? (b) How is Sheol translated in the *King James Version?*
5. What question is raised regarding Sheol and Hades?
6. (a) How does the Bible show that Sheol and Hades mean the same thing? (b) What is shown by the fact that Jesus was in Hades?
7, 8. How does what is said about Jacob and his son Joseph, and about Job, prove that Sheol is not a place of torment?

Psalm 16:10

9 Therefore my heart is glad,
and my glory rejoiceth:
My flesh also shall dwell in
safety.
10 For thou wilt not leave my soul
to Shĕ'ōl;
Neither wilt thou suffer thy
holy one to see corruption.
11 Thou wilt show me the path of
life:
In thy presence is fulness of joy;

Acts 2:31

30 Being therefore a prophet, and
knowing that God had sworn with
an oath to him, that of the fruit of
his loins he would set *one* upon his
throne; 31 he foreseeing *this* spake
of the resurrection of the Christ,
that neither was he left unto
Hā'dēs, nor did his flesh see
corruption. 32 This Jĕ'sus did
God raise up, whereof we all are
witnesses. 33 Being therefore [11]by

American Standard Version

The Hebrew word "Sheol" and the Greek word "Hades"
mean the same thing

to my son into Sheol!" (Genesis 37:35) However, the *King James
Version* here translates Sheol "grave," and the *Douay Version*
translates it "hell." Now, stop for a moment and think. Did
Jacob believe that his son Joseph went to a place of torment
to spend eternity there, and did he want to go there and meet
him? Or, rather, was it that Jacob merely thought that his
beloved son was dead and in the grave and that Jacob himself
wanted to die?

⁸ Yes, good people go to the Bible hell. For example, the good
man Job, who was suffering a great deal, prayed to God: "O
that in Sheol [grave, *King James Version;* hell, *Douay Version*]
you would conceal me, . . . that you would set a time limit for
me and remember me!" (Job 14:13) Now think: If Sheol means
a place of fire and torment, would Job wish to go and spend
his time there until God remembered him? Clearly, Job wanted
to die and go to the grave that his sufferings might end.

⁹ In all the places where Sheol occurs in the Bible it is never
associated with life, activity or torment. Rather, it is often linked
with death and inactivity. For example, think about Ecclesiastes
9:10, which reads: "All that your hand finds to do, do with your
very power, for there is no work nor devising nor knowledge
nor wisdom in Sheol [grave, *King James Version;* hell, *Douay
Version*], the place to which you are going." So the answer
becomes very clear. Sheol and Hades refer not to a place of
torment but to the common grave of all mankind. (Psalm 139:8)

9. (a) What is the condition of those in Sheol? (b) So what are Sheol and Hades?

Good people as well as bad people
go to the Bible hell.

GETTING OUT OF HELL

10 Can people get out of hell? Consider the case of Jonah. When God
had a big fish swallow Jonah to save
him from drowning, Jonah prayed
from the fish's belly: "Out of my
distress I called out to Jehovah, and
he proceeded to answer me. Out of
the belly of Sheol [hell, *King James
Version* and *Douay Version* (2:3)] I

10, 11. Why did Jonah, while in the fish's
belly, say he was in hell?

After he was swallowed by a fish,
why did Jonah say:
'Out of the belly of hell I cried'?

cried for help. You heard my voice."—Jonah 2:2.

[11] What did Jonah mean by *"out of the belly of hell"*? Well, that fish's belly was surely not a place of fiery torment. But it could have become Jonah's grave. In fact, Jesus Christ said regarding himself: "Just as Jonah was in the belly of the huge fish three days and three nights, so the Son of man will be in the heart of the earth three days and three nights."—Matthew 12:40.

[12] Jesus was dead and in his grave for three days. But the Bible reports: "His soul was not left in hell . . . This Jesus hath God raised up." (Acts 2:31, 32, *King James Version*) Similarly, by God's direction Jonah was raised from hell, that is, from what would have been his grave. This happened when the fish vomited him out onto dry land. Yes, people can get out of hell! In fact, the heartwarming promise is that hell (Hades) is to be emptied of all its dead. This can be seen by reading Revelation 20:13, which says: "The sea gave up the dead which were in it; and death and hell [Hades] delivered up the dead which were in them: and they were judged every man according to their works."—*King James Version.*

GEHENNA AND THE LAKE OF FIRE

[13] Yet someone may object, saying: 'The Bible does talk about *hellfire* and the *lake of fire*. Does this not prove that hell is a place of torment?' True, some Bible translations, such as the *King James Version,* speak of "hell fire" and of being "cast into hell, into the fire that shall never be quenched." (Matthew 5:22;

12. (a) What proof is there that those in hell can get out? (b) What further evidence is there that "hell" means the "grave"?

13. What Greek word that occurs 12 times in the Bible is translated "hell" in the *King James Version?*

Mark 9:45) All together there are 12 verses in the Christian Greek Scriptures where the *King James Version* uses "hell" to translate the Greek word *Gehenna.* Is Gehenna really a place of fiery torment, whereas when Hades is translated "hell" it simply means the grave?

[14] Clearly, the Hebrew word *Sheol* and the Greek word *Hades* do mean the grave. Well, then, what does Gehenna mean? In the Hebrew Scriptures Gehenna is "the valley Hinnom." Remember, Hinnom was the name of the valley just outside the walls of Jerusalem where the Israelites sacrificed their children in the fire. In time, good King Josiah

14. What is Gehenna, and what was done there?

Gehenna was a valley outside Jerusalem. It was used as a symbol of everlasting death

had this valley made unfit to be used for such a horrible practice. (2 Kings 23:10) It was turned into a huge garbage, or rubbish, dump.

15 So during the time Jesus was on earth Gehenna was Jerusalem's garbage dump. Fires were kept burning there by the adding of brimstone (sulfur) to burn up the garbage. *Smith's Dictionary of the Bible,* Volume 1, explains: "It became the common lay-stall [garbage dump] of the city, where the dead bodies of criminals, and the carcasses of animals, and every other kind of filth was cast." No live creatures, however, were cast there.

16 Knowing about their city's garbage dump, Jerusalem's inhabitants understood what Jesus meant when he told the wicked religious leaders: "Serpents, offspring of vipers, how are you to flee from the judgment of Gehenna?" (Matthew 23:33) Jesus plainly did not mean that those religious leaders would be tormented. Why, when the Israelites were burning their children alive in that valley, God said that to do such a horrible thing had never come up into his heart! So it was clear that Jesus was using Gehenna as a fitting symbol of complete and everlasting destruction. He meant that those wicked religious leaders were not worthy of a resurrection. Those listening to Jesus could understand that those going to Gehenna, like so much garbage, would be destroyed forever.

17 What, then, is "the lake of fire" mentioned in the Bible book of Revelation? It has a meaning similar to that of Gehenna. It means not conscious torment but everlasting death, or destruction. Notice how the Bible itself says this at Revelation 20:14: "And death and Hades [hell, *King James Version* and *Douay Version*] were hurled into the lake of fire. *This means the second death, the lake of fire.*" Yes, the lake of fire means "second death," the death from which there is no resurrection. It is evident that this "lake" is a symbol, because death and hell (Hades) are thrown into it. Death and hell cannot literally be

---

15. (a) In Jesus' day, for what purpose was Gehenna used? (b) What was never thrown there?
16. What evidence is there that Gehenna was used as a symbol of everlasting destruction?
17. What is "the lake of fire," and what proof is there of this?

burned. But they can, and will, be done away with, or destroyed.

[18] 'Yet the Bible says that the Devil will be tormented forever in the lake of fire,' someone may point out. (Revelation 20:10) What does this mean? When Jesus was on earth jailers were at times called "tormentors." As Jesus said of a certain man in one of his illustrations: "And his lord was wroth, and delivered him to the tormentors, till he should pay all that was due unto him." (Matthew 18:34, *King James Version*) Since those who are thrown into "the lake of fire" go into "second death" from which there is no resurrection, they are, so to speak, jailed forever in death. They remain in death as though in the custody of jailers for all eternity. The wicked, of course, are not literally tormented because, as we have seen, when a person is dead he is completely out of existence. He is not conscious of anything.

THE RICH MAN AND LAZARUS

[19] What, then, did Jesus mean when he said in one of his illustrations: "The beggar died, and was carried by the angels into Abraham's bosom: the rich man also died, and was buried; and in hell [Hades] he lift up his eyes, being in torments, and seeth Abraham afar off, and Lazarus in his bosom"? (Luke 16:19-31, *King James Version*) Since, as we have seen, Hades refers to mankind's grave, and not to a place of torment, it is plain that Jesus was here telling an illustration or a story. As further evidence that this is not a literal account but is an illustration, consider this: Is hell literally within speaking distance of heaven so that such a real conversation could be carried on? Moreover, if the rich man were in a literal burning lake, how could Abraham send Lazarus to cool his tongue with just a drop of water on the tip of his finger? What, then, was Jesus illustrating?

[20] The rich man in the illustration stood for the self-important

---

18. What does it mean that the Devil will be tormented forever in "the lake of fire"?
19. How do we know that Jesus' words about the rich man and Lazarus are an illustration?
20. What is the meaning of the illustration with regard to (a) the rich man? (b) Lazarus? (c) the death of each? (d) the torments of the rich man?

religious leaders who rejected Jesus and later killed him. Lazarus pictured the common people who accepted God's Son. The death of the rich man and of Lazarus represented a change in their condition. This change took place when Jesus fed the neglected Lazarus-like people spiritually, so that they thus came into the favor of the Greater Abraham, Jehovah God. At the same time, the false religious leaders "died" with respect to having God's favor. Being cast off, they suffered torments when Christ's followers exposed their evil works. (Acts 7:51-57) So this illustration does not teach that some dead persons are tormented in a literal fiery hell.

DEVIL-INSPIRED TEACHINGS

[21] It was the Devil who told Eve: "You positively will not die." (Genesis 3:4; Revelation 12:9) But she *did* die; no part of her lived on. That the soul lives on after death is a lie started by the Devil. And it is also a lie, which the Devil has had spread, that the souls of the wicked are tormented in a hell or a purgatory. Since the Bible clearly shows that the dead are unconscious, these teachings could not be true. Actually, neither the word "purgatory" nor the idea of a purgatory is found in the Bible.

[22] We have seen that hell (Sheol, or Hades) is a place of rest in hope for the dead. Both good and bad persons go there, to await the resurrection. We have also learned that Gehenna does not mean a place of torment, but is used in the Bible as a symbol of everlasting destruction. In the same way, "the lake of fire" is not a literal place of fire, but represents the "second death" from which there will be no resurrection. Hell could not be a place of torment because such an idea never came into the mind or heart of God. Additionally, to torment a person *eternally* because he did wrong on earth *for a few years* is contrary to justice. How good it is to know the truth about the dead! It can truly set one free from fear and superstition.—John 8:32.

---

21. (a) What lies has the Devil spread? (b) Why can we be sure that the teaching of purgatory is false?
22. (a) What have we learned from this chapter? (b) What effect has this knowledge had upon you?

Chapter 10

Wicked Spirits Are Powerful

OFTEN PEOPLE say they have talked with the dead. The late James A. Pike, a prominent Episcopalian bishop, said he talked with his dead son, Jim. According to Pike, his son told him: "I have masses of people around me, and hands lifting me up, as it were . . . I was so unhappy until I could make you know."

² Since such experiences are so common, it is evident that many people have spoken with *someone* from the spirit world. *But they have not talked with the dead.* The Bible is very clear when it says: "As for the dead, *they are conscious of nothing at all.*" (Ecclesiastes 9:5) So if it is not the dead who are speaking from the spirit world, who are speaking? Who are pretending to be dead persons?

³ Wicked spirits are. These spirits, or demons, are the angels who joined Satan in rebellion against God. Why do they pretend to be persons who have died? It is to advance the idea that the dead are still living. Wicked spirits have also led many to believe the lie that death is only a change to another life. To spread this lie, wicked spirits provide spirit mediums, fortune-tellers and sorcerers with special knowledge that only *seems* to come from persons who have died.

PRETENDING TO BE DEAD SAMUEL

⁴ There is an example in the Bible of a wicked spirit who pretended to be a dead prophet of God, Samuel. This was in the 40th year of King Saul's reign. A powerful army

1. Why do many persons believe that they can talk with the dead?
2. (a) Why can nobody talk with the dead? (b) So what questions are raised?
3. (a) Who pretend to be dead persons, and why? (b) To whom do wicked spirits often give information?
4. (a) Why was King Saul desperate for help? (b) What was God's law regarding spirit mediums and fortune-tellers?

With whom did
the spirit medium
of En-dor get in touch?

of Philistines had come up against Saul's Israelite army, and he was very much afraid. Saul knew God's law: "Do not turn yourselves to the spirit mediums, and do not consult professional foretellers of events, so as to become unclean by them." (Leviticus 19:31) In time, however, Saul turned away from Jehovah. Therefore Samuel, who at the time was alive, refused any longer to see Saul. (1 Samuel 15:35) And now, in this time of trouble, King Saul was desperate because Jehovah would not listen to his calls for help.

⁵ Saul was so eager to learn about what was going to happen that he went to a spirit medium in En-dor. She was able to bring forth the form of a person that she could see. By her description of the form, Saul identified him as "Samuel." At this the spirit person, pretending to be Samuel, spoke: "Why have you disturbed me by having me brought up?" Saul answered: "I am in very sore straits, as the Philistines are fighting against me." The spirit person replied: "Why, then, do you inquire of me, when Jehovah himself has departed from you and proves to be your adversary?" The wicked spirit person, who was pretending to be the dead Samuel, then went on to tell Saul that he would be killed in the battle with the Philistines.—1 Samuel 28:3-19.

⁶ Obviously, it was not really Samuel that the spirit medium

5. (a) Where did Saul go for help? (b) What was the spirit medium able to do?
6. Why could it not have been Samuel who spoke with Saul?

had contacted. Samuel was dead, and at death a person "goes back to his ground; *in that day his thoughts do perish*." (Psalm 146:4)

A little thinking on the matter further shows that the voice was not really that of dead Samuel. Samuel was God's prophet. So he had opposed spirit mediums. And, as we have seen, while he was alive he had refused to speak any more with disobedient Saul. So, then, if Samuel were still alive, would he allow a spirit medium to arrange for him to meet Saul? Think too: Jehovah had refused to give Saul any information. Could a spirit medium force Jehovah to give Saul a message through dead Samuel? And if the living could actually talk with dead loved ones, surely a God of love would not say that they had become "unclean" because of turning to a spirit medium.

7 The fact is that wicked spirits are out to harm humans, so Jehovah gives warnings to protect his servants. Read the following warning to the nation of Israel. It gives you an idea of methods that the demons use to mislead people. The Bible says: "There should not be found in you . . . anyone who employs divination, a practicer of magic or anyone who looks for omens or a sorcerer, or one who binds others with a spell or anyone who consults a spirit medium or a professional foreteller of events *or anyone who inquires of the dead*. For everybody doing these things is something *detestable* to Jehovah." (Deuteronomy 18:10-12) We should want to find out what wicked spirits are doing to harm people today and how we can protect ourselves from them. But before we learn about this, let us consider when and how the wicked spirits got their start.

---

7. What warning did God give to protect his people against wicked spirits?

ANGELS THAT BECAME WICKED SPIRITS

[8] By lying to Eve in the garden of Eden, a certain angelic creature made himself the wicked spirit Satan the Devil. Afterward he began trying to get other angels also to turn against God. In time he succeeded. Some angels stopped the work that God had given them to do in heaven, and they came down to earth and made for themselves fleshly bodies like those of humans. The Christian disciple Jude wrote about them when he mentioned "the angels that did not keep their original position but forsook their own proper dwelling place." (Jude 6) Why did they come to the earth? What wrong desire did Satan put in their heart to get them to leave the fine positions they had in heaven?

[9] The Bible lets us know when it says: "The sons of the true God began to notice the daughters of men, that they were good-looking; and they went taking wives for themselves, namely,

all whom they chose." (Genesis 6:2) Yes, the angels put on fleshly bodies. Then they came to earth to have sexual relations with beautiful women. But such love affairs were wrong for angels. This was an act of disobedience. The Bible indicates that what they did was just as wrong as the homosexual acts of the people of Sodom and Gomorrah. (Jude 6, 7) What resulted?

8. (a) Who did Satan also get to rebel against God? (b) After stopping their work in heaven, where did they go?

9. (a) Why did the angels come to earth? (b) How does the Bible show that what they did was wrong?

The materialized angels did not drown.
They put aside their fleshly bodies
and returned to heaven

¹⁰ Well, babies were born to these angels and their wives. But the babies were different. They kept growing bigger until they became giants, yes, wicked giants. The Bible calls them "mighty ones who were of old, the men of fame." These giants tried to force everyone to be bad as they were. As a result, the Bible says that "the badness of man was abundant in the earth and every inclination of the thoughts of his heart was only bad all the time." (Genesis 6:4, 5) So Jehovah brought the Flood. The giants, or "Nephilim," and all the wicked people were drowned. But what happened to the angels that had come to earth?

¹¹ They did not drown. They put aside their fleshly bodies and returned to heaven as spirit persons. But they were not allowed to become part of God's organization of holy angels again. Instead, the Bible says that "God did not hold back from punishing the angels that sinned, but, by throwing them

---

10, 11. (a) What kind of children did the angels have? (b) What happened to the giants when the Flood came? (c) What happened to the angels at the time of the Flood?

into Tartarus, delivered them to pits of dense darkness to be reserved for judgment."—2 Peter 2:4.

[12] These wicked angels were not thrown into a literal place called Tartarus. Rather, Tartarus, which is mistranslated "hell" in some Bibles, refers to the abased or fallen condition of these angels. They were cut off from the spiritual light of God's organization, and they have only everlasting destruction awaiting them. (James 2:19; Jude 6) Since the time of the Flood, God has not permitted these demon angels to take on fleshly bodies, so they cannot directly satisfy their unnatural sexual desires. Yet they can still exercise dangerous power over men and women. In fact, with the help of these demons Satan is "misleading the entire inhabited earth." (Revelation 12:9) The great increase today in sexual crimes, violence and other wrongdoing shows our need to be on guard against being misled by them.

HOW WICKED SPIRITS MISLEAD

[13] We learned earlier that Satan, as "the god of this system of things," uses worldly governments and false religion to blind people to Bible truths. (2 Corinthians 4:4) Another important way that wicked spirits mislead men and women is through spiritism. What is spiritism? It is the getting in touch with wicked spirits, either directly or through a human medium. Spiritism brings a person under the influence of the demons. The Bible warns us to keep free from every practice connected with spiritism.—Galatians 5:19-21; Revelation 21:8.

[14] Divination is a very common form of spiritism. It is the practice of trying to find out about the future, or about something unknown, with the help of unseen spirits. This is shown by what the Christian disciple Luke wrote: "A certain servant girl with a spirit, a demon of divination, met us. She used to furnish her masters with much gain by practicing the art of

---

12. (a) What happened to the wicked angels when they returned to heaven? (b) Why can they not take on human bodies again? (c) So what are they now doing?
13. (a) How do wicked spirits mislead? (b) What is spiritism, and what does the Bible say about it?
14. (a) What is divination? (b) What does the Bible say about it?

prediction." The apostle Paul was able to free the girl from the power of this wicked spirit, and no longer was she able to foretell the future.—Acts 16:16-19.

[15] Many persons are interested in spiritism because it is mysterious and strange. It fascinates them. So they become involved with witchcraft, voodooism, hypnotism, magic, astrology, Ouija boards or something else connected with spiritism. They may read books about these things, or go to movies, or watch television programs about them. They may even go to a meeting where a medium seeks to contact the spirit world. But all of this is unwise for a person who wants to serve the true God. It is also dangerous. It can lead to real trouble now. Also, God will judge and cast away from him all practicers of spiritism. —Revelation 22:15.

[16] Even when a person does all he can to keep free from spiritism, he may still come under attack by wicked spirits. Recall that the voice of the Devil himself was heard by Jesus Christ, tempting him to break God's law. (Matthew 4:8, 9) Other servants of God have had such attacks. The apostle Paul said: "We have a wrestling . . . against the wicked spirit forces in the heavenly places." This means that every servant of God must "take up the complete suit of armor from God, that [he] may be able to resist."—Ephesians 6:11-13.

RESISTING WICKED SPIRIT ATTACKS

[17] What should you do if a "voice" from the spirit world speaks to you? What if the "voice" pretends to be a dead relative or a good spirit? Well, what did Jesus do when the "ruler of the demons" spoke to him? (Matthew 9:34) He said: "Go away, Satan!" (Matthew 4:10) You can do that too. Also, you can call on Jehovah for help. Pray out loud and use God's name. Remember that he is more powerful than are wicked spirits. Follow this wise course. Do not listen to such voices from the

---

15. (a) What are some things connected with spiritism? (b) Why is taking part in such things dangerous?
16. How does the Bible show that Christians have a fight against wicked spirits?
17. What should you do if a "voice" from the spirit world speaks to you?

The Bible warns: 'Keep free from all forms of spiritism'

spirit world. (Proverbs 18:10; James 4:7) This does not mean that everyone who hears "voices" is being spoken to by demons. At times the hearing of voices can be traced to certain physical or mental illnesses.

18 Maybe at one time you shared in some practice of spiritism and you now want to break free. What can you do? Well, consider the example of early Christians at Ephesus. After they had accepted the "word of Jehovah" preached by the apostle Paul, the Bible says: "Quite a number of those who practiced magical arts brought their books together and burned them up

18. What example of the early Christians at Ephesus is a good one to follow if a person wants to break free from spiritism?

Those who became Christians in Ephesus
burned their books on spiritism
—a fine example for us today

before everybody." And these books were worth 50,000 pieces of silver! (Acts 19:19, 20) In imitation of those who became Christ's followers at Ephesus, if you have objects in your possession that are directly related to spiritism the wise course is to destroy them no matter how costly they are.

¹⁹ Since there is so much interest today in the strange and mysterious, more and more persons are becoming involved in spiritism. Most of these persons, however, do not know that they are actually becoming involved with wicked spirits. This is not innocent fun. Wicked spirits have power to hurt and harm. They are vicious. And, before Christ jails them in destruction forever, they are doing all they can to bring humans under their wicked power. (Matthew 8:28, 29) So if you want to live forever in happiness on earth after all wickedness is removed, you need to keep free from demon power by keeping away from every kind of spiritism.

19. (a) What do most persons who take part in spiritism not know? (b) If we want to live forever in happiness on earth, what must we do?

Chapter 11

Why Has God
Permitted Wickedness?

WHEREVER you look in the world, there is crime, hatred and trouble. Often it is the innocent who suffer. Some people blame God. They may say: 'If there is a God, why does he permit all these terrible things to happen?'

2 Yet who are doing these wicked things to others? It is *people,* not God. God condemns wicked acts. In fact, much of the suffering on earth would be prevented if people obeyed God's laws. He commands us to love. He forbids murder, stealing, fornication, greed, drunkenness and other acts of wrongdoing that cause humans to suffer. (Romans 13:9; Ephesians 5:3, 18) God made Adam and Eve with a marvelous brain and body and with the ability to enjoy life to the full. He never wanted them or their children to suffer or have trouble.

3 It was Satan the Devil who started wickedness on earth. But Adam and Eve were also to blame. They were not so weak that they could not have resisted when the Devil tempted them. They could have told Satan to "go away," just as the perfect man Jesus later did. (Matthew 4:10) But they did not. As a result, they became imperfect. All their children, including us, have inherited that imperfection, which brought with it sickness, sorrow and death. (Romans 5:12) But why has God permitted suffering to go on?

---

1. (a) What is the situation on earth today? (b) What complaint do some people have?
2. (a) Who are doing wicked things? (b) How might much of the suffering on earth be prevented?
3. (a) Who are responsible for wickedness? (b) What shows that Adam and Eve could have resisted Satan's temptations?

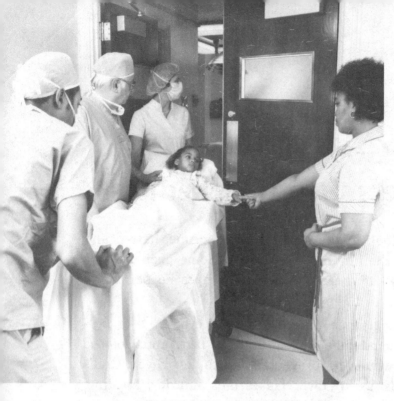

With good reason,
a parent will permit
a beloved child to undergo
a painful operation.
God also has good reasons
for temporarily permitting
humans to suffer

[4] A person may at first think that there could be no reason great enough for God to allow all the human suffering that has been experienced over the centuries. Yet, is it right to reach that conclusion? Have not parents who truly love their children permitted them to undergo a painful operation to correct some problem? Yes, the permission of temporary suffering has often made it possible for children to enjoy better health later on in life. What good has been done by God's permission of wickedness?

AN IMPORTANT ISSUE TO BE SETTLED

[5] The rebellion against God in the garden of Eden raised an important issue or question. We need to examine it in order to understand why God has permitted wickedness. Jehovah told Adam not to eat from a certain tree in the garden. If Adam did, what would happen? God said: "You will positively die." (Genesis 2:17) However, Satan said exactly the opposite. He told Adam's wife, Eve, to go ahead and eat from the forbidden tree.

---

4. What helps us to understand that a loving God would temporarily permit wickedness?
5. (a) How did Satan contradict God? (b) What did Satan promise Eve?

"You positively will *not* die," Satan said. In fact, he went on to tell Eve: "For God knows that in the very day of your eating from it your eyes are bound to be opened and you are bound to be like God, knowing good and bad."—Genesis 3:1-5.

⁶ Eve disobeyed God and ate. Why? Eve believed Satan. She selfishly thought that she would benefit by disobeying God. She reasoned that no longer would she or Adam need to answer to God. No longer would they have to submit to his laws. They could decide for themselves what is "good" and what is "bad." Adam went along with Eve and also ate. Discussing man's original sin against God, a footnote in *The Jerusalem Bible* says: "It is the power of deciding for himself what is good and what is evil and of acting accordingly, a claim to complete moral independence . . . The first sin was an attack on God's sovereignty." That is, it was an attack on God's right to be man's absolute ruler or superior.

Adam and Eve, by eating the forbidden fruit, abandoned God's rulership. They began making their own decisions as to what was good or bad

⁷ So by eating the forbidden fruit, Adam and Eve withdrew themselves from under God's rulership. They went out on their own, doing what was "good" or "bad" according to their own decisions. So the important issue or question raised was: *Does God have the right to be the absolute ruler of humankind?* In other words, is Jehovah the One to decide what is

6. (a) Why did Eve disobey God? (b) What did it mean to eat from the forbidden tree?

7. (a) What issue was raised by man's disobedience? (b) What questions need answering in connection with this issue?

good or bad for humans? Is he the One to say what is right conduct and what is not? Or can man do a better job of governing himself? Whose way of ruling is best? Can humans, under the invisible direction of Satan, rule successfully without Jehovah's direction? Or is God's guidance needed in order to set up a righteous government that will bring lasting peace to the earth? All such questions were raised in this attack on God's sovereignty, on his right to be the only and absolute ruler of humankind.

8 Of course, as soon as the rebellion happened Jehovah could have destroyed the three rebels. There was no question that he was stronger than Satan or Adam and Eve. But destroying them would not have settled matters in the best way. For example, it would not have answered the question of whether humans could successfully rule themselves without help from God. So Jehovah allowed time to settle the important issue that was raised.

SETTLING THE ISSUE

9 Now that time has passed, what has been the result? Well, what would you say? Have the past 6,000 years of history shown that humans have been successful in governing themselves without God's guidance? Have humans provided good government for the blessing and happiness of all? Or has the record of history shown that the prophet Jeremiah's words are correct: "It does not belong to man who is walking even to direct his step"?—Jeremiah 10:23.

10 Throughout history all kinds of governments have been tried, but none have brought security and real happiness to all those living under their rule. Some persons may point to the signs of progress. But can a person speak of true progress when the bow and arrow have been replaced by the atomic bomb, and when the world now is in great fear of another world war? What kind of progress is it when men can walk on the moon but cannot live together in peace on the earth? What good is it for men to build homes equipped with all kinds of modern

8. Why did Jehovah not destroy the rebels right away?
9, 10. What have been the results of humans trying to govern themselves without God's guidance?

conveniences when the families who live in them are torn apart by troubles? Are riots in the streets, the destruction of property and life and the widespread lawlessness things of which to be proud? Not at all! But these are the results of humans trying to rule themselves apart from God.—Proverbs 19:3.

[11] The evidence should be clear to all. Man's efforts to govern himself independently of God have been a terrible failure. They have resulted in great human suffering. "Man has dominated man to his injury," the Bible explains. (Ecclesiastes 8:9) Clearly, humans need God's guidance in governing their affairs. Just as God created man with the need to eat food and drink water, so man was made with the need to obey God's laws. If man ignores God's laws, he will come into difficulty, just as surely

11. So, evidently, what do humans need?

Just as man was created with the need to eat food and drink water, he was also created with the need for God's guidance as he would suffer if he ignored his body's need for food and water.—Proverbs 3:5, 6.

WHY SO LONG?

[12] However, a person might ask, 'Why has God permitted so much time, over 6,000 years now, to settle this issue? Could it not have been settled in a satisfactory way long ago?' Not really. If God had stepped in long ago, the charge could have been made that humans were not given enough time to experiment. But as it is, humans have had plenty of time to develop a government that would satisfy the needs of all its subjects, as well as make scientific discoveries that could contribute to the prosperity of all. Over the centuries humans have tried nearly every form of government. And their progress in the field of science has been remarkable. They have harnessed the atom and traveled to the moon. But what has been the result? Has it brought a grand new system for the blessing of humankind?

[13] Far from it! Instead, there is more unhappiness and trouble on earth than ever before. In fact, crime, pollution, war, family breakdown and other problems have reached such a dangerous stage that scientists believe man's very existence is threatened. Yes, after some 6,000 years of experience in self-rule, and after reaching a peak in scientific "progress," humankind is now facing self-destruction! How clear it is that humans cannot successfully govern themselves apart from God! Nor can anyone now complain that God did not allow enough time to settle this issue.

[14] Surely God has had good reason for permitting humans under the rule of Satan to cause the wickedness that has existed for so long. By his rebellion Satan raised another issue that it has also required time to settle. An examination of this issue will provide further help in our understanding why God has permitted wickedness. You should be especially interested in this issue because you are personally involved.

---

12. Why has God allowed such a long time to settle the issue?
13. (a) In spite of all man's scientific progress, what is the situation today? (b) What does this clearly prove?
14. Why should we be encouraged to examine the other important issue raised by Satan?

Chapter 12

You Are Involved
in a Vital Issue

HOW YOU live your life really does matter. It will mean for you either a happy future or a miserable one. Eventually it will determine whether you pass away with this world or survive its end into God's righteous new order where you can live forever. —1 John 2:17; 2 Peter 3:13.

2 But how you live your life affects more than just yourself. Others are involved. What you do affects them too. For example, if your parents are alive, what you do can bring them either honor or shame. The Bible says: "A wise son is the one that makes a father rejoice, and a stupid son is the grief of his mother." (Proverbs 10:1) More importantly, how you live your life affects Jehovah God. It can either make him rejoice or make him sad. Why? Because of a vital issue in which you are involved.

WILL HUMANS BE FAITHFUL TO GOD?

3 This issue was raised by Satan the Devil. He raised it when he was able to get Adam and Eve to break God's law and thus join him in rebellion against God. (Genesis 3:1-6) This provided Satan with what he felt were grounds for addressing Jehovah with the challenge: 'People serve you only for what they get from you. Just give me the chance and I can turn anybody away from you.' Although these words do not actually appear in the Bible, it is clear that Satan said something like this to God. This is shown in the Bible book of Job.

4 Job was a man who lived many centuries after the rebellion

1, 2. (a) Why does the way you live really matter to you? (b) To whom else does it matter, and why?
3. What challenge did Satan make to Jehovah?
4, 5. (a) Who was Job? (b) What happened in heaven in Job's day?

105

Job met Satan's challenge that nobody would remain faithful to God under test

had taken place in the garden of Eden. <u>He was a righteous and</u> <u>faithful servant of God.</u> But did it really matter to God or to Satan that Job was faithful? The Bible shows that it did. It tells us about an appearance of Satan before Jehovah in the courts of heaven. Notice the subject of their conversation:

⁵ "Now it came to be the day when the sons of the true God entered to take their station before Jehovah, and even Satan proceeded to enter right among them. Then Jehovah said to Satan: 'Where do you come from?' At that Satan answered Jehovah and said: 'From roving about in the earth and from walking about in it.' And Jehovah went on to say to Satan: 'Have you set your heart upon my servant Job, that there is no one like him in the earth, a man blameless and upright, fearing God and turning aside from bad?' "—Job 1:6-8.

⁶ Why did Jehovah mention to Satan that Job was an upright man? Clearly, there was an issue as to whether Job would remain faithful to Jehovah or not. Think about God's question, "Where do you come from?" and Satan's reply, "From roving about in the earth and from walking about in it." This question and Satan's reply showed that Jehovah was permitting Satan free opportunity to carry out his challenge that he could turn anyone away from God. Well, what was Satan's reply to Jehovah's question about Job's faithfulness?

⁷ "At that Satan answered Jehovah and said: 'Is it for nothing that Job has feared God? Have not you yourself put up a hedge about him and about his house and about everything that he has all around? The work of his hands you have blessed, and his livestock itself has spread abroad in the earth. But, for a change, thrust out your hand, please, and touch everything he has and see whether he will not curse you to your very face.' " —Job 1:9-11.

⁸ By his reply Satan was making an excuse for Job's faithfulness to God. 'Job serves you,' Satan argued, 'because of the things you give him, not because he loves you.' Satan also com-

---

6. What issue does the Bible show existed in Job's day?

7, 8. (a) For what reason did Satan say that Job served God? (b) What did Jehovah do to settle the issue?

plained that Jehovah was using his greater power in an unfair way. 'You have always protected him,' he said. So, to settle the issue, Jehovah answered: "Look! Everything that he has is in your hand. Only against him himself do not thrust out your hand!"—Job 1:12.

⁹ Right away Satan began causing trouble for Job. He had all Job's livestock either killed or stolen. Then he saw to it that Job's 10 children were killed. Job lost almost everything, yet he remained faithful to Jehovah. He did not curse God. (Job 1:2, 13-22) But that was not the end of the matter.

¹⁰ Satan again appeared with the other angels before Jehovah. Once again Jehovah asked Satan if he had seen the faithfulness of Job and said: "Even yet he is holding fast his integrity." At that Satan answered: "Skin in behalf of skin, and everything that a man has he will give in behalf of his soul. For a change, thrust out your hand, please, and touch as far as his bone and his flesh and see whether he will not curse you to your very face."—Job 2:1-5.

¹¹ In answer, Jehovah gave Satan permission to do whatever he could to Job, although God said: 'You are not to kill him.' (Job 2:6) So Satan struck Job with a terrible disease. Job's suffering was so great that he prayed to die. (Job 2:7; 14:13, 14) His own wife turned against him, saying: "Curse God and die!" (Job 2:9) But Job refused to do that. "Until I expire I shall not take away my integrity from myself!" he said. (Job 27:5) Job remained faithful to God. So it was proved that Satan was wrong in his challenge that Job only served God for material gain and not out of love. It was also shown that Satan could not turn everybody away from serving God.

¹² How do you suppose Job's faithful course made Jehovah feel? It made him very happy! God's Word urges: "Be wise, my son, and make my heart rejoice, that I may make a reply to

9. What trouble did Satan cause for Job, and with what result?
10. What shows that Satan did not give up?
11. (a) What further trials did Satan cause for Job? (b) What was the outcome?
12. (a) What answer to Satan's challenge did Job provide God? (b) What did Jesus' faithfulness to God prove?

him that is taunting me." (Proverbs 27:11) It is Satan who is taunting Jehovah. And by his faithful course Job made God's heart rejoice. This gave God an answer to Satan's boastful taunt or challenge that humans would not serve Him under test. Many others have also provided God with such an answer. The greatest example was the perfect man Jesus. He held fast his loyalty to God despite all the tests and trials that Satan brought upon him. This proved that the perfect man Adam could have done the same if he had wanted to, and that God was not unrighteous in requiring full obedience from man.

WHERE DO YOU STAND?

[13] What about your life? You may not think that it really matters how you live. But it does. Whether you know it or not, it supports either God's side of the issue or Satan's side. Jehovah cares for you, and he wants to see you serve him and live forever on the paradise earth. (John 3:16) When the Israelites rebelled against God, he was pained or felt hurt. (Psalm 78:40, 41) Is your course of life one that is making God happy or is he pained by it? Of course, to make God happy you need to learn his laws and obey them.

[14] A chief aim of Satan is to get persons to break God's laws that govern the use of their reproductive powers, and his arrangement of marriage and the family. God's laws to protect our happiness say that unmarried persons should not engage in sexual relations, and that married persons should not have sexual relations with anybody else besides their marriage mate. (1 Thessalonians 4:3-8; Hebrews 13:4) When God's law is broken, often children are born without parents who love and want them. Mothers may even have an abortion, killing the children before they can be born. Additionally, many who commit fornication get terrible sexual diseases that can damage children that they may bear. It is an act of unfaithfulness, a crime against

---

13. (a) What does the way you live your life have to do with the issue? (b) How can we make God happy or cause him pain?
14. (a) As regards sexual relations, what laws must we obey to make God happy? (b) Why is breaking such laws a crime?

God, to have sexual relations with someone to whom you are not married. Job said: "If my heart has been enticed toward a woman, and I have lain in wait at my neighbor's door . . . that would be heinous, a crime to be condemned."—Job 31:1, 9, 11, *The New American Bible*.

[15] We should not be surprised that this Devil-ruled world would make it seem normal and right for you to have sexual relations with a person to whom you are not married. But if you do so, whom are you pleasing? Satan, not Jehovah. To make God happy, you must "flee from fornication." (1 Corinthians 6:18) True, it is not always easy to be faithful to God. It was not easy for Job either. But remember, it is *wise* to obey God's laws. You will be happier now if you do. But, more importantly, you will be supporting God's side of the issue and will make him happy. And he will bless you with everlasting life in happiness on earth.

[16] True, Satan was able to reduce Job to poverty and to cause the death of his 10 children. There is no question that this was a deep loss for Job. But when Job proved faithful, God blessed him with twice as much as he had before Satan was permitted to test him. Job also became father to 10 more children. (Job

15. (a) If we commit fornication, whom do we please? (b) Why is it wise to obey God's laws?
16. (a) How was Job blessed for his faithfulness? (b) What can be said about the harm Satan causes, such as the killing of Job's 10 children?

Having sexual relations with someone to whom you are not married is a crime against God

Jehovah blessed Job for his faithfulness with far more than he had before

42:10-17) Furthermore, we can be sure that Job's 10 children who were killed by Satan will be brought back to life in the resurrection of the dead. Truly, there is no harm or trouble that Satan is permitted to cause that our loving Father, Jehovah, will not correct in his own due time.

17 So you will always want to keep in mind that how you live your life really does matter. It matters particularly to Jehovah God and Satan the Devil. This is because you are involved in the issue of whether humans will be faithful to God or not.

17. Why does the way we live really matter?

Chapter 13

God's Government of Peace

HAVE YOU noted that human governments, even those with good intentions, have failed to satisfy the real needs of people? None have solved the problems of crime and racial hatred or have provided proper food and housing for all their people. They have not freed their citizens completely of disease. Nor has any government been able to stop aging or death or to bring the dead to life again. There is not one that has even brought lasting peace and security to its citizens. Governments of men are simply not able to solve the big problems facing people.

[2] Our Creator knows how much we need a righteous government that will make it possible for all people to enjoy a full and happy life. So that is why the Bible tells of a government under God's direction. In fact, this promised government by God is the main message of the Bible.

[3] But you may ask: 'Where does the Bible speak of God's government?' It does so, for example, at Isaiah 9:6, 7. According to the *King James Version,* these verses say: "For unto us a child is born, unto us a son is given: and *the government* shall be upon his shoulder: and his name shall be called Wonderful, Counsellor, The mighty God, The everlasting Father, The Prince of Peace. Of the increase of *his government* and peace there shall be no end."

1. What have human governments failed to do?
2. What is the main message of the Bible?
3. What does Isaiah 9:6, 7 say about God's government?

112

⁴ The Bible is here telling about the birth of a child, a prince. In time this 'son of a king' was to become a great ruler, "The Prince of Peace." He would have charge of a truly wonderful government. This government will bring peace to the whole earth, and the peace will last forever. The child, whose birth was foretold in Isaiah 9:6, 7, was Jesus. When announcing his birth to the virgin girl Mary, the angel Gabriel said of Jesus: "He will rule as king . . . and there will be no end of his kingdom."—Luke 1:30-33.

STRESSING THE KINGDOM'S IMPORTANCE

⁵ While they were on earth, the main work of Jesus Christ and his supporters, was to preach and teach about the coming kingdom of God. (Luke 4:43; 8:1) They make about 140 references to that kingdom in the Bible. Jesus even taught his followers to

4. Who is the child that becomes the ruler of God's government?
5. (a) How is the importance of the Kingdom shown in the Bible? (b) What is God's kingdom, and what will it do?

Jesus sent out his followers to do the important work of preaching about God's kingdom

When on trial for his life, Jesus continued to preach God's kingdom

pray to God: "Thy kingdom come. Thy will be done in earth, as it is in heaven." (Matthew 6:10, *King James Version*) Is this kingdom that Christians pray for really a government? You may not have thought it to be, but it is. God's Son, Jesus Christ, is the King of the Kingdom. And the whole earth will be the territory over which he rules. How fine it will be when people will not be divided into many opposing nations, but all humans will be united in peace under God's Kingdom government!

[6] John the Baptizer started preaching about this government, telling the people: "Repent, for the kingdom of the heavens has drawn near." (Matthew 3:1, 2) Why could John say this? Because Jesus, the One who would become ruler of God's heavenly government, was about to be baptized by him and to be anointed with God's holy spirit. So you can understand why Jesus later told the Pharisees: "Look! the kingdom of God is in your midst." (Luke 17:21) It was because Jesus, whom God had appointed as king, was there with them. During his three and a half years of preaching and teaching, Jesus, by his faithfulness to God unto death, proved his right to be king.

[7] To show that God's kingdom was the important issue during Christ's ministry, let us consider what happened on the last day before his death. The Bible tells us that the people accused Jesus, saying: "This man we found subverting our nation and forbidding the paying of taxes to Caesar and saying he himself is Christ a king." On hearing these things, the Roman governor Pontius Pilate asked Jesus: "Are you the king of the Jews?" —Luke 23:1-3.

[8] Jesus did not answer Pilate's question directly, but said: "My kingdom is no part of this world. If my kingdom were part of this world, my attendants would have fought that I should not be delivered up to the Jews. But, as it is, my kingdom is not from this source." Jesus answered this way because his kingdom

6. When Jesus was on earth, why was the Kingdom said to be "near" and "in your midst"?
7. What shows that the Kingdom was an important issue when Jesus was on earth?
8. (a) How did Jesus answer when he was asked if he was a king? (b) What did Jesus mean when he said that his kingdom was "not from this source"?

was not to be an earthly one. He was to rule from heaven, not as a man from some throne on earth. Since the issue was whether Jesus had the right to rule as king or not, Pilate again asked Jesus: "Well, then, are you a king?"

⁹ Clearly, Jesus was on trial for his life because he had been preaching and teaching about a new government. So Jesus answered Pilate: "You yourself are saying that I am a king. For this I have been born, and for this I have come into the world, that I should bear witness to the truth." (John 18:36, 37) Yes, Jesus had spent his life on earth telling people the wonderful truth about God's Kingdom government. It was his main message. And the Kingdom is still the most important issue today. These questions, however, yet remain: Which government is the most important in a person's life? Is it some government of men, or is it God's kingdom with Christ as ruler?

ARRANGING FOR EARTH'S NEW GOVERNMENT

¹⁰ It was when Satan got Adam and Eve to join him in his rebellion that Jehovah saw the need for a new government over mankind. So right away God told about his purpose to set up such a government. He referred to this government when he pronounced sentence on the serpent, actually telling Satan the Devil: "I shall put enmity between you and the woman and between your seed and her seed. He will bruise you in the head and you will bruise him in the heel."—Genesis 3:14, 15.

¹¹ But you may ask: 'Where is anything said here about a government?' Let us look carefully at this statement and we will see. The scripture says that there was to be enmity, or hatred, between Satan and "the woman." Additionally, there was to be hatred between Satan's "seed," or children, and the woman's "seed," or children. First of all, we need to find out who "the woman" is.

9. (a) What wonderful truth did Jesus make known? (b) What are the big questions today?
10. (a) When did God see the need for a new government? (b) In the Bible, where is the first reference made to this government? (c) Who is represented by the serpent?
11. Between whom was there to be hatred?

¹² She is not an earthly woman. Satan has not had any special hatred toward any human female. Rather, this is a *symbolic* woman. That is, she stands for something else. This is shown in the Bible's last book, Revelation, where more information is given about her. There "the woman" is described as being "adorned with the sun, standing on the moon, and with the twelve stars on her head." To help us to find out who this "woman" represents, note what Revelation goes on to say about her child: "The woman brought *a male child into the world,* the son who was *to rule all the nations with an iron sceptre,* and the child was taken straight up to God and to his throne." —Revelation 12:1-5, *The Jerusalem Bible.*

¹³ Learning who or what the "male child" is will help us to find out whom or what "the woman" represents. The child is not a literal person, just as the woman is not a real human female. The scripture shows that this "male child" is "to rule all the nations." So the "child" represents God's government with Jesus Christ ruling as King. "The woman," therefore, represents God's organization of faithful heavenly creatures. Just as the "male child" came forth from "the woman," so the King, Jesus Christ, came forth from the heavenly organization, (the body of loyal spirit creatures in heaven that work together to carry out God's purpose.) Galatians 4:26 calls this organization "the Jerusalem above." So, then, when Adam and Eve first rebelled against God's rulership, Jehovah made arrangements for a Kingdom government that would serve as a hope for lovers of righteousness.

JEHOVAH REMEMBERS HIS PROMISE

¹⁴ Jehovah did not forget his promise to send a "seed" who would be the ruler of God's government. This ruler would destroy Satan by crushing his head. (Romans 16:20; Hebrews 2:14) Later, Jehovah said that the promised seed would come through

12. What is said about "the woman" in Revelation chapter 12?
13. Whom or what do the "male child" and "the woman" represent?
14. (a) How did Jehovah show that he remembered his promise about a "seed" that would bruise Satan? (b) Who is the promised "seed"?

the faithful man Abraham. Jehovah told Abraham: "By means of your *seed* all nations of the earth will certainly bless themselves." (Genesis 22:18) Who is this "seed" that was promised to come through the line of Abraham? The Bible gives the answer later, saying: "Now the promises were spoken to Abraham and to his seed. It says, not: 'And to seeds,' as in the case of many such, but as in the case of one: *'And to your seed,' who is Christ.* (Galatians 3:16) Jehovah also told Abraham's son Isaac and his grandson Jacob that the "seed" of God's "woman" would come through their line of descent.—Genesis 26:1-5; 28:10-14.

¹⁵ Making clear that this "seed" would be a ruling king, Jacob made this statement to his son Judah: "The scepter [or, ruling authority] will not turn aside from Judah, neither the commander's staff from between his feet, until Shiloh comes; and to him the obedience of the peoples will belong." (Genesis 49:10) Jesus Christ came from the tribe of Judah. He proved to be this "Shiloh" to whom "the obedience of the peoples will belong."—Hebrews 7:14.

¹⁶ Nearly 700 years after the statement to Judah, Jehovah said regarding David of the tribe of Judah: "I have found David my servant . . . And I shall certainly *set up his seed forever and his throne as the days of heaven.*" (Psalm 89:20, 29) When God says the "seed" of David will be set up "forever" and that "his throne" will exist as long "as the days of heaven," what does he mean? Jehovah God is referring to the fact that the Kingdom government in the hands of his appointed ruler, Jesus Christ, will last forever. How do we know?

¹⁷ Well, recall what Jehovah's angel Gabriel told Mary about the child that was to be born to her. He said: "You are to call his name Jesus." But Jesus was not to remain only a child, or even a man, on earth. Gabriel went on to say: "This one will be great and will be called Son of the Most High; and Jehovah God will give him *the throne of David his father,* and he will rule as king over the house of Jacob forever, *and there*

15, 16. What proves that the "seed" was to be a ruling king?
17. How do we know that the promised ruler is Jesus Christ?

How do you view Jesus —as a victorious king or as a helpless baby?

will be no end of his kingdom." (Luke 1:31-33) Is it not truly marvelous that Jehovah has made arrangements to set up a righteous government for the everlasting benefit of those who love and trust him?

18 The time is now near when God's Kingdom government will take action to destroy all governments of the world. Jesus Christ will then go into action as a victorious King. Describing this battle, the Bible says: "In the days of those kings the God of heaven will set up a kingdom that will never be brought to ruin. . . . It will crush and put an end to all these kingdoms, and it itself will stand to times indefinite." (Daniel 2:44; Revelation 19:11-16) With all other governments out of the way, God's government will satisfy the real needs of the people. The Ruler, Jesus Christ, will see to it that no faithful subject of his gets sick, grows old or dies. Crime, poor housing, hunger and all other such problems will be solved. There will come to be true peace and security earth wide. (2 Peter 3:13; Revelation 21:3-5) However, we need to learn more about those who will be rulers in this Kingdom government of God.

18. (a) How does the Bible describe the end of earthly governments? (b) What will God's government do for people?

Chapter 14

Who Go to Heaven, and Why?

MANY PERSONS say, 'All good people go to heaven.' However, when asked _why_ they go to heaven, they may say: 'It is to be with God,' or, 'It is the reward for being good.' What does the Bible teach about this?

2 The Bible makes clear that Jesus was raised from the dead and that he went to heaven. Also, it says that other humans would be taken there. On the night before his death, Jesus told his faithful apostles: "In the house of my Father there are many abodes. Otherwise, I would have told you, because I am going my way to prepare a place for you. Also, if I go my way and prepare a place for you, I am coming again and _will receive you home to myself, that where I am you also may be._"—John 14:1-3.

3 Clearly, Jesus was telling his apostles that they would be taken to heaven to be with him. The apostle Paul often told early Christians about that wonderful hope. For example, he wrote: "As for us, our citizenship exists in the heavens, from which place also we are eagerly waiting for a savior, the Lord Jesus Christ." (Philippians 3:20, 21; Romans 6:5; 2 Corinthians 5:1, 2) Based on such promises, millions of persons have set their hearts on heavenly life. Yet will _all_ good persons go to heaven?

DO ALL GOOD PERSONS GO TO HEAVEN?

4 Shortly after Jesus was raised from the dead, the apostle Peter told a crowd of Jews: "The family head David . . . both deceased and was buried and his tomb is among us to this day. _Actually David did not ascend to the heavens._" (Acts 2:29, 34) So

1. How will many persons answer the question, Who go to heaven, and why?
2, 3. (a) Why can we be sure some humans will go to heaven? (b) What question needs to be answered?
4, 5. What proof is there that David and Job did not go to heaven?

120

the good man David did not go to heaven. What about the righteous man Job?

5 While suffering, Job prayed to God: "O that in Sheol [the grave] you would conceal me, that you would keep me secret until your anger turns back, that you would set a time limit for me and remember me!" Job expected that when he died he would become unconscious in the grave. He knew he would not go to heaven. But he had hope, as he explained: "If an able-bodied man dies can he live again? All the days of my compulsory service [appointed time in the grave] I shall wait, until my relief comes. You will call, and I myself shall answer you."—Job 14:13-15.

6 John, who baptized Jesus, was also a good man. Yet Jesus said: "A person that is a lesser one in the kingdom of the heavens is greater than he is." (Matthew 11:11) This is so because John the Baptizer will not go to heaven. When Jesus was on earth, which was over 4,000 years after the rebellion of Adam and Eve, he said: "No man has ascended into heaven but he that descended from heaven, the Son of man."—John 3:13.

7 Therefore, according to Jesus'

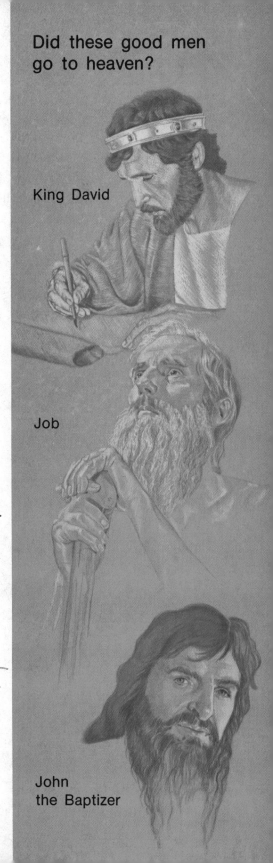

Did these good men go to heaven?

King David

Job

John the Baptizer

6, 7. (a) What shows that no one who died before Christ went to heaven? (b) What will happen to all faithful ones who died before Christ?

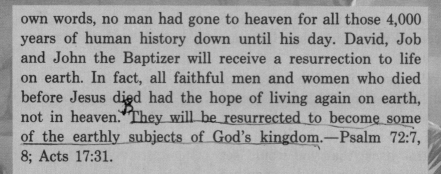

own words, no man had gone to heaven for all those 4,000 years of human history down until his day. David, Job and John the Baptizer will receive a resurrection to life on earth. In fact, all faithful men and women who died before Jesus died had the hope of living again on earth, not in heaven. They will be resurrected to become some of the earthly subjects of God's kingdom.—Psalm 72:7, 8; Acts 17:31.

WHY SOME FAITHFUL ONES GO TO HEAVEN

⁸ Why did Jesus go to heaven? What work does he have to do there? The answers to these questions are impor-

8. The answers to what questions are important, and why?

On his last night with the apostles, Jesus said they would be rulers with him in his Father's kingdom

tant. This is because those who go to heaven will share with Jesus in his work. They go to heaven for that very purpose.

[9] We learned in earlier chapters that Jesus will rule over the paradise new earth as king of God's heavenly government. Long before Jesus came to the earth, the Bible book of Daniel foretold that the "son of man" would be "given rulership." The "Son of man" is Jesus Christ. (Mark 14:41, 62) And Daniel goes on to say: "His rulership is an indefinitely lasting rulership that will not pass away, and his kingdom one that will not be brought to ruin."—Daniel 7:13, 14.

[10] However, it is important to note here in the book of Daniel that the "son of man" is not to rule alone. The Bible says: "And the kingdom and the rulership . . . were given to *the people who are the holy ones of the Supreme One. Their kingdom* is an indefinitely lasting kingdom." (Daniel 7:27) These expressions "the people" and "their kingdom" let us know that others will rule with Christ in God's government.

[11] On the last night that Jesus spent with his faithful 11 apostles he showed that they would be rulers with him in God's kingdom. He told them: "You are the ones that have stuck with me in my trials; and I make a covenant with you, just as my Father has made a covenant with me, for a kingdom." (Luke 22:28, 29) Later, the apostle Paul and Timothy were included in this covenant, or agreement, for a kingdom. For that reason Paul wrote Timothy: "If we go on enduring, we shall also rule together as kings." (2 Timothy 2:12) Also, the apostle John wrote of those who will "rule as kings over the earth" along with Jesus Christ.—Revelation 5:9, 10; 20:6.

[12] So those who go to heaven go there to serve as joint rulers with Christ in God's heavenly government. While Jesus is the main "seed" of promise, God chooses others from among humankind to rule with Jesus in the kingdom. They thus become part of the "seed," as the Bible says: "If you belong to Christ, you

9, 10. According to Daniel, who besides Christ will rule in God's government?
11. What shows that Christ's early followers will rule with him?
12. What fact regarding Abraham's "seed" reveals that Christ will have joint rulers?

re really Abraham's seed, heirs with reference to a promise."
—Galatians 3:16, 29; James 2:5.

HOW MANY GO TO HEAVEN?

[13] Since they are to rule over the earth, it is clear that those
who go to heaven will be tried and tested followers of Christ.
This means that babies or young children, who have not been
fully tested during years of Christian service, will not be tak-
en to heaven. (Matthew 16:24) However, such young ones who
die have the hope of being raised to life on earth. (John 5:28,
29) So the total number who go to heaven will be small when
compared with the many who will receive life on earth under
Kingdom rule. Jesus told his disciples: "Have no fear, *little flock,*
because your Father has approved of giving you the kingdom."
—Luke 12:32.

[14] How small a number will that class of Kingdom rulers be?
Will it include only the apostles and other early followers of
Jesus? No, the Bible shows that the "little flock" will include
more. At Revelation 14:1, 3 the Bible says: "And I saw, and,
look! the Lamb [Jesus Christ] standing upon the [heavenly]
Mount Zion, and with him *a hundred and forty-four thousand* . . .
who have been bought [or, taken] from the earth." Note that
only 144,000 persons are seen with the Lamb, Jesus Christ, on
heavenly Mount Zion. (Hebrews 12:22) So rather than all good
people going to heaven, the Bible reveals that only 144,000 tried
and faithful persons will be taken there to rule with Christ.

WHY CHOSEN FROM THE EARTH

[15] But why does God choose these rulers from among humankind? Why not have angels rule with Christ? Well, it was here
at the earth that Jehovah's right to rule was challenged. It was
here that the faithfulness of men to God could be put to the test
under opposition from the Devil. It was here that Jesus proved
his full loyalty to God under test and gave his life as a ransom

13. (a) Why will babies not go to heaven? (b) How did Jesus describe the number
who receive the Kingdom?
14. How many make up the "little flock" who go to heaven?
15. Why does God choose the Kingdom rulers from among humankind?

for mankind. So it was from the earth that Jehovah arranged to take a "little flock" of persons to be associated with his Son in the heavenly kingdom. They are the ones who, by their faithfulness to God, proved false the Devil's charge that men serve God only for selfish reasons. It is fitting, therefore, that Jehovah uses these humans for his glory.—Ephesians 1:9-12.

[16] Also, think how wonderful it will be to have as rulers persons who proved faithful to God on earth, many of them even sacrificing their lives in behalf of the Kingdom. (Revelation 12:10, 11; 20:4) Angels have not faced such kind of testings. Nor have they experienced the problems common to humankind. So they would not fully understand what it is like to be a sinful human and to have the problems we humans do. But the 144,000 will understand because they have had these very problems. Some of them have had to overcome very sinful practices, and they know how hard it can be to do so. (1 Corinthians 6:9-11) Therefore, they will deal with their earthly subjects in an understanding way.—Hebrews 2:17, 18.

THE CONGREGATION OF GOD

[17] The Bible tells us that Christ is the head of God's congregation, and that its members are subject to Jesus. (Ephesians 5:23, 24) So the word "church," or "congregation of God," does not refer to some building. Rather, it refers to a group of Christians. (1 Corinthians 15:9) Today we may speak of the *congregation* of Christians with whom we associate. In the same way, we read in the Bible about "the congregation of the Laodiceans," and, in the apostle Paul's letter to Philemon, about "the congregation that [was in his] house."—Colossians 4:16; Philemon 2.

[18] However, when the Bible speaks of "the congregation of the living God," it is referring to a particular group of Christ's followers. (1 Timothy 3:15) They are also called "the congregation of the firstborn who have been enrolled in the heavens." (Hebrews 12:23) So this "congregation of God" is made up of

16. Why can we be grateful that the Kingdom rulers have lived on earth?
17. To what does the word "congregation" refer?
18. (a) Who make up "the congregation of the living God"? (b) By what terms is this congregation also referred to in the Bible?

all Christians on earth who have the hope of heavenly life. In all, only 144,000 persons finally make up the "congregation of God." Today only a few of these, a remnant, are still on earth. Christians who hope to live forever on earth look for spiritual guidance from members of this "congregation of the living God." The Bible also refers to this congregation of 144,000 members by such terms as "the bride, the Lamb's wife," "the body of the Christ," "the temple of God," "the Israel of God," and the "New Jerusalem."—Revelation 21:9; Ephesians 4:12; 1 Corinthians 3:17; Galatians 6:16; Revelation 21:2.

THE NEW THING IN GOD'S PURPOSE

[19] Jehovah God did not change his purpose for the earth and mankind on it after Adam started the human race down the path of sin and death. Had God done so, it would have meant that he was not able to carry out his original purpose. His purpose from the beginning was to have an earth-wide paradise filled with happy, healthy people, and that purpose still stands. The only new thing that God introduced was his arrangement for a new government to carry out his purpose. As we have seen, his Son, Jesus Christ, is the main ruler in this government, and 144,000 persons will be taken from among humankind to rule in heaven with him.—Revelation 7:4.

[20] These rulers in heaven will make up the "new heavens" of God's new system. Yet it is clear that if there are to be such righteous rulers over the earth, then there must be those over whom they rule. The Bible refers to these persons as the "new earth." (2 Peter 3:13; Revelation 21:1-4) They will include Job, David and John the Baptizer—yes, all the faithful ones who lived before Christ came to the earth. But there will be many more who will make up the "new earth," including persons who survive the end of this wicked system of things. Will you be one of these survivors? Do you want to be a subject of God's government? If so, there are requirements you must meet.

19. What new thing did God introduce to carry out his original purpose for the earth?
20. (a) Who make up the "new heavens" and the "new earth"? (b) What must you do to become part of the "new earth"?

Chapter 15

Becoming a Subject of God's Government

DO YOU WANT to live forever on earth under God's government? Any person in his right mind would answer, Yes! Wonderful benefits will be enjoyed. But to receive them you cannot simply raise your hand and say: 'I want to be a subject of God's government.' More is needed.

2 For example, suppose you wanted to become a citizen of another country. In order to do so, you would have to meet the requirements set by the rulers of that country's government. But before you could do this, you would have to learn what these requirements are. In a similar way, you need to learn what God requires of those who want to become subjects of his government. And then you need to meet these requirements.

KNOWLEDGE NEEDED

3 A very important requirement for becoming a subject of God's government is the gaining of a knowledge of its "language." Surely this is reasonable. Some human governments also require that new citizens be able to speak their country's language. Well, then, what "language" must those learn who will receive life under God's government?

4 Notice what Jehovah says about this in his Word, the Bible: "For then I shall give to peoples the change to a *pure language*, in order for them all to call upon the name of Jehovah, in order to serve him shoulder to shoulder." (Zephaniah 3:9) This "pure language" is the *truth of God* found in the Bible. In particular, it is the truth about God's Kingdom government. So to become a

1, 2. What is needed to become a subject of God's government?
3. What is one requirement for becoming a subject of God's government?
4. What "pure language" must God's people learn?

subject of God's government, you must learn this "language" by taking in knowledge of Jehovah and his Kingdom arrangement. —Colossians 1:9, 10; Proverbs 2:1-5.

⁵ Today some human governments require that those who receive citizenship know something about the history of their government, as well as facts regarding its operation. Likewise, you should know such things about God's government if you are to become its subject. This knowledge can lead to eternal life. In prayer to his Father, Jesus said: "This means everlasting life, their taking in knowledge of you, the only true God, and of the one whom you sent forth, Jesus Christ."—John 17:3.

⁶ If you have studied the previous chapters of this book, you should by now have taken in much of this all-important knowledge. Have you? Can you show that you have, by answering questions such as the following: When did God first mention his purpose for a Kingdom government? Who were some of God's servants that looked forward to being its earthly subjects? How many rulers, or kings, will God's government have? From where will these kings rule? Who were the first ones chosen to be kings in God's government? How did Jesus prove that he would

5. (a) What should we know about God's government? (b) What knowledge do we need in order to gain everlasting life?
6. (a) What are some questions that subjects of God's government should be able to answer? (b) Can you answer them?

be a good king? Yet, to become a subject of God's government, more is required than simply having knowledge regarding it.

RIGHTEOUS CONDUCT REQUIRED

[7] Governments today require that new citizens meet a certain standard of conduct. For example, they may say that a man can have only one wife and a woman only one husband. Yet some other governments have different laws. They permit their citizens to have more than one marriage mate. What conduct is expected of persons who want to become subjects of God's government? What does God say is right regarding marriage?

[8] In the beginning Jehovah set the standard for marriage when he gave Adam only one wife. God said: "A man will leave his father and his mother and he must stick to his wife and they must become one flesh." (Genesis 2:21-24) Jesus explained that this is the right standard for Christians. (Matthew 19:4-6) Since marriage mates have become "one flesh," they dishonor the marriage if they have sex relations with someone else. This act is called adultery, and God says that he will punish adulterers. —Hebrews 13:4; Malachi 3:5.

[9] On the other hand, many couples live together and have sexual relations, but they do not get married. However, God did not mean for this close relationship between a man and a woman to be on a trial basis. So to live together without getting married is a sin against God, who made the marriage arrangement. It is called fornication. Fornication is the having of sexual relations with any person to whom you are not married. And the Bible says: "This is what God wills, . . . that you abstain from fornication." (1 Thessalonians 4:3-5) So, then, for a single person to have sexual relations with anyone is wrong.

[10] Today many men and women perform sexual acts with persons of their own sex—men with men and women with women.

---

7. As regards human governments, how do requirements for citizenship differ?
8. (a) What is God's standard for marriage? (b) What is adultery, and what does God say about it?
9. (a) What is God's view of persons having sexual relations when they are not married? (b) What is fornication?
10. What other sexual practices are against God's laws?

Such persons are called homosexuals. Sometimes homosexual women are called Lesbians. But God's Word says that what they do is wrong, that it is "obscene." (Romans 1:26, 27) Also, it is against God's law for a person to have sexual relations with an animal. (Leviticus 18:23) Anyone who wants to live under God's government needs to keep away from these immoral practices.

[11] The drinking of wine, beer or liquor in moderation is not against God's law. In fact, the Bible shows that a little wine can be good for a person's health. (Psalm 104:15; 1 Timothy 5:23) But it *is* against God's law to get drunk, or to share in wild parties at which people carry on immoral conduct. (Ephesians 5:18; 1 Peter 4:3, 4) In addition to using alcoholic drinks to get drunk or "high," many persons today use various drugs for this same purpose. Also, for pleasure they may smoke marijuana or tobacco, while others may chew betel nut or coca leaves. But these things make their bodies unclean and harm their health. So if you want to be a subject of God's government, you must keep away from these harmful things.—2 Corinthians 7:1.

[12] It is obvious that human governments do not want criminals as new citizens. And Jehovah has even higher standards. He requires that we "conduct ourselves honestly in all things." (Hebrews 13:18) If persons do not keep God's laws, they will not be permitted to live under his kingdom. Today people often pretend to be honest, but they break many laws. However, God can see all things. Nobody can fool him. (Hebrews 4:13; Proverbs 15:3; Galatians 6:7, 8) So Jehovah will make sure that persons who break his laws, such as those laws against lying and stealing, will not become subjects of his government. (Ephesians 4:25, 28; Revelation 21:8) Yet God is patient and forgiving. So if a wrongdoer stops his bad practices and turns to doing good, God will accept him.—Isaiah 55:7.

[13] But what about keeping the laws of human governments?

---

11. (a) What is God's view of the use of alcoholic drinks? (b) Those who want to be subjects of God's government must keep away from what practices that are damaging to health?

12. (a) What are some dishonest practices that are against God's laws? (b) How can a person who engages in these practices gain God's favor?

13. What view should God's servants have toward the laws of human governments?

As long as the governments of men exist, God requires that his servants be in subjection to these "superior authorities." Taxes should be paid to them, even though the taxes are high and a person may not agree with the way in which the tax money is spent. Also, the laws of the government should be obeyed. (Romans 13:1, 7; Titus 3:1) The only exception to this would be when obedience to the law would cause a person to disobey the law of God. In that case, as Peter and the other apostles said, "We must obey God as ruler rather than men."—Acts 5:29.

¹⁴ God puts a high value on life. Those who want to become subjects of his government must understand this. Obviously, murder is against God's law. But hatred often leads to murder, and even if someone continues to hate his fellowman he cannot be a subject of God's government. (1 John 3:15) It is vital, therefore, to apply what is said in the Bible at Isaiah 2:4 about

14. How can we show that we share God's view of the value of life?

Subjects of God's government must avoid activities condemned by God

not taking up weapons to kill our neighbors. God's Word shows that even the life of an unborn child in its mother's womb is precious to Jehovah. (Exodus 21:22, 23; Psalm 127:3) And yet millions of abortions are performed each year. This destruction of life is against God's law, because the human inside its mother is a living person and should not be destroyed.

15 Yet, of those who would become subjects of God's government, more is required than merely not doing what is wrong or immoral. They must also make a real effort to do kind and unselfish things for others. They must live by the godly rule given by the King, Jesus Christ: "All things, therefore, that you want men to do to you, you also must likewise do to them." (Matthew 7:12) Christ set the example in showing love for others. He even gave his life for humankind, and commanded his followers: "Love one another; just as I have loved you." (John 13:34; 1 John 3:16) It is this kind of unselfish love and concern for others that will make living a real pleasure under the rule of God's kingdom.—James 2:8.

16 The Bible shows that persons must make changes in their life in order to meet the requirements for becoming subjects of God's government. (Ephesians 4:20-24) Are you working to make these changes? Surely it is worth *any* effort to do so! Why so? It will not mean that you will simply have a better life for a *few* years under some *human* government. No, but you will receive *everlasting* life in perfect health on a paradise earth under a government ruled by *God!*

17 Even now, by meeting God's requirements, you will enjoy a happier life. But you may need to make changes. Well, many, many persons who were hateful or greedy have changed. Also, fornicators, adulterers, homosexuals, drunkards, murderers, thieves, drug addicts and users of tobacco have changed their way of life. They have done so by real effort and with God's help. (1 Corinthians 6:9-11; Colossians 3:5-9) So if you

15. What commands of God's King must all Kingdom subjects obey?
16, 17. (a) What good reasons are there for making changes in our life in order to meet God's requirements? (b) Why can we be sure that we can make any necessary changes?

Subjects of God's government must tell others about it

have hard changes to make in order to meet God's requirements, do not give up. You can do it!

LOYALTY TO GOD'S GOVERNMENT

[18] That Jehovah God would require his subjects loyally to support his Kingdom government should not be surprising. Governments of men require the same thing from their citizens. But in what special way does God expect loyal support to be given? By his subjects taking up weapons to fight for his kingdom? No. Rather, like Jesus Christ and his early followers, they must be loyal *spokesmen* or *proclaimers* of God's kingdom. (Matthew 4:17; 10:5-7; 24:14) It is Jehovah's will that everyone may know what his kingdom is and how it will solve mankind's problems. Have you shared things that you have learned from God's Word with relatives, friends and others? It is God's will that you do. —Romans 10:10; 1 Peter 3:15.

[19] Christ and his early followers needed courage to talk to others about the Kingdom, for often they met up with opposition. (Acts 5:41, 42) The same is true today. This Devil-ruled world does not want the good news of the Kingdom to be preached. So the questions are: Where do you stand? Will you give loyal support to God's kingdom? His will is that a great Kingdom witness be given before the end comes. Will you have a share in giving it?

18. In what special way does God expect us to show our loyal support for his kingdom?
19. (a) Why can we expect opposition when we talk to others about God's kingdom? (b) What questions must you answer?

Chapter 16

God's Government Begins Its Rule

FOR THOUSANDS of years persons with faith in God's government have looked forward to the time when it would begin its rule. For example, the Bible says that faithful Abraham "was awaiting the city having real foundations, the builder and maker of which city is God." (Hebrews 11:10) That "city" is God's kingdom. But why is it here called a "city"? This is because in ancient times it was common for a king to rule over a city. So people often thought of a city as a kingdom.

1. (a) To what have persons of faith long looked forward? (b) Why is God's kingdom called a "city"?

"Are you restoring the kingdom to Israel at this time?"

² The kingdom of God was real to Christ's early followers. This is shown by their keen interest in its rule. (Matthew 20:20-23) A question in their minds was: When would Christ and his disciples begin ruling? Once when Jesus appeared to his disciples after his resurrection, they asked: "Lord, are you restoring the kingdom to Israel *at this time?*" (Acts 1:6) So, are you eager to learn when Christ begins to rule as King of God's government, even as Christ's disciples were?

THE GOVERNMENT FOR WHICH CHRISTIANS PRAY

³ Christ taught his followers to pray to God: "Let your kingdom come. Let your will take place, as in heaven, also upon earth." (Matthew 6:9, 10) But someone may ask: 'Has not Jehovah God always ruled as king? And if he has, why pray for his kingdom to come?'

⁴ True, the Bible calls Jehovah the "King of eternity." (1 Timothy 1:17) And it says: "Jehovah himself has firmly established his throne in the very heavens; and over everything his own kingship has held domination." (Psalm 103:19) So Jehovah has always been the Supreme Ruler over all his creations. (Jeremiah 10:10) However, because of the rebellion against his rulership in the garden of Eden, God arranged for a special government. This is the government for which Jesus Christ later taught his followers to pray. Its purpose is to end the problems caused when Satan the Devil and others turned away from God's rulership.

⁵ This new Kingdom government receives its power and right to rule from the Great King, Jehovah God. It is *his* kingdom. Over and over again, the Bible calls it the "kingdom of God." (Luke 9:2, 11, 60, 62; 1 Corinthians 6:9, 10; 15:50) However, since Jehovah has appointed his Son to be its Chief Ruler, it is also referred to as Christ's kingdom. (2 Peter 1:11) As we learned in an earlier chapter, 144,000 persons from among humankind will

2. (a) What shows that the Kingdom was real to Christ's early disciples? (b) What did they want to know about it?

3, 4. (a) What shows that God has always ruled as King? (b) So why did Christ teach his followers to pray for God's kingdom to come?

5. If it is God's kingdom, why is it also called Christ's kingdom and the kingdom of the 144,000?

rule with Christ in this kingdom. (Revelation 14:1-4; 20:6) So the Bible also refers to it as "their kingdom."—Daniel 7:27.

⁶ Some persons say that the Kingdom began its rule in the year that Jesus returned to heaven. They say that Christ began ruling when he poured out the holy spirit on his followers on the day of the Jewish festival of Pentecost in the year 33 C.E. (Acts 2:1-4) But the Kingdom government that Jehovah arranged to end all the problems created by Satan's rebellion *did not begin its rule then*. There is nothing to show that the 'male child,' which is God's government with Christ as ruler, was then born and began its rule. (Revelation 12:1-10) Well, did Jesus in any way have a kingdom in the year 33 C.E.?

⁷ Yes, Jesus then began to rule over his congregation of follow- ers who, in time, were to join him in the heavens. Thus the Bible speaks of them, while they are on earth, as being taken into "the kingdom of the Son of [God's] love." (Colossians 1:13) But this rule, or "kingdom," over Christians with the hope of heavenly life is not the Kingdom government for which Jesus taught his followers to pray. It is a kingdom over only the 144,000 persons who will rule with him in heaven. Down through the centuries *they have been its only subjects*. Thus this rule, or 'kingdom of the Son of God's love,' will end when the last one of these subjects with a heavenly hope dies and joins Christ in heaven. No longer will they be Christ's subjects, but they will then be kings with him in God's long-promised Kingdom government.

BEGINNING OF RULE IN THE MIDST OF ENEMIES

⁸ When Christ returned to heaven after his resurrection, he did not start ruling then as King of God's government. Rather, there was to be a time of waiting, as the apostle Paul explains: "This man [Jesus Christ] offered one sacrifice for sins perpet- ually and sat down at the right hand of God, *from then on awaiting* until his enemies should be placed as a stool for his

6. According to some persons, when did God's kingdom begin to rule?

7. Over whom has Christ been ruling since 33 C.E.?

8. (a) What shows that after Christ's resurrection there would be a time of waiting before he began to rule? (b) What did God say to Christ when it was time for him to rule?

feet." (Hebrews 10:12, 13) When the time came for Christ to begin to rule, Jehovah told him: "Go subduing [or, conquering] in the midst of your enemies."—Psalm 110:1, 2, 5, 6.

⁹ Does it sound strange that anyone would be an enemy of God's government? Yet not everyone wants to live under a government that requires its subjects to do what is right. So after telling how Jehovah and his Son would take over world rulership, the Bible says, *"the nations became wrathful."* (Revelation 11:15, 17, 18) The nations do not welcome God's kingdom because Satan misleads them into opposing it.

¹⁰ When God's government begins its rule, Satan and his angels are still living in heaven. Since they oppose Kingdom rule, right away war breaks out. As a result, Satan and his angels are thrown out of heaven. At this, a loud voice says: "Now have come to pass the salvation and the power and *the kingdom of our God and the authority of his Christ.*" Yes, the rule of God's government begins! And with Satan and his angels removed from heaven, there is rejoicing there. "On this account be glad, you heavens and you who reside in them!" the Bible says.—Revelation 12:7-12.

¹¹ Is this also a happy time for the earth? No! Instead, there is the greatest time of trouble the earth has ever had. The Bible tells us: "Woe for the earth and for the sea, because the Devil has come down to you, having great anger, knowing he has a short period of time." (Revelation 12:12) So this is an important point to remember: *The start of the rule of God's kingdom does not mean immediate peace and security on earth.* True peace will come later when God's kingdom takes full control of the earth. This happens at the end of the "short period of time," when Satan and his angels will be put out of the way so that they can no longer cause trouble for anyone.

¹² But *when* is Satan thrown out of heaven, thus causing trou-

---

9. (a) Why does not everyone want God's kingdom? (b) When God's government begins its rule, what do the nations do?

10, 11. (a) When God's government begins its rule, what happens in heaven? (b) What happens on earth? (c) So what important point do we want to remember?

12. Why can we expect that the Bible would tell us when God's kingdom begins its rule?

ble on earth for "a short period of time"? *When* does God's government begin its rule? Does the Bible give an answer? We should expect that it would. Why? Well, because long in advance the Bible foretold when God's Son would appear first as a human on earth to become the Messiah. In fact, it pointed to the very year that he became the Messiah. What, then, about the even more important coming of the Messiah, or Christ, to begin his Kingdom rule? Surely we would expect that the Bible would also tell us when this would happen!

[13] But a person may ask: 'Where does the Bible foretell the very year the Messiah appeared on earth?' The Bible book of Daniel says: "From the going forth of the word to restore and to rebuild Jerusalem *until Messiah the Leader,* there will be seven weeks, also sixty-two weeks," or all together 69 weeks. (Daniel 9:25) These, however, are not 69 literal weeks, which amount to only 483 days, or a little more than one year. They are *69 weeks of years, or 483 years.* (Compare Numbers 14:34.) The command to restore and rebuild the walls of Jerusalem was given in 455 B.C.E.* (Nehemiah 2:1-8) So these 69 weeks of years ended 483 years later, in 29 C.E. And that is the very year that Jesus came to John to be baptized! On that occasion he was anointed with holy spirit and became the Messiah, or Christ.—Luke 3:1, 2, 21-23.

WHEN GOD'S GOVERNMENT BEGINS ITS RULE

[14] Well, then, where does the Bible foretell the year that Christ begins to rule as king of God's government? It is in this same Bible book of Daniel. (Daniel 4:10-37) There a giant, heaven-high tree is used to represent King Nebuchadnezzar of Babylon. He was the highest human ruler at that time. However, King Nebuchadnezzar was forced to know that someone higher was ruling. This one is "the Most High," or "the King of the heavens," Jehovah God. (Daniel 4:34, 37) So, in a more important

---

* For the historical evidence that this command was given in 455 B.C.E., see the subject "Artaxerxes" in the book *Aid to Bible Understanding,* published by the Watchtower Bible and Tract Society of New York, Inc.

---

13. How does the Bible foretell the very year that the Messiah appeared on earth?
14. What does the "tree" in Daniel chapter four represent?

The tall tree in Daniel chapter 4 represents divine rulership. For a time this was expressed through the kingdom of Judah

way, this heaven-high tree, comes to represent *the supreme rulership of God, particularly in its relationship to our earth.* Jehovah's rulership was expressed for a time through the kingdom that he set up over the nation of Israel. Thus the kings of the tribe of Judah who reigned over the Israelites were said to "sit upon Jehovah's throne."—1 Chronicles 29:23.

[15] According to the Bible account in Daniel chapter four, the heaven-high tree was cut down. However, the stump was left, and bands of iron and of copper were put on it. This would keep the stump from growing until it was God's time to remove the bands and let it start growing again. But how and when was God's rulership cut down?

[16] In due course, the kingdom of Judah that Jehovah had set up became so corrupt that he allowed King Nebuchadnezzar to destroy it, to cut it down. This happened in the year 607 B.C.E. At that time Zedekiah, the last king of Judah to sit on Jehovah's throne, was told: "Lift off the crown. . . . it will certainly become no one's until he comes who has the legal right, and I must give it to him."—Ezekiel 21:25-27.

15. When the "tree" was cut down, why were bands put on it?
16. (a) How and when was God's rulership cut down? (b) What was the last king of Judah to sit on "Jehovah's throne" told?

¹⁷ So God's rulership, as represented by the "tree," was cut down in 607 B.C.E. No longer was there a government to represent God's rulership in the earth. Thus, in 607 B.C.E. a period of time began that Jesus Christ later referred to as *"the appointed times of the nations,"* or, "the times of the Gentiles." (Luke 21:24; *King James Version*) During these "appointed times" God did not have a government to represent his rulership in the earth.

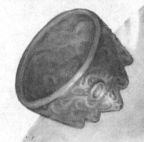

607 B.C.E.

¹⁸ What was to happen at the end of these "appointed times of the nations"? Jehovah was to give the power to rule to the One "who has the legal right." This One is Jesus Christ. So if we can find out when "the appointed times of the nations" end, we will know when Christ begins to rule as king.

¹⁹ According to Daniel chapter four, these "appointed times" would be "*seven times.*" Daniel shows that there would be "seven times" during which God's rulership, as represented by the "tree," would not be in operation over the earth. (Daniel 4:16, 23) How long are these "seven times"?

---

17. What period of time began in 607 B.C.E.?
18. What was to happen at the end of "the appointed times of the nations"?
19. For how many "times" would God's rulership over the earth be interrupted?

The tree was cut down when the kingdom of Judah was destroyed

In 607 B.C.E. God's kingdom of Judah fell.
In 1914 C.E. Jesus Christ began to rule
as king of God's heavenly government

1914 C.E.

October, 607 B.C.E.—October, 1 B.C.E. = **606 YEARS**
October, 1 B.C.E.—October, 1914 C.E. = **1,914 YEARS**

SEVEN GENTILE TIMES = 2,520 YEARS

[20] In Revelation chapter 12, verses 6 and 14, we learn that 1,260 days are equal to "a time [that is, 1 time] and times [that is, 2 times] and half a time." That is a total of 3½ times. So "a time" would be equal to 360 days. Therefore, "seven times" would be 7 times 360, or 2,520 days. Now if we count a day for a year, according to a Bible rule, the "seven times" equal *2,520 years.*—Numbers 14:34; Ezekiel 4:6.

[21] We have already learned that "the appointed times of the nations" began in the year 607 B.C.E. So by counting 2,520 years from that date, we come down to 1914 C.E. That is the year these "appointed times" ended. Millions of people still living remember the things that happened in 1914. In that year, World War I began a period of terrible trouble that has continued to our day. *This means that Jesus Christ began to rule as king of God's heavenly government in 1914.* And because the Kingdom has already started its rule, how timely it is that we pray for it to "come" and wipe Satan's wicked system of things from the earth!—Matthew 6:10; Daniel 2:44.

[22] Yet a person may ask: 'If Christ has already returned to rule in his Father's kingdom, why do we not see him?'

20. (a) How long is one "time"? (b) How long are the "seven times"? (c) Why do we count a day for a year?
21. (a) When do "the appointed times of the nations" begin and end? (b) When does God's government begin its rule? (c) Why is it still proper to pray for God's kingdom to come?
22. What question may some ask?

Chapter 17

Christ's Return— How Seen?

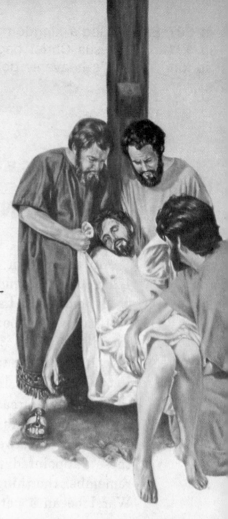

"I AM COMING AGAIN." (John 14:3) Jesus Christ made this promise to his apostles when he was with them the night before his death. You will probably agree that never has there been a greater need for the peace, health and life that Christ's return in Kingdom power will bring to humankind. But *how* does Christ return? Who see him, and in what way?

2 At his return, Christ does not come to live on earth. Rather, those who are to rule as kings with him are taken to live with him in heaven. Jesus told his apostles: "I am coming again and will receive you home to myself, that where I am you also may be." (John 14:3) So, when Christ returns, those who are taken to heaven become spirit persons, and they see Christ in his glorified spirit body. (1 Corinthians 15:44) But do the rest of humankind, who do not go to heaven, see Christ when he returns?

Christ gave up his body as a sacrifice. He could never take it back and become a man again

WHY HE COULD NOT RETURN AS A HUMAN

3 That same night Jesus went on to say to his apostles: "A little longer and *the world will behold me no more.*" (John 14:19)

1. (a) What promise did Christ make? (b) What need is there for Christ's return?
2. (a) When he returns, where does Christ take his anointed followers, including his apostles, to live? (b) What kind of bodies do they have there?
3. What Bible evidence shows that humans will never see Christ again?

The "world" refers to humankind. So Jesus here plainly said that people on earth would not see him again after his death. The apostle Paul wrote: "Even if we have known Christ according to the flesh, certainly we now know him so no more." —2 Corinthians 5:16.

⁴ Yet many persons believe that Christ will return in the same human body in which he was put to death, and that all those living on earth will see him. The Bible, however, says that Christ returns in glory with all the angels, and that he sits "down on his glorious throne." (Matthew 25:31) If Jesus were to come and sit as a man on an earthly throne, he would be lower in station than the angels. But he comes as the mightiest and most glorious of all these spirit sons of God and is therefore invisible, just as they are.—Philippians 2:8-11.

⁵ On the other hand, over 1,900 years ago it was necessary for Jesus to lower himself and become a man. He needed to give his perfect human life as a ransom for us. Jesus once explained it this way: "The bread that I shall give is my flesh in behalf of the life of the world." (John 6:51) Jesus thus gave up his fleshly body in sacrifice for humankind. For how long was that sacrifice to be in effect? The apostle Paul answers: "We have been sanctified through the offering of the body of Jesus Christ *once for all time*." (Hebrews 10:10) Having given up his flesh for the life of the world, Christ could never take it again and become a man once more. For that basic reason his return could never be in the human body that he sacrificed once for all time.

FLESHLY BODY NOT TAKEN TO HEAVEN

⁶ However, many persons believe that Christ took his fleshly body to heaven. They point to the fact that when Christ was raised from the dead, his fleshly body was no longer in the tomb. (Mark 16:5-7) Also, after his death Jesus appeared to his disciples in a fleshly body to show them that he was alive. Once He even had the apostle Thomas put his hand into

4. What shows that Christ returns as a mighty invisible spirit person?
5. Why could Christ not return in a human body?
6. Why do many persons believe that Christ took his fleshly body to heaven?

the hole in His side so that Thomas would believe that He had actually been resurrected. (John 20:24-27) Does this not prove that Christ was raised alive in the same body in which he was put to death?

7 No, it does not. The Bible is very clear when it says: "Christ died once for all time concerning sins . . . , *he being put to death in the flesh, but being made alive in the spirit.*" (1 Peter 3:18) Humans with

Why did Mary Magdalene mistake Jesus for a gardener after his resurrection?

flesh-and-blood bodies cannot live in heaven. Of the resurrection to heavenly life, the Bible says: "It is sown a physical body, it is raised up a spiritual body. . . . *flesh and blood cannot inherit God's kingdom.*" (1 Corinthians 15:44-50) Only spirit persons with spiritual bodies can live in heaven.

8 Well, then, what happened to Jesus' fleshly body? Did not the disciples find his tomb empty? They did, because God removed Jesus' body. Why did God do this? It fulfilled what had been written in the Bible. (Psalm 16:10; Acts 2:31) Thus Jehovah saw fit to remove Jesus' body, even as he had done before with Moses' body. (Deuteronomy 34:5, 6) Also, if the body had been left in the tomb, Jesus' disciples could not have understood that he had been raised from the dead, since at that time they did not fully appreciate spiritual things.

9 But since the apostle Thomas was able to put his hand into the hole in Jesus' side, does that not show that Jesus was raised from the dead in the same body that was nailed to the stake? No, for Jesus simply materialized or took on a fleshly body, as

7. What proves that Christ went to heaven as a spirit person?
8. What happened to Christ's human body?
9. How was it possible for Thomas to put his hand into a wound in the materialized body of the resurrected Jesus?

angels had done in the past. In order to convince Thomas of who He was, He used a body with wound holes. He appeared, or seemed to be, fully human, able to eat and drink, just as did the angels that Abraham once entertained.—Genesis 18:8; Hebrews 13:2.

[10] While Jesus appeared to Thomas in a body similar to the one in which He was put to death, He also took on different bodies when appearing to His followers. Thus Mary Magdalene at first thought that Jesus was a gardener. At other times his disciples did not at first recognize him. In these instances it was not his personal appearance that served to identify him, but it was some word or action that they recognized.—John 20:14-16; 21:6, 7; Luke 24:30, 31.

[11] For 40 days after his resurrection, Jesus made appearances in a fleshly body to his disciples. (Acts 1:3) Then he left for heaven. But some may ask: 'Did not the two angels present tell the apostles that Christ "will come thus in the same manner as you have beheld him going into the sky"?' (Acts 1:11) Yes, they did. But notice that they said *"in the same manner,"* not in the same body. And what was the manner of Jesus' leaving? It was quiet, without public display. Only his apostles knew about it. The world did not.

[12] Consider how the Bible describes the manner in which Jesus left his apostles on his way to heaven: "While they were looking on, he was lifted up and a cloud caught him up from their vision." (Acts 1:9) So when Jesus began going into the sky, a cloud hid him from the literal eyesight of his apostles. The departing

Into what fleshly body did the resurrected Jesus ask Thomas to put his hand?

10. What shows that Jesus put on different physical bodies?
11, 12. (a) In what *manner* did Christ leave the earth? (b) So in what manner should we expect Christ's return?

Jesus, therefore, became invisible to them. They could not see him. Then in his spiritual body he ascended to heaven. (1 Peter 3:18) Thus his return also would be invisible, in a spiritual body.

HOW SEEN BY EVERY EYE

[13] How, then, are we to understand the words of Revelation 1:7? There the apostle John writes: "Look! He is coming with the clouds, and *every eye will see him,* and those who pierced him; and all the tribes of the earth will beat themselves in grief because of him." Here the Bible speaks of seeing, not with physical eyes, but in the sense of *discerning* or *perceiving.* Thus, when a person comprehends or understands a matter, he may say, 'I see it.' The Bible, in fact, speaks of "the eyes of your understanding." (Ephesians 1:18, *King James Version*) So the expression "every eye will see him" means that everyone will then understand or recognize that Christ is present.

[14] Those who actually "pierced" Jesus are no longer alive on earth. So they represent persons who, by hurting Christ's present-day followers, copy the conduct of those first-century men. (Matthew 25:40, 45) The time will soon come for Christ to execute such wicked ones. They have been warned in advance about this. When this execution takes place, they will "see" or recognize what is happening. And their grief will indeed be great!

DOES CHRIST COME BACK TO EARTH?

[15] To return does not always mean that one goes to a literal place. Thus sick persons are said to 'return to health.' And a former ruler may be said to 'return to power.' In a similar way, God told Abraham: "I shall return to you, next year at this time, and Sarah will have a son." (Genesis 18:14; 21:1) Jehovah's return meant, not literally returning, but *turning his attention* to Sarah to do what he had promised.

---

13. How are we to understand the statement that "every eye will see" Christ when he comes with the clouds?
14. (a) Who are meant by "those who pierced him"? (b) Why will there be great grief when everyone finally recognizes Christ's presence?
15. In what way is the word "return" often used?

[16] In the same way, Christ's return does not mean that he literally comes back to this earth. Rather, it means that he takes Kingdom power toward this earth and turns his attention to it. He does not need to leave his heavenly throne and actually come down to earth to do this. As we have seen in the previous chapter, Bible evidence shows that in the year 1914 C.E. God's time arrived for Christ to return and begin ruling. It was then that the cry was heard in heaven: "Now have come to pass the salvation and the power and the kingdom of our God and the authority of his Christ."—Revelation 12:10.

[17] Since Christ's return is invisible, is there a way to confirm that it has really occurred. Yes, there is. Christ himself gave a visible "sign" by which we may know that he is invisibly present and the end of the world is near. Let us examine that "sign."

Christ was to return in the same manner that he left the earth. In what manner did he leave?

---

16. (a) In what way does Christ return to earth? (b) When did Christ return, and what then came to pass?
17. Since Christ's return is invisible, what did he give so that we could know that he had returned?

Chapter 18

"The End of the World" Is at Hand!

WHEN JESUS CHRIST threw Satan and his angels out of heaven and began his Kingdom rule, it meant that the end of Satan and his wicked system was near. (Revelation 12:7-12) But how could Christ's followers on earth know that this event in heaven, unseen to their eyes, had taken place? How could they know that Christ was invisibly present in Kingdom power and that "the end of the world" was near? They could know by checking to see if the "sign" that Jesus gave was being fulfilled.

2 Shortly before Jesus' death, while he was sitting on the Mount of Olives, four of his apostles came to ask him for a "sign." This is the way their question has been read, in the *King James Version,* by millions of people: "Tell us, when shall these things be? and what shall be the sign of thy coming, and the end of the world?" (Matthew 24:3) But what do these expressions, *"thy coming"* and *"the end of the world,"* really mean?

3 The Greek word here translated "coming" is *parousia,* and it means "presence." So, then, when the "sign" is seen, this means we would know that Christ is present though unseen, that he has already come in Kingdom power. The expression "end of the world" is also very misleading. It does not mean the end of the earth, but, rather, the end of Satan's system of things. (2 Corinthians 4:4) The apostles' question therefore accurately reads: "Tell us, When will these things be, and what will be

1. How would Christ's earthly followers know when he had begun to rule in heaven?

2. What question did Christ's disciples ask him?

3. (a) What do the expressions *"thy coming"* and *"the end of the world"* really mean? (b) How, then, is the question asked by Christ's disciples correctly translated?

the sign of *your presence* and of *the conclusion of the system of things?"*—Matthew 24:3, *New World Translation.*

4 Jesus did not give just one event as "the sign." He told of many happenings and situations. Other Bible writers besides Matthew mentioned additional events that would mark the "last days." All these things that were foretold would take place during the time that Bible writers called the "last days." (2 Timothy 3:1-5; 2 Peter 3:3, 4) These happenings would be like the different lines that make up a person's fingerprint, a print that cannot belong to any other person. The "last days" contain their own pattern of marks, or happenings. These form a positive "fingerprint" that cannot belong to any other time period.

5 In chapter 16 of this book we considered Bible evidence that Christ returned and began ruling in the midst of his enemies in the year 1914. Now take a careful look at the various features of "the sign" of Christ's presence and further evidence of the "last days" of Satan's wicked system of things. As you examine these foretold things on the next four pages, note how they have been undergoing fulfillment since 1914.

---

4. (a) What makes up "the sign" that Jesus gave? (b) In what way can "the sign" be compared to a fingerprint?
5, 6. As you examine 11 evidences of the "last days" on the following pages, what do you understand about "the conclusion of the system of things"?

Jesus told his disciples what would be visible proof of his invisible presence in Kingdom power

"NATION WILL RISE AGAINST NATION AND KINGDOM AGAINST KINGDOM."—Matthew 24:7.

Surely you have seen this part of the "sign" being fulfilled since 1914! In that year World War I began. Never in history had there been such a terrible war. It was *total* war. World War I was much greater than all the major wars fought during the 2,400 years before 1914. Yet only 21 years after that war ended, World War II began. And it was four times as destructive as World War I.

Terrible wars continue to be fought. Since World War II ended in 1945, more than *25 million persons* have been killed in some 150 wars fought around the globe. On any given day, there have been, on the average, 12 wars going on somewhere in the world. And there is the continual threat of another world war. The United States alone has enough nuclear weapons to destroy every man, woman and child on earth 12 times over!

"THERE WILL BE FOOD SHORTAGES."—Matthew 24:7.

Following World War I came the greatest famine in all history. In northern China alone 15,000 died *every day* from starvation. But the shortage of food was even greater after World War II. A fourth of the world was then starving! And ever since, food has remained scarce for many people on earth.

"Every 8.6 seconds someone in an underdeveloped country dies as a result of illness caused by malnutrition," said the New York *Times* in 1967. Millions still die of starvation —some *50 million* a year! By 1980, about one fourth of the people on earth (1,000,000,000 persons) were hungry because they could not get enough to eat. Even in places where food is plentiful, many are too poor to buy it.

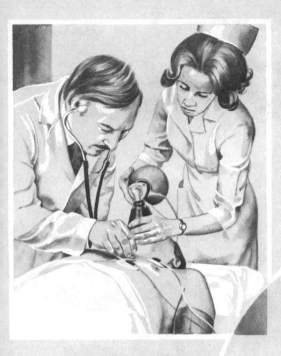

"IN ONE PLACE AFTER ANOTHER PESTILENCES."—Luke 21:11.

Right after World War I more people died of the Spanish flu than had died of any disease epidemic in the history of mankind. The death toll was some *21 million* people! Yet pestilence and disease continue to rage. Millions die each year from heart trouble and cancer. Venereal disease is spreading rapidly. Other terrible diseases, such as malaria, snail fever and river blindness, occur in country after country, especially in Asia, Africa and Latin America.

"THERE WILL BE . . . EARTHQUAKES IN ONE PLACE AFTER ANOTHER."—Matthew 24:7.

From 1914 until now, there have been many more major earthquakes than in any other like period in recorded history. For over 1,000 years, from the year 856 C.E. to 1914, there were only 24 major earthquakes, causing some 1,973,000 deaths. But in the 63 years from 1915 to 1978, a total of some 1,600,000 persons died in 43 great earthquakes.

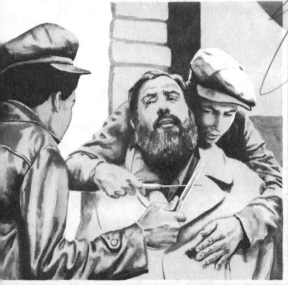

"INCREASING OF LAWLESSNESS." —Matthew 24:12.

From all over the world come reports of increasing lawlessness and crime. Crimes of violence, such as murder, rape and robberies, are now running wild. In the United States alone, a serious crime is committed, on the average, about *every second*. In many places no one feels safe on the streets, even during the daytime. At night people stay in their homes behind locked and barricaded doors, afraid to go outside.

"MEN BECOME FAINT OUT OF FEAR."—Luke 21:26.

Fear is probably the biggest single emotion in people's lives today. Not long after the exploding of the first nuclear bombs, atomic scientist Harold C. Urey said: "We will eat fear, sleep fear, live in fear and die in fear." For much of humankind this is what is happening. And it is not simply because of the ever-present threat of nuclear warfare. People also fear crime, pollution, disease, inflation and many other things that threaten their security and their very lives.

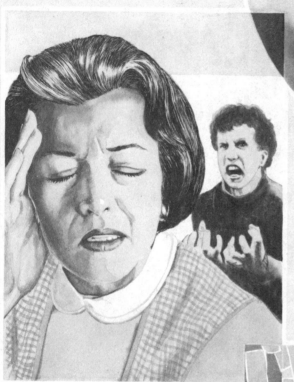

'DISOBEDIENCE TO PARENTS.'
—2 Timothy 3:2.

Parents today often have little control over their children. Youths rebel against all authority. So every country on earth is affected by the plague of youth crime. More than half of all serious crimes in some countries are committed by children 10 to 17 years of age. Murder, rape, assault, robbery, burglary, car theft—all these things children are doing. Never in history has disobedience to parents been so common.

"LOVERS OF MONEY."
—2 Timothy 3:2.

Wherever you look today you can see acts of greed. Many will do practically anything for money. They will steal or even kill. It is not unusual for greedy persons to produce and sell products that are known, in one way or another, to make others sick or to kill them. Either openly, or by the way they live, people are saying of money: 'This is my god.'

"LOVERS OF PLEASURES RATHER THAN LOVERS OF GOD." —2 Timothy 3:4.

Most people today think only of doing what pleases them or their families, not what pleases God. Particularly do many love what God condemns, including fornication, adultery, drunkenness, drug abuse and other so-called pleasures. Even pleasures that, in themselves, can be wholesome are put ahead of any effort to learn about God and serve him.

"HAVING A FORM OF GODLY DEVOTION BUT PROVING FALSE TO ITS POWER."—2 Timothy 3:5.

World leaders and common people alike often make an outward show of being godly. They may attend church services and make contributions to religious causes. Those in government may put their hand on a Bible when they take office. But often it is simply *"a form of godly devotion."* Just as the Bible foretold, the true worship of God is not really a force in most people's lives today. They are not motivated by a real power for good.

"RUINING THE EARTH." —Revelation 11:18.

The air we breathe, the water we drink and the land our food is grown on are being polluted. It is so serious that scientist Barry Commoner warned: "I believe that continued pollution of the earth, if unchecked, will eventually destroy the fitness of this planet as a place for human life."

[6] After considering the foregoing, is it not clear that "the sign" Christ gave and the evidences foretold by his disciples are now being fulfilled? Although there are many other proofs, those listed here should be enough to show that we really are living in the time the Bible foretold as the "last days."

[7] Yet some persons may say: 'Such things as wars, famines, pestilences and earthquakes have occurred often throughout history. So it would not be hard to foretell that they would occur again.' But think: The Bible not only foretold these things, but indicated that they would occur on a *worldwide scale*. Also, the Bible said that *all these things* would happen upon the generation that was alive in 1914. Yet what were prominent world leaders foretelling just before 1914? They were saying that conditions promising world peace were never more favorable. Yet the terrible troubles the Bible foretold began right on time, in 1914! In fact, world leaders now say that 1914 was a turning point in history.

[8] After drawing attention to the many things that have marked the period from 1914 onward, Jesus said: "This generation will by no means pass away until all these things [including the end of this system] occur." (Matthew 24:34, 14) Which generation did Jesus mean? He meant the generation of people who were living in 1914. Those persons yet remaining of that generation are now very old. However, some of them will still be alive to see the end of this wicked system. So of this we can be certain: Shortly now there will be a sudden end to all wickedness and wicked people at Armageddon.

---

7. (a) What makes the Bible prophecies regarding Christ's presence and the "last days" so remarkable? (b) In contrast with what the Bible foretold, what were world leaders forecasting just prior to 1914?
8. (a) Which generation did Jesus indicate would see the end of this system of things? (b) So of what can we be certain?

1914

ARMAGEDDON

Some of the generation living in 1914 will see the end of the system of things and survive it

Chapter 19

After Armageddon,
a Paradise Earth

"ARMAGEDDON" is a frightening word to many. Often world leaders use it to refer to a possible World War III. However, the Bible speaks of Armageddon as the place of a righteous war fought by God. (Revelation 16:14, 16, *King James Version*) This war of God will prepare the way for a righteous new order.

2 Unlike the wars of men, which kill both the good and the bad, Armageddon will destroy only the bad. (Psalm 92:7) Jehovah God will be the Judge, and he will remove any who *willfully* refuse to obey his righteous laws. Today many persons see nothing wrong with such things as fornication, getting drunk, lying or cheating. But, according to God, these things are wrong. So at Armageddon he will not save those who continue to do them. (1 Corinthians 6:9, 10; Revelation 21:8) Knowing God's laws on these matters, it is important for persons who may be practicing such bad things to change their ways.

3 After Armageddon no part of this wicked world will remain. Only persons who serve God will continue to live. (1 John 2:17) Jesus Christ compared the situation to that of Noah's day. (Matthew 24:37-39; 2 Peter 3:5-7, 13; 2:5) After Armageddon, God's kingdom will be the only government ruling over the earth. Satan and his demons will be gone. (Revelation 20:1-3) Consider, on the following pages, some of the blessings that the Bible indicates obedient people will enjoy.

1. (a) What is a common view of Armageddon? (b) What does the Bible say about it?
2. (a) Who will be destroyed at Armageddon? (b) So what practices should we wisely avoid?
3. (a) To what did Jesus compare the end of the present world? (b) What will happen to Satan and his demons? (c) According to scriptures on following pages, what kind of conditions will be enjoyed on the paradise earth?

ALL HUMANKIND AT PEACE

"There has been a child born to us, there has been a son given to us; and the princely rule will come to be upon his shoulder. And his name will be called . . . Prince of Peace. To the abundance of the princely rule and to peace there will be no end."—Isaiah 9:6, 7.

"In his days the righteous one will sprout, and the abundance of peace until the moon is no more. And he will have subjects from sea to sea and from the River to the ends of the earth."—Psalm 72:7, 8.

NO MORE WAR

"Come, you people, behold the activities of Jehovah, how he has set astonishing events on the earth. He is making wars to cease to the extremity of the earth."—Psalm 46:8, 9.

FINE HOMES AND ENJOYABLE WORK FOR EVERYONE

"They will certainly build houses and have occupancy . . . They will not build and someone else have occupancy; they will not plant and someone else do the eating . . . the work of their own hands my chosen ones will use to the full. They will not toil for nothing, nor will they bring to birth for disturbance; because they are the offspring made up of the chosen ones of Jehovah, and their descendants with them."—Isaiah 65:21-23.

CRIME, VIOLENCE AND WICKEDNESS GONE

"For evildoers themselves will be cut off . . . And just a little while longer, and the wicked one will be no more; and you will certainly give attention to his place, and he will not be."—Psalm 37:9, 10.

"As regards the wicked, they will be cut off from the very earth; and as for the treacherous, they will be torn away from it."—Proverbs 2:22.

ALL THE EARTH A PARADISE

Jesus said: "You will be with me in Paradise." —Luke 23:43.

"The righteous themselves will possess the earth, and they will reside forever upon it." —Psalm 37:29.

PLENTY OF GOOD THINGS FOR ALL TO EAT

"Jehovah of armies will certainly make for all the peoples . . . a banquet of well-oiled dishes, a banquet of wine kept on the dregs, of well-oiled dishes filled with marrow."—Isaiah 25:6.

"There will come to be plenty of grain on the earth; on the top of the mountains there will be an overflow." "The earth itself will certainly give its produce; God, our God, will bless us." —Psalm 72:16; 67:6.

⁴ Surely you want to live on the paradise earth like the garden in which the first man Adam was created. (Genesis 2:8; Luke 23:43) Think of it—no more war, crime or violence. You will be able to walk anywhere at any time of the day or night without fear of being harmed. The wicked simply will no longer be. —Psalm 37:35-38.

⁵ This means that there will be no dishonest politicians and greedy business leaders to oppress the people. Nor will people be burdened with high taxes to pay for military weapons. Never again will anyone be without good food and comfortable housing because he cannot afford them. Unemployment, inflation and high prices will be no more. The troubles that cause suffering to families today will no longer exist. All will have pleasant work to do, and they will be able to see and enjoy the results of their labors.

⁶ First of all, those who survive Armageddon will have the work of cleaning up the earth and clearing away the ruins of this old system. And then they will have the privilege, under the direction of the Kingdom rule, of cultivating the earth and making it a beautiful place in which to live. What a happy work that will be! God will bless everything that is done. He will provide the right kind of climate to grow crops and raise livestock, and he will see to it that these are protected from disease and harm.

⁷ This promise of the loving Creator, as given through the Bible psalmist, will be fulfilled: "You are opening your hand and satisfying the desire of every living thing." (Psalm 145:16) Yes, all the proper desires of God-fearing persons will be completely satisfied. We cannot even imagine how wonderful life will be in paradise on earth. Telling about God's arrangement for blessing his people, the apostle Peter wrote: "There are *new heavens*

4, 5. (a) What conditions will no longer exist on the paradise earth? (b) What will people be able to do that, in many places, they cannot do today?
6. (a) What work will Armageddon survivors do? (b) How will God bless the work that is done?
7. (a) What promise of God will be fulfilled? (b) What do Christians await according to God's promise?

and a *new earth* that we are awaiting according to [God's] promise, and in these *righteousness* is to dwell."—2 Peter 3:13; Isaiah 65:17; 66:22.

[8] What are these "new heavens"? They are not new physical heavens. God made our physical heavens perfect, and they bring him glory. (Psalm 8:3; 19:1, 2) The "new heavens" refer to a new rulership over the earth. The "heavens" now are made up of man-made governments. At Armageddon these will pass away. (2 Peter 3:7) The "new heavens" that will replace them will be God's heavenly government. Its king will be Jesus Christ. But ruling with him as part of the "new heavens" will be 144,000 of his faithful followers.—Revelation 5:9, 10; 14:1, 3.

[9] What, then, is the "new earth"? It is not a new planet. God made this planet Earth just right for humans to live on, and it is his will that it remain forever. (Psalm 104:5) The "new earth" refers to a new group or society of people. The Bible often uses the word "earth" in such a way. For example, it says: "All the earth [meaning, the people] continued to be of one language." (Genesis 11:1) The "earth" that will be destroyed are the people that make themselves part of this wicked system of things. (2 Peter 3:7) The "new earth" that replaces them will be made up of true servants of God who have separated themselves from this world of wicked people.—John 17:14; 1 John 2:17.

[10] Right now people of all races and nationalities who will make up part of the "new earth" are being gathered into the Christian congregation. The unity and peace that exist among them is only a small preview of what will make living on the paradise earth after Armageddon such a pleasure. Truly, God's kingdom will bring to pass what no human government could even hope to do. Just consider a few of such blessings on the following pages.

---

8. (a) Why do we not need new physical heavens? (b) What are the "new heavens"?
9. (a) What is the "new earth"? (b) What is the earth that will be destroyed?
10. (a) Who are now being gathered, and into what? (b) According to the scriptures on the following pages, what will be done on the paradise earth that human governments cannot do?

A LOVING BROTHERHOOD OF ALL HUMANKIND

"God is not partial, but in every nation the man that fears him and works righteousness is acceptable to him."—Acts 10:34, 35.

"Look! a great crowd, which no man was able to number, *out of all nations and tribes and peoples and tongues* . . . They will hunger no more nor thirst anymore."—Revelation 7:9, 16.

PEACE BETWEEN PEOPLE AND ANIMALS

"The wolf will actually reside for a while with the male lamb, and with the kid the leopard itself will lie down, and the calf and the maned young lion and the well-fed animal all together; and a mere little boy will be leader over them."—Isaiah 11:6; Isaiah 65:25.

NO MORE SICKNESS, OLD AGE OR DEATH

"At that time the eyes of the blind ones will be opened, and the very ears of the deaf ones will be unstopped. At that time the lame one will climb up just as a stag does, and the tongue of the speechless one will cry out in gladness."—Isaiah 35:5, 6.

"And God himself will be with them. And he will wipe out every tear from their eyes, and death will be no more, neither will mourning nor outcry nor pain be anymore. The former things have passed away."—Revelation 21:3, 4.

THE DEAD ARE BROUGHT BACK TO LIFE

"The hour is coming in which all those in the memorial tombs will hear his voice and come out."—John 5:28, 29.

"The sea gave up those dead in it, and death and Hades gave up those dead in them."—Revelation 20:13.

¹¹ How much better the paradise under God's kingdom will be than anything this old system can bring! True, some people today have made the place where they live into what looks like a paradise. But the people who live together in these places may be mean and selfish, and may even hate one another. And, in time, they get sick, grow old and die. After Armageddon, however, the paradise on earth will include much more than simply beautiful homes, gardens and parks.

¹² Think of it. People of all races and nationalities will learn to live together as one family of brothers and sisters. They will truly love one another. None will be selfish or unkind. No one will hate another person just because of his race, color, or the place that he comes from. Prejudice will cease to exist. Everyone on earth will become a true friend and neighbor of everyone else. Truly, it will be a paradise in a spiritual way. Would you like to live in this paradise under the "new heavens"?

¹³ Today people talk a lot about living together in peace, and have even set up a "United Nations" organization. Yet people and nations are divided as never before. What is needed? The hearts of people need to change. But it is simply impossible for the governments of this world to perform such a miracle. The Bible's message about God's love, however, *is* doing it.

¹⁴ Upon learning about the righteous new system, the hearts of many people are being moved to love God. And so they begin to act also in a loving way toward others, just as God does. (1 John 4:9-11, 20) This means a big change in their lives. Many who were mean and hateful, like vicious animals, thus have become meek and peaceable. Like obedient sheep, they are gathered into the Christian flock.

¹⁵ For over 1,900 years there was a gathering together of the "little flock" of 144,000 Christians who will rule with Christ. Only a few of these are left on earth; most are already ruling with

11. What often ruins the kind of paradise that people now make?
12, 13. (a) What conditions of peace will exist after Armageddon? (b) What is needed to bring about these conditions?
14. What is happening now to prove that these paradise conditions will be realized?
15. (a) What two groups of Christians are there? (b) Who will be the first ones to make up the "new earth"?

Christ in heaven. (Luke 12:32; Revelation 20:6) But speaking of other Christians, Jesus said: "I have other sheep, which are not of this fold [of the "little flock"]; those also I must bring, and they will listen to my voice, and they will become one flock, one shepherd." (John 10:16) A "great crowd" of these "other sheep" are now being gathered. They will make up the first ones of the "new earth." Jehovah will protect them through "the great tribulation" at the end of this wicked system to live on into the earthly paradise.—Revelation 7:9, 10, 13-15.

[16] After Armageddon another miracle will add to the paradise conditions. Animals such as lions, tigers, leopards and bears, which now can be dangerous, will be at peace. How fine then to take a walk in the woods and to be joined for a while by a lion at your side, and perhaps later by a big bear! Never again will anybody need to fear another living thing.

[17] Yet no matter how beautiful the homes and gardens, how kind and loving the people, or how friendly the animals, if we got sick, grew old and died there would still be sadness. But who can bring perfect health to all? Human governments have failed to wipe out cancer, heart troubles and other diseases. Yet even if they were to do so, doctors admit that this would not stop people from aging. We would still grow old. In time our eyes would grow dim, our muscles would weaken, our skin would wrinkle and the organs inside our bodies would break down. Death would follow. How sad!

[18] After Armageddon, in the paradise earth, a grand miracle by God will change all of that, for the Bible promise is: "No resident will say: 'I am sick.'" (Isaiah 33:24) When Jesus Christ was on earth he proved his power to heal all kinds of sickness and disease, which result because of the sin we inherited from Adam. (Mark 2:1-12; Matthew 15:30, 31) Aging will also be stopped under Kingdom rule. The old will even grow young again. Yes, 'a man's flesh will become fresher than in his youth.' (Job 33:25) What a thrill it will be then to wake up each morn-

16. What miracle will make living with the animals a pleasure?
17, 18. (a) What cause for sadness will no longer exist in the paradise earth? (b) Why can we be sure that perfect health will be enjoyed by all?

ing and realize that you are in better health than you were the day before!

[19] Surely no one living in youthful, perfect health in the paradise earth will ever want to die. And nobody will need to die! Their receiving the benefits of the ransom sacrifice will mean at last enjoying God's grand gift of "everlasting life by Christ Jesus our Lord." (Romans 6:23) As the Bible says, Christ "must rule as king until God has put all enemies under his feet. As the last enemy, death is to be brought to nothing."—1 Corinthians 15:25, 26; Isaiah 25:8.

[20] Even persons now dead will enjoy the paradise earth. They will return to life! So, at that time, instead of announcements of deaths, there will be joyful reports about those who have been resurrected. How wonderful to welcome back from the grave dead fathers, mothers, children and other loved ones! No funeral parlors, graveyards or tombstones will remain to spoil the beauty of the paradise earth.

[21] Who will govern or direct activities on the paradise earth? All laws and instructions will come from the "new heavens" above. But on earth there will be faithful men appointed to see that these laws and instructions are carried out. Because these men represent the heavenly kingdom in a special way, the Bible calls them "princes." (Isaiah 32:1, 2; Psalm 45:16) Even in the Christian congregation today men are appointed by God's holy spirit to care for and direct its activities. (Acts 20:28) After Armageddon we can be confident that Christ will see to it that the right men are appointed to represent the Kingdom government, for then he will be taking a direct hand in earth's affairs. How can you show that you are eagerly awaiting God's "new heavens" and "new earth"? By doing everything you can to meet the requirements for living in that righteous new system. —2 Peter 3:14.

---

19. What last enemy will be brought to nothing, and how?
20. Who, besides persons now living, will enjoy the paradise earth, and how will that be possible?
21. (a) Who will help to see that the laws and instructions of the "new heavens" are carried out? (b) How can we show that we really want the "new heavens" and the "new earth"?

Chapter 20

Resurrection—
For Whom, and Where?

GOD'S SERVANTS have always believed in the resurrection. Of Abraham, who lived 2,000 years before Jesus was born as a human, the Bible says: "He reckoned that God was able to raise him [his son Isaac] up even from the dead." (Hebrews 11:17-19) Later God's servant Job asked: "If an able-bodied man dies can he live again?" In answer to his own question, Job said to God: "You will call, and I myself shall answer you." Thus he showed that he believed in the resurrection.—Job 14:14, 15.

² When Jesus Christ was on earth, he explained: "That the dead are raised up even Moses disclosed, in the account about the thornbush, when he calls Jehovah 'the God of Abraham and God of Isaac and God of Jacob.' He is a God, not of the dead, but of the living, for they are all living to him." (Luke 20:37, 38) In the Christian Greek Scriptures the word "resurrection" is used more than 40 times. Indeed, the resurrection of the dead is a main Bible teaching.—Hebrews 6:1, 2.

³ When her brother Lazarus died, Jesus' friend Martha showed faith in the resurrection. On hearing that Jesus was coming, Martha ran out to meet him. "Lord, if you had been here my brother would not have died," she said. Seeing her sorrow, Jesus comforted her with the words: "Your brother will rise." Martha answered: "I know he will rise in the resurrection on the last day."—John 11:17-24.

⁴ Martha had strong reasons for her faith in the resurrection. She knew, for example, that many years earlier God's prophets Elijah and Elisha, with God's power, had each resurrected a

1, 2. How do we know that ancient servants of God believed in the resurrection?
3. What faith in the resurrection did Martha express?
4-6. What reasons did Martha have for believing in the resurrection?

166

"I know he will rise in the resurrection"

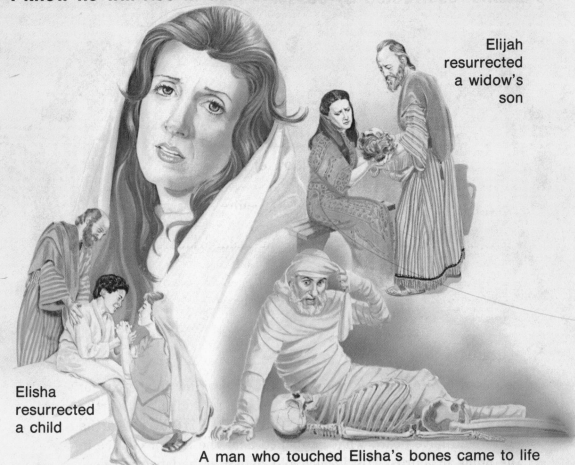

Elijah resurrected a widow's son

Elisha resurrected a child

A man who touched Elisha's bones came to life

child. (1 Kings 17:17-24; 2 Kings 4:32-37) And she knew that a dead man had come to life when he was thrown into a pit and touched the bones of dead Elisha. (2 Kings 13:20, 21) But what had strengthened her faith in the resurrection the most was what Jesus himself had taught and done.

⁵ Martha may have been present in Jerusalem less than two years before, when Jesus spoke of the part that he would have in resurrecting the dead. He said: "For just as the Father raises the dead up and makes them alive, so the Son also makes those alive whom he wants to. Do not marvel at this, because the hour is coming in which all those in the memorial tombs will hear his voice and come out."—John 5:21, 28, 29.

⁶ Up until the time Jesus spoke those words, there is no Bible record that he had resurrected anyone. But shortly afterward

Persons resurrected by Jesus:

Widow of Nain's son

Lazarus

Jairus' daughter

he raised to life a young man, the son of a widow in the city of Nain. The news of this was carried south to Judea, so Martha was sure to have heard about it. (Luke 7:11-17) Later, Martha also would have heard what happened near the Sea of Galilee in the home of Jairus. His 12-year-old daughter had become very sick and had died. But when Jesus arrived at Jairus' home, he went over to the dead child, and said: "Girl, get up!" And she did!—Luke 8:40-56.

7 Still Martha did not expect Jesus to resurrect her brother at this time. That is why she said: "I know he will rise in the resurrection on the last day." However, to impress on Martha the part he has in raising the dead, Jesus said: "I am the resurrection and the life. He that exercises faith in me, even though he dies, will come to life; and everyone that is living and exercises faith in me will never die at all." Jesus was soon afterward taken to the tomb where Lazarus had been laid. "Lazarus, come on out!" he cried. And Lazarus, who had been dead four days, came out!—John 11:24-26, 38-44.

7. What proof did Jesus give Martha that he can resurrect the dead?

Others who were resurrected:

Dorcas

Jesus himself

Eutychus

⁸ A few weeks later Jesus himself was killed and placed in a tomb. But he was there only parts of three days. The apostle Peter explains why, saying: "This Jesus God resurrected, of which fact we are all witnesses." The religious leaders could not stop God's Son from coming out of the tomb. (Acts 2:32; Matthew 27:62-66; 28:1-7) There can be no doubt that Christ was raised from the dead, for afterward he showed himself alive to many of his disciples, once to some 500 of them. (1 Corinthians 15:3-8) So strongly did Jesus' disciples believe in the resurrection that they were willing to face even death to serve God.

⁹ Further proof that the dead can be raised was given later through the apostles Peter and Paul. First, Peter resurrected Tabitha, also called Dorcas, of the city of Joppa. (Acts 9:36-42) And then Paul brought back to life young Eutychus, who had died when he fell from a third-floor window while Paul was speaking. (Acts 20:7-12) Surely these nine resurrections recorded in the Bible give certain proof that the dead can be brought back to life!

---

8. What evidence is there that Jesus was resurrected?
9. What nine persons does the Bible say were resurrected?

WHO WILL BE RESURRECTED?

[10] In the beginning it was not God's purpose to resurrect anyone, because if Adam and Eve had remained faithful no one would have had to die. But then Adam's sin brought imperfection and death upon everyone. (Romans 5:12) So to make it possible for any of Adam's children to enjoy everlasting life, Jehovah God arranged for the resurrection. But what determines whether a person is resurrected or not?

[11] The Bible explains: "There is going to be a resurrection of both the *righteous* and the *unrighteous*." (Acts 24:15) This may surprise some. 'Why bring the *"unrighteous"* back to life?' they may wonder. What happened while Jesus was

Where is the Paradise that Jesus promised the evildoer?

hanging on the torture stake will help us to answer this question.

[12] These men next to Jesus are criminals. One of them has just finished insulting him, saying: "You are the Christ, are you not? Save yourself and us." However, the other criminal believes Jesus. He turns to him and says: "Remember me when you get into your kingdom." At that, Jesus promises: "Truly I tell you today, You will be with me in Paradise."—Luke 23:39-43.

[13] But what does Jesus mean when he says: "You will be with me in Paradise"? Where is Paradise? Well, where was the paradise God made at the beginning? It was on earth, was it not? God put the first human pair in the beautiful paradise called the garden of Eden. So when we read that this former

10, 11. (a) Why did God arrange for the resurrection? (b) According to Acts 24:15, what two classes of people will be resurrected?
12, 13. (a) What promise did Jesus make to a criminal? (b) Where is the "Paradise" Jesus spoke about?

criminal will be in Paradise, we should picture in our minds this earth made into a beautiful place in which to live, for the word "paradise" means "garden" or "park."—Genesis 2:8, 9.

[14] Jesus Christ, of course, will not be right here on earth with the former criminal. No, Jesus will be in heaven ruling as king over the earthly Paradise. So he will be with that man in the sense that He will raise him from the dead and care for his needs, both physical and spiritual. But why will Jesus permit a man who was a criminal to live in Paradise?

[15] It is true that this man did bad things. He was "unrighteous." Also, he was ignorant of God's will. But would he have been a criminal if he had known about God's purposes? To find out, Jesus will resurrect this unrighteous man, as well as thousands of millions of others who died in ignorance. For instance, in past centuries many people died who did not know how to read and who had never seen a Bible. But they will be raised from Sheol, or Hades. Then, in the paradise earth, they will be taught God's will, and they will have the opportunity to prove that they really do love God by doing his will.

[16] This does not mean that everyone will receive a resurrection. The Bible shows that Judas Iscariot, who betrayed Jesus, will not. Because of his willful wickedness, Judas is called "the son of destruction." (John 17:12) He went to the symbolic Gehenna from which there is no resurrection. (Matthew 23:33) Persons who willfully do what is bad after knowing God's will may be sinning against the holy spirit. And God will not resurrect those who sin against his holy spirit. (Matthew 12:32; Hebrews 6:4-6; 10:26, 27) However, since God is the Judge, there is no reason for us to try to figure out whether certain wicked people in the past or in modern times will be resurrected or not. God knows who is in Hades and who is in Gehenna. For our part, we should do everything we can to be the kind of persons that God wants in his new system.—Luke 13:24, 29.

---

14. In what way will Jesus be with the former criminal in Paradise?
15. Why are the "unrighteous" resurrected?
16. (a) Who of the dead will not be resurrected? (b) Why should we not try to judge matters? (c) What should be our main concern?

[17] The fact is that not all who receive everlasting life will need to be resurrected. Many servants of God now living in these "last days" of this system of things will live through Armageddon. And then, as part of the righteous "new earth," they will never need to die. What Jesus said to Martha can in a literal way be true of them: "And everyone that is living and exercises faith in me will never die at all."—John 11:26; 2 Timothy 3:1.

[18] Who are the "righteous" that are to be resurrected? These will include faithful servants of God who lived before Jesus Christ came to earth. Many of these persons are mentioned by name in Hebrews chapter 11. They did not hope to go to heaven, but hoped to live again on earth. Also among the "righteous" to be resurrected are faithful servants of God who have died in recent years. God will see to it that their hope of living forever on earth is realized by raising them from the dead.

WHEN AND WHERE RESURRECTED

[19] Jesus Christ is spoken of as "the first to be resurrected from the dead." (Acts 26:23) This means that he was the first to be resurrected of those who would not have to die again. Also, he was the first to be raised as a spirit person. (1 Peter 3:18) But the Bible tells us that there would be others, saying: "Each one in his own rank: Christ the firstfruits, afterward those who belong to the Christ during his presence." (1 Corinthians 15:20-23) So in the resurrection some would be raised up before certain others.

[20] "Those who belong to the Christ" are the 144,000 faithful disciples chosen to rule with him in the Kingdom. Of their heavenly resurrection, the Bible says: "Happy and holy is anyone having part in *the first resurrection;* over these the second death has no authority, but they will . . . rule as kings with him for the thousand years."—Revelation 20:6; 14:1, 3.

---

17. Who will not need to be resurrected to enjoy everlasting life?
18. Who are the "righteous" that will be resurrected?
19. (a) In what sense was Jesus the first to be resurrected? (b) Who are resurrected next?
20. (a) Who are "those who belong to the Christ"? (b) What resurrection do they have?

21 So following the resurrection of Christ, the 144,000 are the next to be raised. They have part in "the first resurrection," or "the earlier resurrection." (Philippians 3:11) When does this take place? "During his presence," the Bible says. As we have learned in earlier chapters, Christ's presence began in the year 1914. So the "day" for "the first resurrection" of faithful Christians to heaven has already come. No doubt the apostles and other early Christians have already been raised to heavenly life. —2 Timothy 4:8.

22 But there are Christians living now during Christ's invisible presence who have this same hope of ruling in heaven with Christ. They are the remaining ones, a remnant of the 144,000. When are they resurrected? They do not need to sleep in death, but they are raised immediately when they die. The Bible explains: "We shall not all fall asleep in death, but we shall all be changed, in a moment, in the twinkling of an eye, during the last trumpet. For the trumpet will sound, and the dead will be raised."—1 Corinthians 15:51, 52; 1 Thessalonians 4:15-17.

23 Of course, this "first resurrection" to heavenly life is unseen to human eyes. It is a resurrection to life as spirit creatures. The Bible describes the change to spirit life this way: "It is sown in corruption, it is raised up in incorruption. It is sown in dishonor, it is raised up in glory. . . . It is sown a physical body, it is raised up a spiritual body."—1 Corinthians 15:42-44.

24 However, the very expression "first resurrection" shows that another one will follow. This is the resurrection to life on the paradise earth of both righteous and unrighteous persons. This will occur after Armageddon. It will be a "better resurrection" than that of the boys resurrected by Elijah and Elisha and of others once resurrected on earth. Why? Because if those resurrected after Armageddon choose to serve God they will never need to die again.—Hebrews 11:35.

21. (a) When does "the first resurrection" begin? (b) Who no doubt have been raised already to heavenly life?
22. (a) Who else will have part in "the first resurrection"? (b) When are they resurrected?
23. How does the Bible describe the change to spirit life?
24. (a) What resurrection follows "the first resurrection"? (b) Why is it called a "better resurrection"?

A MIRACLE OF GOD

²⁵ After a person dies, what is resurrected? It is not the same body that died. The Bible shows this when it describes the resurrection to heavenly life. (1 Corinthians 15:35-44) Even those who are resurrected to life on earth do not receive the same body they had when they lived before. That body probably decayed and returned to the ground. In time the elements of the dead body may have become a part of other living things. So God resurrects not the same *body* but the same *person* that died. To persons who go to heaven, he gives a new spiritual body. To those who are raised to live on earth, he gives a new physical body. This new physical body will no doubt be similar to the one the person had before he died so that he will be recognized by those who knew him.

²⁶ The resurrection is indeed a wonderful miracle. The person that died may have built up a great amount of experience and knowledge and many memories over a lifetime. He developed a personality that made him different from any other person that ever lived. Yet Jehovah God remembers every detail, and will restore this complete person when He resurrects him. As the Bible says of the dead to be resurrected: "They are all living to him." (Luke 20:38) Humans can record voices and pictures of people, and play them back long after the people have died. But Jehovah can, and actually will, bring back to life all persons who are living in his memory!

²⁷ The Bible tells us much more about life in Paradise after the dead are resurrected. For example, Jesus spoke of persons coming out, some to "a resurrection of life" and others to "a resurrection of judgment." (John 5:29) What did he mean? And will the situation be any different for the "righteous" that are resurrected from what it will be for the "unrighteous"? A consideration of Judgment Day will answer such questions for us.

---

25. (a) Why is it not the body that died that is resurrected? (b) What is resurrected, and what is given to those who are resurrected?
26. (a) Why is the resurrection such a wonderful miracle? (b) What inventions of humans can help us to understand God's great ability to remember people who have died?
27. What questions regarding the resurrection will we have answered later?

Chapter 21

Judgment Day and Afterward

WHAT PICTURE does Judgment Day call to your mind? Some imagine a great throne, and in front of it a long line of persons who have been resurrected from the dead. As each person passes before the throne, he is judged by his past deeds, all of which are written down in the Judge's book. Based on the things he did, the person is sent either to heaven or to a fiery hell.

² The Bible, however, gives a much different picture of Judgment Day. It is not a day to be dreaded or feared. Note what the Bible says of God: "He has set a day in which he purposes to judge the inhabited earth in righteousness by a man whom he has appointed." (Acts 17:31) This judge appointed by God is, of course, Jesus Christ.

³ We can be sure that Christ will be fair and just in his judgment. A prophecy regarding him at Isaiah 11:3, 4 assures us of this. So, contrary to popular opinion, he will not judge persons on the basis of their past sins, many of which may have been committed in ignorance. The Bible explains that at death a person is set free or released from any sins he has committed. It says: "He who has died has been acquitted from his sin." (Romans 6:7) This means that when a person is resurrected he will be judged on the basis of what he does *during Judgment Day*, not on what he did before he died.

⁴ Judgment Day, therefore, is not a literal 24-hour day. The Bible makes this clear when it speaks of those who will share with Jesus Christ in doing the judging. (1 Corinthians 6:1-3) "I

1. What is a common view of Judgment Day?
2. (a) Who has arranged for Judgment Day? (b) Whom did he appoint as judge?
3. (a) Why can we be sure Christ will be fair in his judgment? (b) On what basis will people be judged?
4. (a) How long will Judgment Day be? (b) Who will be judges with Christ?

saw thrones," the Bible writer says, "and there were those who sat down on them, and power of judging was given them." These judges are Christ's faithful anointed followers who, as the Bible goes on to say, "came to life and ruled as kings with the Christ for a thousand years." So Judgment Day will be 1.000 years long. It is the same 1,000-year period during which Christ and his 144,000 faithful anointed followers will rule as "new heavens" over the "new earth." —Revelation 20:4, 6; 2 Peter 3:13.

[5] Look at these pages. They give some idea of how wonderful Judgment Day will be for

5, 6. (a) How did a Bible psalmist describe Judgment Day? (b) What will life be like on earth during Judgment Day?

humankind. The Bible psalmist wrote of that glorious time: "Let the open field exult and all that is in it. At the same time let all the trees of the forest break out joyfully before Jehovah. For he has come; for he has come to judge the earth. He will judge the productive land with righteousness and the peoples with his faithfulness."—Psalm 96:12, 13.

[6] During Judgment Day those who survive Armageddon will work to make the earth a paradise. Into this paradise the dead will be welcomed back. (Luke 23:43) What happiness there will be when families long separated by death are joined together again! Yes, how pleasant to live in peace, to enjoy good health and to receive instruction regarding God's purposes! The Bible says: "When there are judgments from you for the earth, righteousness is what the inhabitants of the

productive land will certainly learn." (Isaiah 26:9) During Judgment Day all the people will learn about Jehovah, and they will be given every opportunity to obey and serve him.

7 It is under such paradise conditions that Jesus Christ and his 144,000 associate kings will judge humankind. People who choose to serve Jehovah will be in a position to receive everlasting life. But, even under these best of circumstances, some will refuse to serve God. As the Scriptures say: "Though the wicked one should be shown favor, he simply will not learn righteousness. In the land of straightforwardness he will act unjustly." (Isaiah 26:10) So after being given full opportunity to change their ways and to learn righteousness, such wicked ones will be destroyed. Some will be put to death even before Judgment Day ends. (Isaiah 65:20) They will not be permitted to remain to corrupt or spoil the paradise earth.

8 Will it be more difficult for some of the resurrected dead to learn and practice righteousness than it will be for others? When Jesus Christ was on earth, he showed that it would be. Most of the persons to whom he and his disciples preached

7. During Judgment Day, what will happen to those who choose to serve God and to those who refuse to do so?

8. How did Jesus show that during Judgment Day it would be more difficult for some to practice righteousness than it would be for others?

For whom will it be harder on Judgment Day?

People who heard Jesus

Those destroyed in Sodom and Gomorrah

did not listen. They rejected Jesus as the Messiah, even a hearing his preaching and seeing him perform miracles. W sending out his disciples to preach, Jesus said of a city that would reject their message: "Truly I say to you, it will be more endurable for the land of Sodom and Gomorrah on Judgment Day than for that city."—Matthew 10:15.

⁹ By saying this, Jesus showed that at least some of the unrighteous people of ancient Sodom and Gomorrah will be present on earth during Judgment Day. Although they had been very immoral, we can expect that some of them will be resurrected. (Genesis 19:1-26) Jehovah in his mercy will bring them back so that they will have an opportunity to learn about his purposes. But Jesus' words also show that some of the unrighteous ones to whom he and his disciples personally preached will be present during Judgment Day. They, too, will be resurrected and be given further opportunity to learn God's purposes. For whom will it be more difficult to accept Christ as king at that time? For the people of ancient Sodom or for those who had rejected the preaching of Jesus and his disciples?

¹⁰ It will be more difficult for those who personally rejected Jesus. Speaking of Capernaum, one of the cities where he performed miracles, Jesus said: "If the powerful works that took place in you had taken place in Sodom, it would have remained until this very day. Consequently I say to you people, It will be more endurable for the land of Sodom on Judgment Day than for you." (Matthew 11:22-24) Yes, during Judgment Day it will be even more difficult for those from Capernaum to admit their mistakes and to accept and serve Christ as king than it will be for the people of ancient Sodom to learn righteousness.

¹¹ So it will be easier for certain "unrighteous" resurrected ones to learn about God and serve him than it will be for certain other "unrighteous" ones. (Matthew 12:41, 42) What, then, about the "righteous" who are resurrected—persons such as Abraham,

9, 10. (a) What unrighteous people will be resurrected during Judgment Day? (b) Why will it be more difficult for some unrighteous ones than for other unrighteous ones?

11. Why will it be easier on Judgment Day for the "righteous" than for any of the "unrighteous"?

Isaac, Job, Deborah, Ruth, Daniel and others? Before their death they all looked forward to the coming of the Messiah. How glad they will be during Judgment Day to learn about him, and that he is ruling in heaven! So it will be much easier for these "righteous" persons to practice righteousness at that time than for any of the "unrighteous" to do so.—Acts 24:15.

RESURRECTIONS OF "LIFE" AND OF "JUDGMENT"

[12] In describing the situation on Judgment Day, Jesus said: "Those in the memorial tombs will hear his voice and come out, those who did good things to a *resurrection of life,* those who practiced vile things to a *resurrection of judgment.* . . . just as I hear, I judge; and the judgment that I render is righteous, because I seek, not my own will, but the will of him that sent me." (John 5:28-30) What is this *"resurrection of life,"* and what is the *"resurrection of judgment"?* And who receive them?

[13] We have clearly seen that when the dead come forth from the grave, they are not judged by their past deeds. Rather, they are judged on the basis of what they do during Judgment Day. So when Jesus mentioned "those who did good things" and "those who practiced vile things," he was referring to the good things and bad things that they would do *during Judgment Day.* Because of the good things they do, many of those resurrected will progress to human perfection by the end of the 1,000-year Judgment Day. Thus their return from the dead will prove to be a "resurrection of life," for they will attain to *perfect life* without sin.

[14] On the other hand, what about those 'who practiced vile or bad things' during Judgment Day? Their return from the dead will prove to be a "resurrection of judgment." What does this mean? It means a judgment or condemnation to death. So these persons will be destroyed either during or by the close of Judgment Day. The reason is that they do bad things; they stubbornly refuse to learn and practice righteousness.

12. According to John 5:28-30, who receive a "resurrection of life," and who receive a "resurrection of judgment"?
13. What does it mean for a person to receive a "resurrection of life"?
14. What does it mean for a person to receive a "resurrection of judgment"?

WHEN THE JUDGMENT DAY BEGINS

[15] The apostle John saw in vision what takes place immediately before Judgment Day. He wrote: "I saw a great white throne and the one seated on it. From before him *the earth and the heaven fled away,* . . . And I saw the dead, the great and the small, standing before the throne . . . And the dead were judged." (Revelation 20:11, 12) So before Judgment Day begins, this present system of things made up of "the earth and the heaven" will pass away. Only those serving God will survive, while all the wicked are destroyed at Armageddon.—1 John 2:17.

[16] Thus, it is not only the resurrected "dead" who will be judged during Judgment Day. The "living" who survive Armageddon, as well as any children they may have, also will be judged. (2 Timothy 4:1) In his vision John saw how they are judged. "And scrolls were opened," he wrote. "And the dead were judged out of those things written in the scrolls according to their deeds. And the sea gave up those dead in it, and death and Hades gave up those dead in them, and they were judged individually according to their deeds."—Revelation 20:12, 13.

[17] What are the "scrolls" that are opened from which "the dead" as well as "the living" are judged? Evidently they will be something in addition to our present Holy Bible. They are inspired writings or books that contain Jehovah's laws and instructions. By reading these all people on earth will be able to know God's will. Then, on the basis of the laws and instructions in these "scrolls," everyone on earth will be judged. Those who obey the things written therein will receive the benefits of Christ's ransom sacrifice, and they will gradually grow to human perfection.

[18] By the end of the 1,000-year Judgment Day nobody on earth will be in a dying condition because of Adam's sin. Truly, in the fullest sense everyone will have come to life. This is

---

15. What happens just before Judgment Day begins?
16. (a) Who besides the dead will be judged during Judgment Day? (b) From what will they be judged?
17. What are the "scrolls" from which the "living" and the "dead" will be judged?
18. (a) What will be the situation at the end of Judgment Day? (b) In what way do the "dead" come to life at the end of the 1,000 years?

what the Bible refers to when it says: "The rest of the dead [those besides the 144,000 who go to heaven] did not come to life until the thousand years were ended." (Revelation 20:5) The reference here to "the rest of the dead" does not mean that others are resurrected at the end of the 1,000-year Judgment Day. Rather, it means that all persons come to life in that they finally reach human perfection. They will be in the same perfect condition as were Adam and Eve in the garden of Eden. What will happen then?

AFTER JUDGMENT DAY

[19] Having done all that God has given him to do, Jesus Christ "hands over the kingdom to his God and Father." This is at the end of the 1,000-year Judgment Day. By then all enemies will have been put out of the way. The last of these is the death inherited from Adam. It will be destroyed! Then the Kingdom becomes the property of Jehovah God. He rules it directly as King.—1 Corinthians 15:24-28.

[20] How will Jehovah determine whose names are to be written in the "scroll of life," or "the book of life"? (Revelation 20:12, 15) It will be by a test upon humankind. Remember how Adam and Eve failed under such a test, and how Job, when tested, kept integrity. But most humans that live to the end of the 1,000 years will never have had their faith tested. Before they were resurrected they were ignorant of Jehovah's purposes. They were part of Satan's wicked system of things; they were "unrighteous." Then, after their resurrection, it was easy for them to serve Jehovah because of living in Paradise without any opposition from the Devil. But will these billions of humans, who are then perfect, serve Jehovah if Satan is given the opportunity to try to stop them from further doing so? Can Satan do to them what he did to the perfect Adam and Eve?

[21] To settle such questions, Jehovah lets Satan and his demons

---

19. What does Christ do at the end of Judgment Day?
20. (a) What will Jehovah do to determine whose names are to be written in "the book of life"? (b) Why is a final test of humankind fitting?
21. (a) How will Jehovah have humankind tested? (b) When the test is completed, what will happen to all those involved?

loose from the abyss where they have been for the 1,000 years. What is the result? The Bible shows that Satan is successful in turning some persons away from serving Jehovah. These will be as "the sand of the sea," meaning that their number is undetermined. After this test is carried out, Satan and his demons, and also those who do not pass the test, are thrown into the symbolic "lake of fire," which is the second (eternal) death. (Revelation 20:7-10, 15) But those whose names are found written in "the book of life" will remain in the glorious earthly paradise. Having their names written in "the book of life" means that Jehovah judges them to be perfectly righteous in heart, mind and body and thus worthy of living forever in paradise on earth.

THE PRESENT DAY OF JUDGMENT

22 So the Bible gives information about events over 1,000 years into the future. And it shows that there is no reason to fear what lies ahead. But the question is: Will you be there to enjoy the good things that Jehovah God has in store? This will depend on whether you survive an earlier judgment day, namely, the *present* "day of judgment and of destruction of the ungodly men."—2 Peter 3:7.

23 Yes, since Christ returned and sat down on his heavenly throne, all humankind has been on judgment. This present "day of judgment" comes before the 1,000-year Judgment Day begins. During the present judgment people are being separated as "goats" to Christ's left hand or as "sheep" to his right. The "goats" will be destroyed because they fail to help Christ's anointed "brothers" in their service to God. In time, these "goats" show themselves to be unrepentant sinners, wicked, hardened in their practice of unrighteousness. The "sheep," on the other hand, will be blessed with life under the Kingdom rule because they support Christ's "brothers" in every way. —Matthew 25:31-46.

---

22. To live to see Judgment Day and the final test of humankind, what must we now survive?

23. (a) Into what two classes are people now being separated? (b) What will happen to each class, and why?

Chapter 22

Identifying the True Religion

THERE CAN be no doubt as to who were practicing true religion in the first century. It was the followers of Jesus Christ. These all belonged to the one Christian organization. What about today? How can those practicing true religion be identified?

² Explaining how we can do this, Jesus said: "By their fruits you will recognize them. . . . Every good tree produces fine fruit, but every rotten tree produces worthless fruit; . . . Really, then, by their fruits you will recognize those men." (Matthew 7:16-20) What fine fruits would you expect true worshipers of God to produce? What should they be saying and doing now?

SANCTIFYING GOD'S NAME

³ True worshipers of God would act in harmony with the Model Prayer that Jesus gave his followers. The first thing Jesus there mentioned was this: "Our Father in the heavens, let your name be sanctified." Another Bible version puts these words this way: "May your name be held holy." (Matthew 6:9, *Jerusalem Bible*) What does it mean to sanctify, or to hold holy, God's name? How did Jesus do it?

⁴ Jesus showed how he did it when he said in prayer to his Father: "I have made your name manifest to the men you gave me out of the world." (John 17:6) Yes, Jesus made God's name, Jehovah, known to others. He did not fail to use that name. Jesus knew that it was his Father's purpose for His name to be

1. Who were practicing true religion in the first century?
2. How can those practicing true religion be identified?
3, 4. (a) What was the first request made in Jesus' Model Prayer? (b) How did Jesus sanctify God's name?

If you were to talk to someone about Jehovah and his kingdom, with what religion would people associate you?

glorified in all the earth. So he set the example in proclaiming that name and holding it holy.—John 12:28; Isaiah 12:4, 5.

⁵ The Bible shows that the very existence of the true Christian congregation is connected with God's name. The apostle Peter explained that God "turned his attention to the nations to take out of them a *people for his name*." (Acts 15:14) So God's true people must treat his name as holy and make it known throughout the earth. In fact, knowing that name is necessary for salvation, as the Bible says: "For 'everyone who calls on the name of Jehovah will be saved.' "—Romans 10:13, 14.

⁶ Now, then, who today treats God's name as holy and makes it known over all the earth? The churches in general avoid the use of the name Jehovah. Some have even removed it from their translations of the Bible. However, if you were to talk to your neighbors and often refer to Jehovah, using his name, with what organization do you think they would associate you? There is only one people that is really following Jesus' example in this regard. Their main purpose in life is to serve God and bear witness to his name, just as Jesus did. So they have taken the Scriptural name "Jehovah's Witnesses."—Isaiah 43:10-12.

---

5. (a) How is the Christian congregation connected with God's name? (b) What must we do if we are to gain salvation?
6. (a) Are the churches in general holding God's name holy? (b) Are there any who bear witness to the name of God?

PROCLAIMING GOD'S KINGDOM

[7] In the Model Prayer that Jesus gave, he also showed the importance of God's kingdom. He taught people to pray: "Let your kingdom come." (Matthew 6:10) Over and over again Jesus emphasized the Kingdom as the only solution for mankind's troubles. He and his apostles did this by preaching to people about that kingdom "from village to village" and "from house to house." (Luke 8:1; Acts 5:42; 20:20) God's kingdom was the theme of their preaching and teaching.

[8] What about our day? What is the central teaching of God's true Christian organization? In prophesying of these "last days," Jesus said: "This good news of the kingdom will be preached in all the inhabited earth for a witness to all the nations; and then the end will come." (Matthew 24:14) So the Kingdom must be the main message of God's people today.

[9] Ask yourself: If a person comes to your door and he speaks about God's kingdom as the true hope for humankind, with what organization do you associate that person? Have people of any religion other than Jehovah's Witnesses talked to you about God's kingdom? Why, very few of them even know what it is!

---

7. How did Jesus show the importance of God's kingdom?
8. How did Jesus show what the main message of his true followers would be in these "last days"?
9. What people today are preaching the Kingdom message?

Does a person
respect
God's
Word
if he
fails to
live by it?

They are silent about God's government. Yet that government is world-shaking news. The prophet Daniel foretold that this kingdom 'would crush and put an end to all other governments and it alone would rule the earth.'—Daniel 2:44.

RESPECT FOR GOD'S WORD

[10] Another way in which those who are practicing true religion can be identified is by their attitude toward the Bible. Jesus at all times showed respect for God's Word. Time and again he appealed to it as the final authority on matters. (Matthew 4:4, 7, 10; 19:4-6) Jesus also showed respect for the Bible by living in accord with its teachings. Never did he downgrade the Bible. Rather, he condemned those who failed to teach in harmony with the Bible and who tried to weaken the force of its teachings by putting forth their own ideas.—Mark 7:9-13.

[11] How do the churches of Christendom measure up to Christ's example in this regard? Do they have deep respect for the Bible? Many clergymen today do not believe the Bible accounts of Adam's fall into sin, the flood of Noah's day, Jonah and the big fish, and others. They also say that man got here by evolution, not by direct creation of God. Are they thereby encouraging respect for God's Word? Also, some church leaders argue that sex relations outside of marriage are not wrong, or that even homosexuality or polygamy can be proper. Would you say that they are encouraging people to use the Bible as their guide? They certainly are not following the example of God's Son and his apostles.—Matthew 15:18, 19; Romans 1:24-27.

[12] There are church members who have the Bible and even study it, but the way they live their lives shows that they are not following it. Of persons like that, the Bible says: "They publicly declare they know God, but they disown him by their works." (Titus 1:16; 2 Timothy 3:5) If church members who gamble, get drunk or do other wrongs are permitted to remain

10. How did Jesus show respect for God's Word?
11. What attitude toward God's Word do the churches often show?
12. (a) Why is the worship of many who even have the Bible not pleasing to God? (b) If willful wrongdoers are permitted to remain in good standing in a church, what must we conclude?

in good standing within their church, what does this show? It is evidence that their religious organization is not approved by God.—1 Corinthians 5:11-13.

[13] If you have given thought to the previous chapters of this book, considering the Bible texts found there, you have come to know the basic teachings of God's Word. But what if the teachings of the religious organization with which you are associating are not in harmony with those of God's Word? Then you have a serious problem. It is the problem of deciding whether to accept the truthfulness of the Bible or to reject it in favor of teachings that the Bible does not support. What you do, of course, must be your own decision. However, you should weigh matters carefully. This is because the decision you make will affect your standing with God and your prospects of living forever in paradise on earth.

KEEPING SEPARATE FROM THE WORLD

[14] Yet another identifying mark of those who practice true religion is that, as Jesus said, "they are no part of the world." (John 17:14) This means that true worshipers keep separate from the corrupt world and its affairs. Jesus Christ refused to become a political ruler. (John 6:15) You can appreciate why keeping separate from the world is so important when you remember that the Bible says Satan the Devil is the ruler of the world. (John 12:31; 2 Corinthians 4:4) The seriousness of this matter is further seen from the Bible statement: "Whoever, therefore, wants to be a friend of the world is constituting himself an enemy of God."—James 4:4.

[15] Do the facts show that the churches in your community take this matter to heart? Are the clergy as well as the members of the congregations really "no part of the world"? Or are they deeply involved in the nationalism, politics and class struggles

13. What serious decision must a person make if he has found that the teachings of his church do not all line up with the Bible?
14. (a) What is another identifying mark of true religion? (b) Why is it so important that true worshipers meet this requirement?
15. (a) Are the churches with which you are acquainted really "no part of the world"? (b) Do you know of a religion that meets this requirement?

Jesus refused to become a political ruler

of the world? These questions are not hard to answer, since the activities of the churches are widely known. On the other hand, it is also easy to check the activities of Jehovah's Witnesses. By doing so, you will find that they really do follow the example of Christ and his early followers by keeping separate from the world, its political affairs and its selfish, immoral, violent ways.—1 John 2:15-17.

LOVE AMONG THEMSELVES

[16] A most important way in which Christ's true disciples can be identified is by the love they have among themselves. Jesus said: "By this all will know that you are my disciples, if you have love among yourselves." (John 13:35) Do the religious organizations with which you are acquainted have this love? What do they do, for example, when the countries in which they live go to war against one another?

[17] You know what usually happens. At the command of worldly men the members of the various religious organizations go out on the battlefield and slaughter their fellow believers of another country. Thus Catholic kills Catholic, Protestant kills Protestant and Muslim kills Muslim. Do you think such a course is according to God's Word and really shows the spirit of God?—1 John 3:10-12.

[18] How do Jehovah's Witnesses measure up in this matter of showing love to one another? They do not follow the course of worldly

16. What is an important way that true disciples of Christ can be identified?
17. How do religious organizations and their members measure up in meeting the requirement to show love among themselves?
18. How do Jehovah's Witnesses measure up in this matter of showing love to one another?

You are warmly invited to attend
the meetings of Jehovah's Witnesses

religions. They do not slaughter fellow believers on battlefields. They have not been guilty of living a lie by saying, "I love God," while hating their brother of another nationality, tribe or race. (1 John 4:20, 21) But they also show love in other ways. How? By the way they deal with their neighbors and by their loving efforts to help others to learn about God.—Galatians 6:10.

ONE TRUE RELIGION

[19] It is only logical that there would be one true religion. This is in harmony with the fact that the true God is a God, "not of disorder, but of peace." (1 Corinthians 14:33) The Bible says that actually there is only "one faith." (Ephesians 4:5) Who, then, are the ones who form the body of true worshipers today?

[20] We do not hesitate to say that they are Jehovah's Witnesses. For you to be convinced of this we invite you to become better acquainted with them. The best way to do this is to attend their meetings at the Kingdom Hall of Jehovah's Witnesses. Since the Bible shows that practicing true religion brings great contentment now and opens the way to enjoy everlasting life in paradise on earth, it surely will be worth your while to make such an investigation. (Deuteronomy 30:19, 20) You have our warm invitation to do so. Why not investigate now?

---

19. Why is it both logical and Scriptural to say that there is just one true religion?
20. (a) In the light of the evidence, whom does this book point to as the true worshipers today? (b) Is that what you believe? (c) What is the best way to get well acquainted with Jehovah's Witnesses?

Chapter 23

God's Visible Organization

WHY CAN WE be certain that God has a visible organization? One reason is that he has an invisible organization. Jehovah created cherubs, seraphs and many other angels to do his will in the heavens. (Genesis 3:24; Isaiah 6:2, 3; Psalm 103:20) Jesus Christ is the Archangel over and above all of these. (1 Thessalonians 4:16; Jude 9; Revelation 12:7) The Bible describes the angels as being organized into "thrones or lordships or governments or authorities." (Colossians 1:16; Ephesians 1:21) All of them serve at Jehovah's command, unitedly doing the work he has for them to do.—Daniel 7:9, 10; Job 1:6; 2:1.

[2] We also get an idea of the importance God puts on organization when we consider his material creations. For example, there are thousands of billions of stars in the universe that are arranged in huge groups called galaxies. These galaxies travel through space in an orderly way, and so do the individual stars and planets within these galaxies. Our planet Earth, for instance, each year makes a trip around the sun, which is our nearest star, in exactly 365 days, 5 hours, 48 minutes and 45.51 seconds. Yes, the material universe is highly organized!

[3] Does this marvelous organization among God's invisible creations and in his material universe teach us something? Yes, it teaches us that Jehovah is a God of organization. Surely, then, such a God would not leave humans on earth who really love him without guidance and organization.

1. What does the Bible say about God's invisible organization?
2. How does the way that God created our material universe show that he puts great importance on organization?
3. What does the fine organization among God's invisible creations and in his material universe teach us?

At the time of the Flood,
did God have more than one organization?

GOD'S VISIBLE ORGANIZATION—PAST AND PRESENT

⁴ The Bible shows that Jehovah has always guided his servants in an organized way. For example, men of faith such as Abraham led their families and servants in worshiping Jehovah. Jehovah made known his will for Abraham by speaking with him. (Genesis 12:1) And God instructed him to pass this information on to others, saying: "I have become acquainted with [Abraham] in order that he may command his sons and his household after him so that they shall keep Jehovah's way." (Genesis 18:19) Here was an orderly arrangement for a group of people to worship Jehovah properly.

⁵ Later, when the Israelites increased in numbers and became millions, Jehovah did not let each one worship in his own way, separate from any organized arrangement. No, the Israelites were formed into a nation of organized worshipers. The nation of Israel was called "Jehovah's congregation." (Numbers 20:4; 1 Chronicles 28:8) If you were a true worshiper of Jehovah back then, you had to be part of that congregation of worshipers, not separate from it.—Psalm 147:19, 20.

⁶ What was the situation in the first century? The Bible shows that Jehovah's favor was upon the followers of his Son Jesus

4, 5. How do we know that God led his people in an organized way in the days of Abraham and of the nation of Israel?
6. (a) How did God show that his favor was on Christ's followers? (b) What evidence is there that Christians were organized for worship?

Christ. Jehovah poured out his holy spirit upon them. To show that he was now using this Christian organization rather than the nation of Israel, he gave certain early Christians power to heal the sick, raise the dead and to perform other miracles. You cannot read the Christian Greek Scriptures without being impressed by the fact that Christians were organized for worship. In fact, they were commanded to meet together for this purpose. (Hebrews 10:24, 25) So if you were a true worshiper of Jehovah in the first century, you had to be a part of his Christian organization.

[7] Did Jehovah ever use more than one organization during any period of time? In Noah's day only Noah and those with him inside the ark had God's protection and survived the floodwaters. (1 Peter 3:20) Also, in the first century there were not two or more Christian organizations. God dealt with just the one. There was just the "one Lord, *one faith,* one baptism." (Ephesians 4:5) Likewise in our day Jesus Christ foretold that there would be only one source of spiritual instruction for God's people.

[8] When telling of his presence in Kingdom power, Jesus said: "Who really is the faithful and discreet slave whom his master appointed over his domestics, to give them their food at the proper time? Happy is that slave if his master on arriving finds him doing so. Truly I say to you, He will appoint him over all his belongings." (Matthew 24:45-47) On his return in Kingdom power in the year 1914, did Christ find a "faithful and discreet slave" class providing spiritual "food," or information? Yes, he found such a "slave" made up of the remaining ones on earth of his 144,000 "brothers." (Revelation 12:10; 14:1, 3) And since 1914 millions of persons have accepted the "food" they provide, and have begun practicing true religion along with them. This organization of God's servants is known as Jehovah's Witnesses.

[9] Jehovah's Witnesses look to God and his Word for direction

7. How do we know that Jehovah did not use more than one organization in any particular period?
8. How did Jesus show that there would be just one visible organization of God on earth in our day?
9. (a) Why do God's servants bear the name Jehovah's Witnesses? (b) Why do they call their places of worship Kingdom Halls?

in all that they do. Their very name Jehovah's Witnesses shows that their main activity is to witness about the name and kingdom of Jehovah God, even as Christ did. (John 17:6; Revelation 1:5) Also, they call the place where they meet for worship the Kingdom Hall because God's kingdom by the Messiah, or Christ, is the theme of the entire Bible. Since it is clear that first-century Christianity had God's approval, Jehovah's Witnesses pattern their organization after it. Let us look briefly at that early Christian organization and then note the similarities with God's visible organization today.

THE FIRST-CENTURY PATTERN

[10] Wherever there were Christians in the first century, they gathered together in groups for worship. These congregations met regularly for fellowship and study. (Hebrews 10:24, 25) Their main activity was to preach and teach about God's kingdom, even as Christ did. (Matthew 4:17; 28:19, 20) If a member of the congregation turned to a bad way of life, he was put out of the congregation.—1 Corinthians 5:9-13; 2 John 10, 11.

[11] Were those Christian congregations in the first century independent of one another, with each making its own decisions on matters? No, the Bible shows that they were united in the one Christian faith. All the congregations received guidance and direction from the same source. Thus, when a dispute arose over the matter of circumcision, congregations or individuals did not decide for themselves what to do. No, but, instead, the apostle Paul, Barnabas and others were directed to "go up to the apostles and older men in Jerusalem regarding this dispute." When these mature men, with help from God's Word and his "holy spirit," made their decision, they sent out faithful men to inform the congregations.—Acts 15:2, 27-29.

[12] What resulted from the congregations' receiving this theocratic, or God-given, guidance and direction? The Bible says:

---

10. What were some features of the first-century Christian organization?
11, 12. (a) What proves that early Christian congregations received guidance and direction from the apostles and "older men" in Jerusalem? (b) What is meant by "theocratic" direction? (c) What was the result of the congregations' accepting such direction?

"Now as they [the apostle Paul and his companions] traveled on through the cities they would deliver to those there for observance the decrees that had been decided upon by the apostles and older men who were in Jerusalem. Therefore, indeed, the congregations continued to be made firm in the faith and to increase in number from day to day." (Acts 16:4, 5) Yes, all the congregations cooperated with what that body of older men in Jerusalem had decided, and they grew stronger in the faith.

THEOCRATIC DIRECTION TODAY

[13] God's visible organization today also receives theocratic guidance and direction. At the headquarters of Jehovah's Witnesses in Brooklyn, New York, there is a governing body of older Christian men from various parts of the earth who give the needed oversight to the worldwide activities of God's people. This governing body is made up of members of "the faithful and discreet slave." It serves as a spokesman for that faithful "slave."

[14] The men of that governing body, like the apostles and older men in Jerusalem, have many years of experience in God's service. But they do not rely on human wisdom in making decisions. No, being governed theocratically, they follow the example of the early governing body in Jerusalem, whose decisions were based on God's Word and were made under the direction of holy spirit.—Acts 15:13-17, 28, 29.

DIRECTING A WORLDWIDE ORGANIZATION

[15] Jesus Christ gave an idea of the size of the organization that God would have on earth during this time of the end when he said: "This good news of the kingdom will be preached in *all the inhabited earth* for a witness to *all the nations;* and then the end will come." (Matthew 24:14) Think of the tremendous amount of work needed to tell earth's thousands of millions

13. (a) From what place on earth and through what body of men does God's visible organization today receive guidance? (b) What relationship does the governing body have to "the faithful and discreet slave"?
14. Upon what does the governing body of God's people rely in making its decisions?
15. Why do Jesus' words at Matthew 24:14 show that God would have a large organization on earth during the time of the end?

The EXECUTIVE OFFICES

WORLD HEADQUARTERS OF JEHOVAH'S WITNESSES

Computer Systems

Rotary Printing

Book Bindery

Shipping

BROOKLYN PRINTERY

Brazil

England

of people about the established kingdom of God. Is the modern-day Christian organization, which looks to its governing body for guidance and direction, equipped to do this great work?

[16] Jehovah's Witnesses are now preaching the Kingdom message in over 200 lands and islands of the sea throughout the earth. To help the more than 2,300,000 Kingdom publishers (in 1981) to accomplish this work, large printing factories have been established in many countries. Here Bibles and Bible literature are produced in very large quantities. Every day, on the average, over one million *Watchtower* and *Awake!* magazines are printed and shipped from these factories.

South Africa

Wallkill, New York

Canada

[17] All this Bible literature is prepared in order to help persons to grow in knowledge of Jehovah's grand purposes. In fact, the words "Announcing Jehovah's Kingdom" are part of the title of the magazine *The Watchtower*. You are invited to share in distributing this Bible literature and to explain to others the Bible truths it contains. For example, is there someone with whom you can share the vital information that you have learned from this book, *You Can Live Forever in Paradise on Earth?*

16. (a) Why have Jehovah's Witnesses established many large printing factories? (b) What is produced in these factories?
17. (a) Why is this Bible literature prepared? (b) What are you invited to do?

Polo Grounds

Yankee Stadium

Some of the 253,922 at a convention of Jehovah's Witnesses in New York

¹⁸ As in the first century, God's organization today is *an organization of dedicated and baptized Kingdom preachers*. And it is set up to help all its members to share in this preaching activity. These persons need a great deal of encouragement and spiritual strengthening, since Satan and those whom he is able to influence oppose the Kingdom message. Such opposers had Jesus killed for preaching it, and the Bible warns that his followers would be persecuted too.—John 15:19, 20; 2 Timothy 3:12.

¹⁹ As in the first century so today "older men," or elders, are appointed to help and strengthen each congregation. They can help you also with Bible counsel to cope with various problems. These elders also protect "the flock of God." Thus, if a member of the congregation turns to a bad way of life and refuses to change, the "older men" see to it that such a one is put out, or disfellowshipped, from the congregation. Thus a healthy,

18. (a) What kind of organization is God's organization today? (b) Why do God's people now need much encouragement?
19. (a) Who are provided now to help and to strengthen God's people? (b) How is the congregation protected from bad influences that could corrupt it?

spiritually clean congregation is maintained.—Titus 1:5; 1 Peter 5:1-3; Isaiah 32:1, 2; 1 Corinthians 5:13.

[20] Likewise, just as the governing body in Jerusalem sent out special representatives, such as Paul and Silas, to deliver instructions and give encouragement to God's people, so today's governing body does in this time of the end. (Acts 15:24-27, 30-32) About twice a year an experienced minister, called a circuit overseer, is directed to spend a week with each congregation in his circuit.

[21] There are well over 43,000 congregations of Jehovah's Witnesses throughout the world, and these are divided into circuits made up of about 20 congregations each. When visiting the congregations in his circuit, the circuit overseer builds up the Kingdom witnesses by going right along with them in their preaching and teaching activity. Besides stimulating them in this way, he offers suggestions to help them to improve in their ministry.—Acts 20:20, 21.

[22] Further encouragement and strengthening are provided as, usually twice a year, the congregations in each circuit meet together for a two-day circuit assembly. On these occasions there may be anywhere from two or three hundred up to 2,000 or more persons present. You are invited to attend the next one in your area. We feel sure that you will find the assembly spiritually refreshing and personally beneficial.

[23] Then, once a year, a much larger gathering called a district convention may be held for several days. Why not make a real effort to attend and see for yourself how pleasant and spiritually rewarding such a convention can be? Some years, instead of district conventions, there have been larger national or international conventions. The largest ever held in one location was in New York City's Yankee Stadium and Polo Grounds for eight

20. (a) Who in the first century were sent out by the governing body in Jerusalem, and for what reason? (b) Who are sent out by the governing body today?
21. How does the circuit overseer help the congregations of God's people?
22. (a) What further arrangement for strengthening God's people is made twice a year? (b) What invitation is extended to you?
23. (a) What other gatherings are held once each year? (b) What was the size of one of these conventions?

days in 1958. On that occasion 253,922 persons were present for the public talk "God's Kingdom Rules—Is the World's End Near?" Since then no place has been big enough to handle such huge crowds, so arrangements have been made for facilities in many principal cities to be used for large conventions.

MEETINGS WITHIN THE CONGREGATIONS

²⁴ The governing body of Jehovah's Witnesses also arranges for the unified program of Bible instruction that is held in all the congregations of Jehovah's people. Each congregation has five meetings a week. These are the Theocratic Ministry School, Service Meeting, Public Meeting, *Watchtower* study and congregation book study. Since you may not as yet have become acquainted with these meetings, we will briefly describe them.

²⁵ The Theocratic Ministry School is designed to help students to become more effective in speaking to others about God's kingdom. From time to time, those enrolled give short talks on Bible subjects to the entire group. Then an experienced elder offers suggestions for improvement.

²⁶ Generally on the same evening a Service Meeting is also held. The outline for this meeting is published in *Our Kingdom Ministry,* a monthly publication of two or more pages edited by the governing body. During this meeting practical suggestions and demonstrations on effective ways of talking to others about the Kingdom message are presented. In like manner, Christ encouraged his followers and gave them instructions on how to carry out their ministry.—John 21:15-17; Matthew 10:5-14.

²⁷ The Public Meeting and also the *Watchtower* study are usually held on Sunday. Special efforts are made to invite newly interested persons to the Public Meeting, which is a Bible talk by a qualified minister. The *Watchtower* study is a question-and-answer discussion of a Bible article presented in a recent issue of the *Watchtower* magazine.

24. What five weekly meetings are held by the congregations of God's people?
25, 26. What purpose do the Theocratic Ministry School and Service Meeting serve?
27, 28. What kind of meetings are the Public Meeting, *Watchtower* study and congregation book study?

A program of Bible instruction is enjoyed at meetings of Jehovah's Witnesses

²⁸ While the whole congregation may meet at a Kingdom Hall for the meetings outlined above, smaller groups assemble in private homes for the weekly congregation book study. A Bible study aid, such as this book you are reading, is used as the basis for that Bible discussion, which may last up to one hour.

²⁹ In addition to these regular meetings, Jehovah's Witnesses hold a special meeting each year on the anniversary of Jesus' death. When first arranging for this memorial of his death, Jesus said: "Keep doing this in remembrance of me." (Luke 22:19, 20) During a simple ceremony Jesus used wine and unleavened bread as symbols of the life that he was about to sacrifice for humankind. So at this yearly Memorial meal the remaining ones on earth of the 144,000 anointed followers of Christ show forth their heavenly hope by partaking of the bread and wine.

³⁰ The millions of others who attend this Memorial in Kingdom Halls around the earth are glad to be observers. They also are reminded of what Jehovah God and Jesus Christ did to

29. (a) What memorial do true Christians observe each year? (b) Who properly partake of the bread and the wine?
30. (a) Who else properly attend the Memorial, and what are their prospects? (b) How are such persons described by Jesus?

make possible their deliverance from sin and death. But instead of looking forward to heavenly life, they rejoice in the prospect of living forever in paradise on earth. They are like John the Baptizer, who spoke of himself as a "friend of the bridegroom" rather than part of Christ's composite bride of 144,000 members. (John 3:29) These millions of persons are part of the "other sheep" of whom Jesus spoke. They are not members of the "little flock." However, as Jesus said, they serve unitedly with those of the "little flock," so that all "become one flock."—John 10:16; Luke 12:32.

SERVING GOD WITH HIS ORGANIZATION

[31] How clear it is that, as in times past, Jehovah God has a visible organization today! He is now using it to train people for life in his righteous new system. However, we cannot be part of God's organization and, at the same time, be part of false religion. God's Word says: "Do not become unevenly yoked with unbelievers. For what fellowship do righteousness and lawlessness have? Or what sharing does light have with darkness? . . . Or what portion does a faithful person have with an unbeliever?" So God commands: "Therefore get out from among them, and separate yourselves."—2 Corinthians 6:14-17.

[32] What does it mean to "get out from among them"? Well, we could not be obeying that command by remaining a part of, or giving support to, a religious organization other than the one Jehovah God is using. So if any of us still belong to such a religious organization, we need to serve notice that we are withdrawing from it. If we now get out from among those who practice false religion and take positive action to serve God with his visible theocratic organization, we will be among those of whom God says: "I shall reside among them and walk among them, and I shall be their God, and they will be my people." —2 Corinthians 6:16.

31. What evidence is there that God does not approve of those who remain a part of false religion and yet also try to be part of his organization?
32. (a) If we are to "get out from among them," what must we do? (b) What blessing will we receive if we take positive action to serve God with his visible theocratic organization?

Chapter 24

Are We Under the Ten Commandments?

WHAT LAWS does Jehovah God want us to obey? Must we keep what the Bible calls "the law of Moses" or, sometimes, "the Law"? (1 Kings 2:3; Titus 3:9) This is also called "the law of Jehovah," because he is the One who gave it. (1 Chronicles 16:40) Moses merely delivered the Law to the people.

² The law of Moses consists of more than 600 individual laws, or commandments, including the 10 main ones. As Moses said: "He [Jehovah] commanded you to perform, even ten commandments; and he wrote them upon two tables of stone." (Deuteronomy 4:13; Exodus 31:18, *King James Version*) But to whom did Jehovah give the Law, including the Ten Commandments? Did he give it to all humankind? What was the purpose of the Law?

TO ISRAEL FOR A SPECIAL PURPOSE

³ The Law was not given to all humankind. Jehovah made a covenant, or an agreement, with the descendants of Jacob, who

1. What law did Moses deliver to the people?
2. Of what is this law made up?
3. How do we know that the Law was given only to Israel?

THE TEN COMMANDMENTS

1. "I am Jehovah your God . . . You must not have any other gods against my face.
2. "You must not make for yourself a carved image or a form like anything that is in the heavens above or that is on the earth underneath or that is in the waters under the earth. You must not bow down to them nor be induced to serve them . . .
3. "You must not take up the name of Jehovah your God in a worthless way . . .
4. "Remembering the sabbath day to hold it sacred, you are to render service and you must do all your work six days. But the seventh day is a sabbath to Jehovah your God. You must not do any work, you nor your son nor your daughter . . .
5. "Honor your father and your mother in order that your days may prove long upon the ground that Jehovah your God is giving you.
6. "You must not murder.
7. "You must not commit adultery.
8. "You must not steal.
9. "You must not testify falsely as a witness against your fellowman.
10. "You must not desire [covet] your fellowman's house. You must not desire [covet] your fellowman's wife, nor his slave man nor his slave girl nor his bull nor his ass nor anything that belongs to your fellowman."—Exodus 20:2-17.

became the nation of Israel. Jehovah gave his laws to this nation *only*. The Bible makes this clear at Deuteronomy 5:1-3 and Psalm 147:19, 20.

⁴ The apostle Paul asked the question: "Why, then, the Law?" Yes, for what purpose did Jehovah give his law to Israel? Paul answered: "To make transgressions manifest, until the seed should arrive to whom the promise had been made . . . Consequently the Law has become our tutor [or, teacher] leading to Christ." (Galatians 3:19-24) The special purpose of the Law was to protect and guide the nation of Israel so that they might be ready to accept Christ when he arrived. The many sacrifices required by the Law reminded the Israelites that they were sinners who needed a Savior.—Hebrews 10:1-4.

"CHRIST IS THE END OF THE LAW"

⁵ Jesus Christ, of course, was that promised Savior, even as the angel proclaimed at his birth. (Luke 2:8-14) So when Christ came and gave his perfect life as a sacrifice, what happened to the Law? It was removed. "We are no longer under a tutor," Paul explained. (Galatians 3:25) The removal of the Law was a relief to the Israelites. It had shown them up as sinners, for all of them fell short of keeping that Law perfectly. "Christ by purchase released us from the curse of the Law," Paul

The Law served as a wall between the Israelites and other peoples

4. Why was the Law given to the nation of Israel?
5. When Christ came and died for us, what happened to the Law?

said. (Galatians 3:10-14) So the Bible also says: "Christ is the end of the Law."—Romans 10:4; 6:14.

⁶ The Law actually served as a barrier or "wall" between the Israelites and other peoples who were not under it. By the sacrifice of his life, however, Christ "abolished . . . the Law of commandments consisting in decrees, that he might create the two peoples [Israelite and non-Israelite] in union with himself." (Ephesians 2:11-18) Concerning the action that Jehovah God himself took toward the law of Moses, we read: "He kindly forgave us all our trespasses and blotted out the handwritten document against us, which consisted of decrees [including the Ten Commandments] and which was in opposition to us [because of condemning the Israelites as sinners]; and He has taken it out of the way by nailing it to the torture stake." (Colossians 2:13, 14) So, with the perfect sacrifice of Christ, the Law was brought to an end.

⁷ Some persons, however, say that the Law is divided into two parts: The Ten Commandments, and the rest of the laws. The rest of the laws, they say, are what ended, but the Ten Commandments remain. Yet this is not true. In his Sermon on the Mount Jesus quoted from the Ten Commandments as well as other parts of the Law and made no distinction between them. Jesus thus showed that the law of Moses was not divided into two parts.—Matthew 5:21-42.

⁸ Notice, too, what the apostle Paul was inspired by God to write: *"Now we have been discharged from the Law."* Was it only the laws other than the Ten Commandments that Christians were discharged from? No, for Paul goes on to say: "Really I would not have come to know sin if it had not been for the Law; and, for example, I would not have known covetousness if the Law had not said: 'You must not covet.'" (Romans 7:6, 7; Exodus 20:17) Since "You must not covet" is the last one of the Ten Commandments, it follows that the Israelites were discharged from the Ten Commandments also.

6. (a) What was the effect upon Israelites and non-Israelites when the Law ended, and why? (b) What action did Jehovah take toward the Law?
7, 8. What proves that the Law was not divided into two parts?

⁹ Does this mean that the law to keep a weekly Sabbath, which is the fourth of the Ten Commandments, was also removed? Yes, it does. What the Bible says at Galatians 4:8-11 and Colossians 2:16, 17 shows that Christians are not under God's law given to the Israelites, with its requirement to keep the weekly Sabbath and to observe other special days in the year. That keeping a weekly Sabbath is not a Christian requirement can also be seen from Romans 14:5.

LAWS THAT APPLY TO CHRISTIANS

¹⁰ Does this mean that, since Christians are not under the Ten Commandments, they do not need to observe any laws? Not at all. Jesus introduced a "new covenant," based on the better sacrifice of his own perfect human life. Christians come under this new covenant and are subject to Christian laws. (Hebrews 8:7-13; Luke 22:20) Many of these laws have been taken from the law of Moses. This is not unexpected or unusual. A similar thing often happens when a new government takes over the rule of a country. The constitution under the old government might be canceled and replaced, but the new constitution may keep many of the laws of the old one. In a similar way, the Law covenant came to an end, but many of its basic laws and principles were adopted into Christianity.

¹¹ Note how this is the case as you read the Ten Commandments on page 203, and then compare them with the following Christian laws and teachings: "It is Jehovah your God you must worship." (Matthew 4:10; 1 Corinthians 10:20-22) "Guard yourselves from idols." (1 John 5:21; 1 Corinthians 10:14) "Our Father in the heavens, let your name be sanctified [not treated in a worthless way]." (Matthew 6:9) "Children, be obedient to your parents." (Ephesians 6:1, 2) And the Bible makes clear that murder, committing adultery, stealing, lying and coveting are also against the laws for Christians.—Revelation 21:8; 1 John

9. What shows that the weekly Sabbath law was also done away with?
10. (a) Christians are under what laws? (b) From where were many of these laws taken, and why is it reasonable that they were taken from there?
11. What laws or teachings given to Christians are very similar to the Ten Commandments?

3:15; Hebrews 13:4; 1 Thessalonians 4:3-7; Ephesians 4:25, 28; 1 Corinthians 6:9-11; Luke 12:15; Colossians 3:5.

[12] Although Christians are not commanded to keep a weekly Sabbath, we learn something from that arrangement. The Israelites rested in a literal way, but Christians must rest in a spiritual way. How? Because of faith and obedience true Christians leave off doing selfish works. These selfish works include efforts to establish their own righteousness. (Hebrews 4:10) This spiritual rest is observed not only one day a week but for all seven days. The requirement of the literal Sabbath law to set aside one day for spiritual interests protected the Israelites from selfishly using all their time to seek their own material advantage. Applying this principle every day in a spiritual way is an even more effective guard against materialism.

[13] So Christians are urged to "fulfill the law of the Christ," rather than to keep the Ten Commandments. (Galatians 6:2) Jesus gave many commands and instructions, and by our obeying them we are keeping or fulfilling his law. In particular, Jesus stressed the importance of love. (Matthew 22:36-40; John 13:34, 35) Yes, to love others is a Christian law. It is the basis of the entire law of Moses, as the Bible says: "The entire Law stands fulfilled in one saying, namely: 'You must love your neighbor as yourself.' "—Galatians 5:13, 14; Romans 13:8-10.

[14] The law given through Moses, with its Ten Commandments, was a righteous set of laws from God. And even though we are not under that law today, the divine principles behind it are still of great value to us. By studying and applying them we will grow in appreciation for the great Lawgiver Jehovah God. But especially should we study and apply in our lives Christian laws and teachings. Love for Jehovah will move us to obey all that he now requires of us.—1 John 5:3.

12. How is the principle of the Sabbath law carried over into the Christian arrangement?
13. (a) What law are Christians urged to fulfill, and how do they fulfill it? (b) What law did Jesus stress? (c) What law is the basis of the entire law of Moses?
14. (a) What good will result by our studying and applying the principles of the law of Moses? (b) What will love move us to do?

For Satan's World, or for God's New System?

ARE YOU FOR God's righteous new system, and do you want it to come? Are you against Satan, and do you want his world to end? You may say, Yes, to both questions. But is that enough? There is an old saying that actions speak louder than words. If you believe in God's new system, <u>it is the way you live your life</u> that will really prove it.—Matthew 7:21-23; 15:7, 8.

² The fact is, your way of life can be pleasing to only one of two masters. Either you are serving <u>Jehovah God or Satan the Devil.</u> A principle found in the Bible helps us to appreciate this. It says: "Do you not know that if you keep presenting yourselves to anyone as slaves to obey him, you are slaves of him because you obey him?" (Romans 6:16) Whom do you obey? Whose will do you do? Regardless of your answer, if you follow the unrighteous ways of the world you cannot be serving the true God, Jehovah.

SATAN'S WORLD—WHAT IS IT?

³ Jesus called <u>Satan</u> "the ruler of this world." And the apostle John said that "the whole world is lying in the power of the wicked one." (John 12:31; 1 John 5:19) Note that in prayer to God Jesus did not include his disciples as part of Satan's world. He said: "<u>I make request concerning them [his disciples];</u> <u>I make request, *not concerning the world* . . . They are no part of the world, just as I am no part of the world.</u>" (John 17:9, 16;

1. What really proves that you are for God's new system?
2. (a) Who are the two masters that we can serve? (b) What shows whose slave, or servant, we are?
3. (a) Whom does the Bible show is ruler of the world? (b) In prayer, how did Jesus show a difference between the world and his disciples?

15:18, 19) From this it is clear that true Christians are to keep separate from the world.

4 But to what was Jesus referring when he said *"the world"*? In the Bible the expression "the world" sometimes simply means humankind in general. God sent his Son to give his life as a ransom for this world of humankind. (John 3:16) Yet Satan has organized most of humankind in opposition to God. So *Satan's world is this organized human society that exists apart from or outside of God's visible organization.* It is this world from which true Christians must be separate.—James 1:27.

5 Satan's world—his organized human society—is made up of various closely connected parts. An important part is false religion. In the Bible false religion is represented as a "great harlot," or prostitute, with the name "Babylon the Great." She is a world empire, as shown by the fact that she "has a kingdom over the kings of the earth." (Revelation 17:1, 5, 18) But what proves that Babylon the Great is a *religious* world empire?

6 Since "the kings of the earth" are said to 'commit fornication' with her, Babylon the Great could not be a political world empire. And since the "traveling merchants" of the earth stand at a distance and mourn at her destruction, she is not a commercial world empire. (Revelation 17:2; 18:15) However, that she is really a religious empire is shown by the Bible's statement that by means of her "spiritistic practice all the nations were misled." —Revelation 18:23.

7 Also proving that Babylon the Great is a religious empire is her relationship to a "wild beast." In the Bible such beasts represent political governments. (Daniel 8:20, 21) Babylon

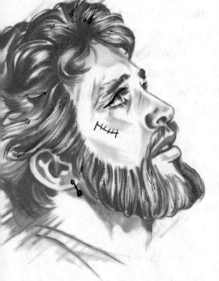

What is the world that Jesus would not pray for and that his disciples are no part of?

---

4. (a) At John 3:16, to whom does the expression "the world" refer? (b) What is "the world" from which Christ's followers have to separate?

5. What is an important part of the world, and how is it represented in the Bible?

6, 7. (a) What proves that Babylon the Great is a religious empire? (b) What relationship has false religion had with political governments?

the Great is described as "sitting upon a scarlet-colored wild beast . . . that had seven heads and ten horns." She has thus been trying to exercise influence over this "wild beast," or world government. (Revelation 17:3) And it is a fact that throughout history religion has been mixed up with politics, often telling governments what to do. She has indeed exercised "a kingdom over the kings of the earth."—Revelation 17:18.

[8] These political governments make up another important part of Satan's world. As we have already noted, they are represented in the Bible as beasts. (Daniel 7:1-8, 17, 23) That these beastlike governments receive their power from Satan is shown by a vision written down by the apostle John: "I saw a wild beast ascending out of the sea, with ten horns and seven heads . . . And the dragon gave to the beast its power." (Revelation 13:1, 2; 12:9) Further proof that these kingdoms, or governments, are part of Satan's world is the fact that Satan tempted Jesus by offering these kingdoms to him. Satan could not have done this if he had not been the ruler of them.—Matthew 4:8, 9.

[9] Yet another prominent part of Satan's world is the greedy and oppressive commercial system, which is referred to at Revelation 18:11 as "traveling merchants." This commercial system promotes a selfish desire in people to obtain the things it produces, even though they may not need them and may be even better off without them. At the same time the greedy commercial system hoards food in storehouses but allows millions of people to starve to death because they cannot pay for the food. On the other hand, military weapons capable of destroying the whole human family are produced and sold for profit. Thus Satan's commercial system, along with false religion and the political governments, promotes selfishness, crime and terrible wars.

[10] The organized human society under Satan the Devil is indeed wicked and corrupt. It is opposed to God's righteous laws, and

8. What is another important part of Satan's world, and how are they represented in the Bible?

9. (a) How is another part of Satan's world described at Revelation 18:11? (b) What does it do and promote, proving that Satan is behind it?

10, 11. (a) What is another feature of Satan's world? (b) What Bible warnings are there against getting involved in this feature?

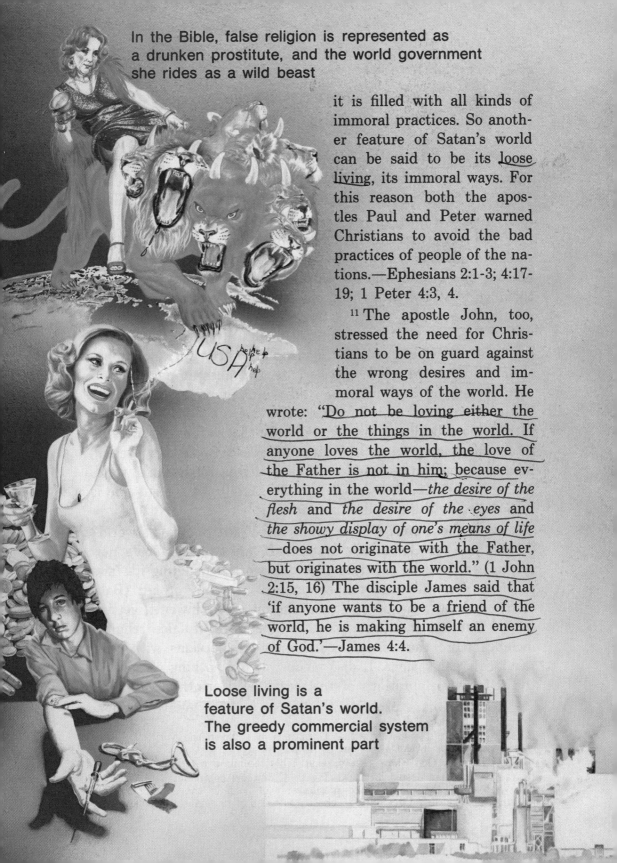

In the Bible, false religion is represented as a drunken prostitute, and the world government she rides as a wild beast

it is filled with all kinds of immoral practices. So another feature of Satan's world can be said to be its loose living, its immoral ways. For this reason both the apostles Paul and Peter warned Christians to avoid the bad practices of people of the nations.—Ephesians 2:1-3; 4:17-19; 1 Peter 4:3, 4.

11 The apostle John, too, stressed the need for Christians to be on guard against the wrong desires and immoral ways of the world. He wrote: "Do not be loving either the world or the things in the world. If anyone loves the world, the love of the Father is not in him; because everything in the world—*the desire of the flesh* and *the desire of the eyes* and *the showy display of one's means of life*—does not originate with the Father, but originates with the world." (1 John 2:15, 16) The disciple James said that 'if anyone wants to be a friend of the world, he is making himself an enemy of God.'—James 4:4.

Loose living is a feature of Satan's world. The greedy commercial system is also a prominent part

HOW TO AVOID BEING PART OF THE WORLD

[12] As long as Satan's world exists, Christians must live in it. Jesus showed this when he prayed to his Father: "I request you, not to take them out of the world." But then Jesus added regarding his followers: "They are no part of the world." (John 17:15, 16) How is it possible to be *in Satan's world* but still *be no part of it?*

[13] Well, you live in among the people who make up today's organized human society. These people include fornicators, greedy persons and others who do wicked things. You may work with them, go to school with them, eat with them, and share in other such activities with them. (1 Corinthians 5:9, 10) You are even to love them, as God does. (John 3:16) But a true Christian does not love the wicked things the people do. He does not adopt their attitudes, actions or goals in life. He takes no part in their corrupt religion and politics. And while he must often work in the commercial world to make a living, he does not engage in dishonest business practices; nor is the gaining of material things his main goal in life. Since he is for God's new system, he avoids the bad association of those living for Satan's world. (1 Corinthians 15:33; Psalm 1:1; 26:3-6, 9, 10) As a result, he is *in Satan's world* but still is *no part of it.*

[14] What about you? Do you want to be part of Satan's world? Or are you for God's new system? If you are for God's new system, you will be separate from the world, including its false religion. You will heed the command: "Get out of her [Babylon the Great], my people." (Revelation 18:4) However, getting out of Babylon the Great, the world empire of false religion, includes more than simply cutting off connections with false religious organizations. It also means having nothing to do with the religious celebrations of the world.—2 Corinthians 6:14-18.

[15] Christmas is a prominent religious holiday today. But his-

---

12, 13. (a) How did Jesus show that Christians must be in the world? (b) How is it possible to be in the world but be no part of it?

14. If you are for God's new system, what Bible command will you obey?

15. (a) Rather than Jesus' birth, what were Christians commanded to observe? (b) What shows that Jesus could not have been born in the cold of winter? (c) Why was the date December 25 chosen as the day to celebrate Jesus' birth?

Since at Jesus' birth shepherds were still
in the fields with their flocks at night,
he could not have been born on December 25

tory shows that it was not a celebration observed by the very
early Christians. Jesus told his followers to observe a memorial
of his death, not of his birth. (1 Corinthians 11:24-26) The fact
is, December 25 is not the date of Jesus' birth. It could not
have been, since the Bible shows that at the time of his birth
shepherds were still in the fields at night. They would not have
been there in the cold, rainy season of winter. (Luke 2:8-12)
Actually December 25 was chosen as the date to celebrate Jesus'
birth because, as *The World Book Encyclopedia* explains: "The
people of Rome already observed it as the Feast of Saturn,
celebrating the birthday of the sun."

¹⁶ Easter is another prominent religious holiday. The Holy
Week in some Latin-American countries is similar. But Easter
was not celebrated by early Christians either. It, too, had its
beginnings in non-Christian celebrations. *The Encyclopædia Britannica* says: "There is no indication of the observance of the
Easter festival in the New Testament." Yet does it really matter
that Christmas and Easter are not Christian celebrations but
actually had their beginnings with worshipers of false gods? The
apostle Paul warned against mixing the true and the false, saying
that even "a little leaven ferments the whole lump." (Galatians

16. (a) What other prominent religious holiday had non-Christian beginnings?
(b) For what good reasons do true Christians not celebrate Christmas and Easter?

5:9) He told some early Christians that it was wrong for them to observe days that had been kept under the law of Moses but that had been canceled by God for Christians. (Galatians 4:10, 11) How much more important it is for true Christians today to keep away from holidays that God never said should be observed and that came from false religion!

17 Other holidays of the world honor famous men. Still others honor and exalt nations or worldly organizations. But the Bible warns against giving worshipful honors to humans, or trusting in human organizations to accomplish what only God can do. (Acts 10:25, 26; 12:21-23; Revelation 19:10; Jeremiah 17:5-7) So holidays that tend to exalt a man or a human organization are not in harmony with God's will, and true Christians will not share in them.—Romans 12:2.

18 Many objects have been made by men that people are told to honor or worship. Some of these are made of metal or wood. Others are made of cloth and may have sewed or painted on

17. (a) What is wrong with holidays that honor famous men or nations? (b) How does the Bible show what course Christians should take?
18. (a) What objects have men made to honor or worship? (b) What does God's law say about giving worshipful honor to an object?

God's servants refused to worship an image set up by a king. What would you do in a similar situation?

them a picture of something in heaven or on earth. A nation may pass a law that says everyone should give worshipful honor to such an object. But God's law says that his servants should not. (Exodus 20:4, 5; Matthew 4:10) What have God's people done in such a situation?

[19] In ancient Babylon King Nebuchadnezzar built a huge image of gold and commanded that everyone bow down to it. 'Whoever does not,' he said, 'will be thrown into the burning fiery furnace.' The Bible tells us that three young Hebrews, Shadrach, Meshach and Abednego, refused to do what the king commanded. Why? Because it involved worship, and their worship belonged only to Jehovah. God approved of what they did, and he saved them from the anger of the king. In fact, Nebuchadnezzar came to see that these servants of Jehovah were no danger to the State, so he passed a law to protect their freedom. (Daniel 3:1-30) Do you not admire the faithfulness of these young men? Will you show that you really are for God's new system by obeying all of God's laws?—Acts 5:29.

[20] Satan, of course, does not want us to serve Jehovah. He wants us to serve him. So he tries to get us to do what he wants, since he knows that we become the slaves, or servants, of whomever we obey. (Romans 6:16) Through various means, including television, movies, certain forms of dancing and immoral literature, Satan encourages sexual relations between unmarried persons, as well as adultery. Such conduct is made to seem acceptable, even proper. However, this is against God's laws. (Hebrews 13:4; Ephesians 5:3-5) And a person who engages in such conduct is actually showing that he is for Satan's world.

[21] There are other practices that Satan's world has made popular but that are against God's laws. Getting drunk on alcoholic beverages is one of them. (1 Corinthians 6:9, 10) Another is the use of such drugs as marijuana and heroin for pleasure, as well

19. (a) What did the king of Babylon command everyone to do? (b) Whose example do Christians do well to follow?
20. What are various means that Satan uses to try to get us to break God's laws on sexual morality?
21. What are other practices that, if a person engages in them, will show that he is for Satan's world?

as the use of tobacco. These things are harmful to the body and are unclean. Their use is clearly in violation of God's instruction to "cleanse ourselves of every defilement of flesh and spirit." (2 Corinthians 7:1) The smoking of tobacco also harms the health of those nearby who must breathe the smoke, so the smoker is violating God's law that states that a Christian should love his neighbor.—Matthew 22:39.

[22] Another common practice in various parts of the world is the eating of blood. Thus animals not properly bled are eaten or the blood may be drained out and used as food in a meal. Yet God's Word forbids the eating of blood. (Genesis 9:3, 4; Leviticus 17:10) What, then, about taking a blood transfusion? Some persons may reason that getting a blood transfusion is not actually "eating." But is it not true that when a patient is unable to take food through his mouth, the doctor often recommends feeding him by the same method in which a blood transfusion is given? The Bible tells us to "*abstain* from . . . blood." (Acts 15:20, 29) What does this mean? If a doctor were to tell you to abstain from alcohol, would that simply mean that you should not take it through your mouth but that you could transfuse it directly into your veins? Of course not! So, too, 'abstaining from blood' means not taking it into your body at all.

[23] You need to show Jehovah God that you are for his new system and are no part of this world. This requires a decision. The decision that you need to make is to serve Jehovah, to do his will. You cannot be undecided, as some Israelites in ancient times were. (1 Kings 18:21) For remember, if you are not serving Jehovah, then you are serving Satan. *You* may say you are for God's new system, but what is your *conduct* saying? Being for God's new system involves avoiding all practices that God condemns and that will not be in his righteous new system.

22. (a) What does the Bible say about blood? (b) Why is taking a blood transfusion not actually different from "eating" blood? (c) What shows that 'abstaining from blood' means not to take it into your body at all?

23. (a) What decision do you need to make? (b) What will show the decision that you have made?

Chapter 26

The Fight to Do What Is Right

AS LONG AS Satan's world exists, Christians must fight to keep free from its wicked influence. The apostle Paul wrote: "Put on the complete suit of armor from God that you may be able to stand firm against the [crafty acts] of the Devil." (Ephesians 6:11-18) However, our fight is not only against Satan and his world; it is also against our own desires to do what is bad. The Bible says: "The inclination of the heart of man is bad from his youth up."—Genesis 8:21; Romans 5:12.

² Because of the sin inherited from the first man Adam, our hearts may crave to do what is bad. If we give in to that craving, we will not receive everlasting life in God's new system. So we need to *fight* to do what is right. Even the apostle Paul had such a fight, as he explained: "When I wish to do what is right, what is bad is present with me." (Romans 7:21-23) You, too, may find this fight a hard one. At times a powerful conflict may be going on within you. What will you then decide to do?

³ You have come to know of God's wonderful promises about living forever under perfect conditions on earth. You believe these promises, and you want these good things for yourself. So you know that it is in your *lasting* best interest to serve God. But in your heart you may desire things that you know are bad. At times you may have a strong desire to commit fornication, to steal, or to take part in other wrongdoing. Some persons studying this book may actually be engaging in such bad practices, though they know that these things are condemned by God. The fact that they do wrong when they wish to do right

1. What two things must Christians fight against?
2. (a) Why do we often have a strong desire to do wrong? (b) Why should we fight wrong desires?
3. (a) What inner conflict do many persons have? (b) What Bible truth is demonstrated by the fact that many do wrong when they wish to do right?

217

demonstrates the Bible truth: "The heart is more treacherous than anything else and is desperate."—Jeremiah 17:9.

THE FIGHT CAN BE WON

[4] This does not mean, however, that a person has no control over his strong desires to do wrong. If you really want to, you can strengthen your heart so that it will lead you in a right way. But it is up to you to do this. (Psalm 26:1, 11) Nobody else can win the fight for you. So, first of all, continue to take in life-giving Bible knowledge. (John 17:3) Yet more is needed than simply getting that knowledge into your head. It must also sink into your heart. You must come to have a deep feeling about what you are learning so that you really want to act upon it.

[5] But how can you gain heart appreciation for God's laws? You need to meditate, or think deeply, about them. For example, ask yourself: What difference does obeying God really make? Then look at the lives of people who have ignored his laws, such as the 19-year-old girl who wrote: "I have had a venereal disease three times. The last time it cost me my right to bear children because I had to have a hysterectomy." It is truly sad to consider all the trouble that is caused when people disobey God's laws. (2 Samuel 13:1-19) A woman who had committed fornication sadly said: "It's just not worth the pain and emotional breakdown that comes with disobedience. I'm suffering for that now."

[6] Yet you will hear people say that fornication, as well as getting drunk and taking drugs, is fun. But the so-called fun is only temporary. Do not be misled into a course of action that will rob you of true and lasting happiness. Think of Moses who was raised as "the son of the daughter of Pharaoh." He lived in the richness of the royal household there in ancient Egypt. However, the Bible says that, when he grew up, he chose "to be ill-treated with the people of God rather than to have *the*

---

4. (a) Whether the fight is won or lost depends upon whom? (b) What is required to win the fight to do what is right?
5. How can you gain heart appreciation for God's laws?
6. (a) Why is pleasure that may come from doing what is bad not worth it? (b) What kind of life could Moses have enjoyed in Egypt?

temporary enjoyment of sin." (Hebrews 11:24, 25) So there must have been enjoyment or fun in the immoral, loose-living way of life that apparently existed among the Egyptian royal household. Why, then, did Moses turn away from all of it?

⁷ It is because Moses believed in Jehovah God. And he knew about something far better than any temporary enjoyment of sin that he might experience in the Egyptian royal household. The Bible says: "*He looked intently toward the payment of the reward.*" Moses meditated, or thought deeply, about the things that God had promised. He had faith in God's purpose to create a righteous new system. His heart was touched by Jehovah's great love and care for humankind. It was not simply that Moses had *heard* or *read* about Jehovah. The Bible says that "he continued steadfast *as seeing the One who is invisible.*" (He-

7. Why did Moses turn away from "the temporary enjoyment of sin" in the Egyptian royal household?

Since there was enjoyment in the life-style of ancient Egypt, why did Moses reject it?

brews 11:26, 27) Jehovah was real to Moses, and so were his promises of everlasting life.

8 Is that true of you? Do you view Jehovah as a real Person, as a Father who loves you? When you read about his promises to provide everlasting life in Paradise on earth, do you picture yourself being there enjoying these blessings? (See pages 156 to 162.) To win the fight against the many pressures to do wrong, we need to have a close relationship with Jehovah. And we need to look, as Moses did, "intently toward the payment of the reward." A 20-year-old youth, who was faced with the temptation to commit fornication, had Moses' viewpoint. He said: "My hope for everlasting life was too valuable to lose for a few moments of immorality." Is that not the right attitude to have?

David kept looking; he did not avoid the situation that led to immorality

LEARNING FROM THE MISTAKES OF OTHERS

9 You can never let down your guard in this fight, as King David once did. He happened one day to be looking from his rooftop, and in the distance he saw beautiful Bath-sheba bathing herself. Rather than turn away before improper thoughts grew in his heart, he kept looking. His desire to have sexual relations with Bath-sheba became so strong that he had her brought to his palace. Later, since she had become pregnant, and he was

8. (a) To win in the fight to do right, what do we need? (b) What viewpoint, as expressed by a youth, would we be wise to have?

9. In what way did King David fail in the fight to do what is right?

unable to have their adultery covered up, he arranged to have her husband killed in battle.—2 Samuel 11:1-17.

[10] That indeed was a terrible sin. And David really suffered for it. Not only was he greatly distressed by what he had done, but Jehovah punished him with trouble in his household for the rest of his life. (Psalm 51:3, 4; 2 Samuel 12:10-12) David's heart was more treacherous than he had realized; his wrong desires overpowered him. Afterward he said: "Look! With error I was brought forth with birth pains, and in sin my mother conceived me." (Psalm 51:5) But the bad thing David did with Bath-sheba did not have to happen. His problem was that he kept looking; he did not avoid the situation that caused his sexual appetite to grow for another man's wife.

[11] We should learn from David's experience to be on guard against situations that excite improper sexual feelings. For example, what will happen if you read books and watch television programs and movies that put emphasis on sex? Sexual desires will likely be stimulated. So avoid activities and entertainment that work up "sexual appetite." (Colossians 3:5; 1 Thessalonians 4:3-5; Ephesians 5:3-5) Do not put yourself in a situation with another person that can lead to fornication. A 17-year-old wisely commented: "Anyone can say, 'we know when to stop.' True, a person may *know* when, but how many

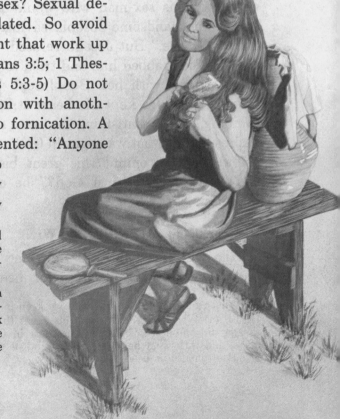

10. (a) How was David punished for his sin? (b) What could have prevented David's falling into adultery?

11. (a) What should we learn from David's experience? (b) What activities would you say can work up "sexual appetite"? (c) As one youth stated, what does the wise person avoid?

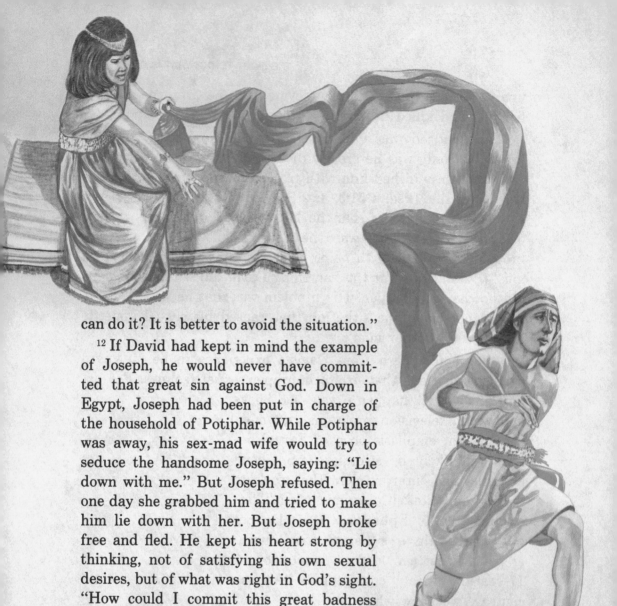

can do it? It is better to avoid the situation."

¹² If David had kept in mind the example of Joseph, he would never have committed that great sin against God. Down in Egypt, Joseph had been put in charge of the household of Potiphar. While Potiphar was away, his sex-mad wife would try to seduce the handsome Joseph, saying: "Lie down with me." But Joseph refused. Then one day she grabbed him and tried to make him lie down with her. But Joseph broke free and fled. He kept his heart strong by thinking, not of satisfying his own sexual desires, but of what was right in God's sight. "How could I commit this great badness and actually sin against God?" he asked. —Genesis 39:7-12.

HELP THAT YOU NEED TO WIN

¹³ To win this fight you must let Bible knowledge sink down into your heart so

12. What example of Joseph should we keep in mind? 13, 14. (a) What is needed to win this fight? (b) What change did those who became Christians in Corinth make, and with what help? (c) What kind of persons had Paul and Titus been?

Joseph fled from the immoral advances of Potiphar's wife

that you are moved to act upon it. But you also need to associate with God's people, to become a part of Jehovah's visible organization. With its help, no matter how deeply you may have been involved in wrongdoing, you can change. Concerning persons in ancient Corinth who changed, the apostle Paul wrote: "Do not be misled. Neither fornicators, nor idolaters, nor adulterers, nor men kept for unnatural purposes, nor men who lie with men, nor thieves, nor greedy persons, nor drunkards, nor revilers, nor extortioners will inherit God's kingdom. *And yet that is what some of you were.* But you have been washed clean."—1 Corinthians 6:9-11.

¹⁴ Think of that! Some of those early Christians had formerly been fornicators, adulterers, homosexuals, thieves and drunkards. But with help from the Christian organization they changed. The apostle Paul himself had once practiced bad things. (1 Timothy 1:15) To his fellow Christian, Titus, he wrote: "For even we were once senseless, disobedient, being misled, *being slaves to various desires and pleasures.*"—Titus 3:3.

¹⁵ When Paul became a Christian, was it then easy for him to do what is right? No. Paul had a lifelong battle against the wrong desires and pleasures to which he had once been a slave. He wrote: "I [beat] my body and lead it as a slave, that, after I have preached to others, I myself should not become disapproved somehow." (1 Corinthians 9:27) Paul 'got tough' with himself. He would force himself to do what is right, even when his body desired to do wrong. And if you do as he did, you also can win this fight.

¹⁶ If you are finding it hard to overcome some bad habit, attend the next large assembly of Jehovah's Witnesses. You will no doubt be impressed by the clean conduct and the joy of those present. Yet many of these persons were once part of this world in which fornication, adultery, drunkenness, homosexuality, smoking, drug addiction, theft, fraud, lying and gambling are so very common. Many of them once practiced these things.

---

15. (a) What shows that it was not easy for Paul to do what is right? (b) How can we benefit from Paul's example?
16. What modern-day examples can help us to win the fight to do right?

(1 Peter 4:3, 4) Also, as you associate with Jehovah's Witnesses at smaller congregation meetings, which should be done without delay, you will be among persons who have fought to overcome the same bad practices and desires that you may now be fighting against. So take courage! They are winning the fight to do what is right. So can you with God's help.

[17] If you have been studying the Bible for some time now with Jehovah's Witnesses, you no doubt have attended meetings at the Kingdom Hall. Make such meeting attendance a regular habit. All of us need the spiritual encouragement received from such Christian association. (Hebrews 10:24, 25) Get to know the "older men," or elders, of the congregation. Their responsibility is to "shepherd the flock of God." (1 Peter 5:1-3; Acts 20:28) So do not hesitate to go to them if you need help to overcome some habit that is contrary to God's laws. You will find them to be loving, kind and considerate.—1 Thessalonians 2:7, 8.

[18] The pressure to do wrong is on us, not only from Satan's world but from within our sinful selves. So to be faithful to God is a daily fight. But how good that the fight will not continue forever! Soon Satan will be removed and his entire wicked world will be destroyed. Then, in God's new system near at hand, there will be righteous conditions that will make our course much easier. Eventually all traces of sin will be gone, and no longer will there be this hard fight to do what is right.

[19] Think regularly about the blessings of that new system. Yes, put on "as a helmet the hope of salvation." (1 Thessalonians 5:8) May your attitude be that of the young woman who said: "I think of everything that Jehovah has done for me and promised me. He hasn't given up on me. He has blessed me in so many ways. I know he wants only the best for me, and I want to please him. Eternal life is worth any effort." If we faithfully pursue righteousness, 'all the good promises that Jehovah has made' toward those who love him will come true.—Joshua 21:45.

---

17. (a) What association is necessary if we are to win the fight? (b) From whom can you receive help with problems?
18. What future prospect provides strength to carry on in the fight?
19. Why should you be willing to put forth any effort to please Jehovah?

Chapter 27

How to Gain Help Through Prayer

TO KEEP FREE from the world's wicked influence, Christians especially need the help received through prayer. Jesus said: "The Father in heaven [will] give holy spirit to those asking him." (Luke 11:13) We need God's holy spirit, or active force, even as we need to study his Word and to associate with his organization. But to receive holy spirit, we must pray for it.

Prayer is respectful speech to God. It can be in the form of a request, such as when asking God for things. But prayer can also be an expression of thanks or praise to God. (1 Chronicles 29:10-13) In order to have a good relationship with our heavenly Father, we must regularly talk to him in prayer. (Romans 12:12; Ephesians 6:18) His active force, which is received by our asking for it, can strengthen us to do his will despite any troubles or temptations that Satan or his world may bring upon us.—1 Corinthians 10:13; Ephesians 3:20.

You may be having a real fight to get rid of some habit or practice that is not pleasing to God. If so, seek Jehovah's help. Turn to him in prayer. The apostle Paul did, and he wrote: "For all things I have the strength by virtue of him who imparts power to me." (Philippians 4:13; Psalm 55:22; 121:1, 2) A woman who broke free from a course of immorality said: "He is the only one who has the power to help you get out of that situation. You have to have that personal relationship with Jehovah, and the only way to keep that personal relationship is to pray."

1. What help do we need from God, and how do we receive it?
2. (a) What is prayer? (b) What are various forms of prayer? (c) Why is prayer important?
3. (a) What strength can we receive from God? (b) How only can we maintain a good relationship with God?

By praying to God.

⁴ Yet a person may say: 'I have prayed for God's help many times, but I still cannot keep from doing wrong.' Persons who smoke have said this. When such a man was asked: "When do you pray?" he answered: "In the evening before going to bed, in the morning when getting up, and after I weaken and take a smoke, I tell Jehovah that I am sorry for what I have done." His friend said: "The time that you really need God's help is the moment that you are reaching for a smoke, is it not? That is the time you should pray to Jehovah to strengthen you." When the man did, he received help to stop smoking.

⁵ This is not to say that prayer to God, along with study of his Word and association with his visible organization, will make it easy for you to do what is right. It still requires effort; yes, a hard fight, which may even include suffering. (1 Corinthians 9:27) Bad habits can result in a terrible craving for what is bad. *So suffering usually results when a person withdraws from sinful activity*. Are you willing to suffer in order to do what is right? —1 Peter 2:20, 21.

PRAYERS THAT GOD HEARS

⁶ Many persons find it hard to pray. "I am having trouble praying to someone I can't see," confessed a young woman. Since no human has seen God, we need faith in order to pray and to be heard by God. We need to believe that Jehovah really exists and that he can do what we ask. (Hebrews 11:6) If we have that kind of faith, and if we approach God with a sincere heart, we can be sure that he will help us. (Mark 9:23) Thus, even though the Roman army officer Cornelius was not at the time part of God's organization, when he sincerely prayed for guidance, God answered his prayer.—Acts 10:30-33.

⁷ Some persons have a hard time expressing themselves in words. However, this should not keep them from speaking to

4. How did a man receive strength to break free from the smoking habit?
5. (a) What does it require to serve God properly? (b) What indicates that suffering is often involved in withdrawing from sinful activity?
6. (a) Why do many find it hard to pray? (b) What do we need in order for our prayers to be heard?
7. (a) What kind of prayers please God? (b) To what kind of prayers will God not listen?

God in prayer. We can be sure that he knows our needs and will understand what we want to say. (Matthew 6:8) Think about it: Which expression do you most appreciate from a child—his simple, sincere thanks or the special words someone told him to say? Our Father in heaven likewise appreciates simple, sincere expressions from us. (James 4:6; Luke 18:9-14) No special words or religious language are needed. He will not even listen to those who pray in unusual or high-sounding language to impress others, or who say the same things over and over again in an insincere way.—Matthew 6:5, 7.

⁸ Even when you pray silently, God can hear. When Nehemiah did, God acted upon his sincere request, and likewise with Hannah. (Nehemiah 2:4-8; 1 Samuel 1:11-13, 19, 20) Nor is a person's physical position when praying the important thing. You can pray while in any position, at any time and at any place. However, the Bible shows that a position of humility,

8. (a) What shows that God can hear prayers said silently? (b) Does the Bible indicate that we must pray in any certain position or place?

What should one do
when tempted to smoke—
pray for help or give in?

Rick & Deanne

such as bowing the head or kneeling, is appropriate. (1 Kings 8:54; Nehemiah 8:6; Daniel 6:10; Mark 11:25; John 11:41) And Jesus indicated that it is good when personal prayers can be said in a place of privacy, unseen to men.—Matthew 6:6.

⁹ Prayer is part of our worship. For this reason our prayers should be addressed only to our Creator, Jehovah God, not to anyone else. (Matthew 4:10) And the Bible shows that Christians must approach God through Jesus, who gave his life to take away our sins. This means we should say our prayers in the name of Jesus.—John 14:6, 14; 16:23; Ephesians 5:20; 1 John 2:1, 2.

¹⁰ However, are all prayers pleasing to Jehovah? The Bible says: "He that is turning his ear away from hearing the law —even his prayer is something detestable." (Proverbs 28:9; 15:29; Isaiah 1:15) Therefore if we want God to hear our prayers, a basic requirement is that we do his will, that we obey his laws. Otherwise God will not listen to us, just as an upright person would not listen to a radio program that he considers immoral. The Bible says: "Whatever we ask we receive from him, *because we are observing his commandments and are doing the things that are pleasing in his eyes.*"—1 John 3:22.

¹¹ This means that we must work at what we pray for. For example, it would be wrong for a person to ask God for his help to stop using tobacco or marijuana and then go out and buy these things. Nor could he ask Jehovah to help him to avoid immorality and then read literature and watch movies and television programs that feature immorality. Or if gambling is a person's weakness, he could not pray for God to help him to stop and then visit racetracks or other such places where gambling is carried on. For our prayers to be heard by God, we need to show him by our actions that we really mean what we say.

¹² What, then, are personal things that we can include in

9. (a) To whom should all our prayers be directed, and why? (b) For our prayers to be acceptable to God, in whose name should they be offered?
10. (a) Whose prayers are not pleasing to God? (b) What basic requirement must we meet if our prayers are to be heard by God?
11. What does it mean to work at what we pray for?
12. (a) What are things that we can include in our prayers? (b) In order for our prayers to be pleasing to God, what must we learn?

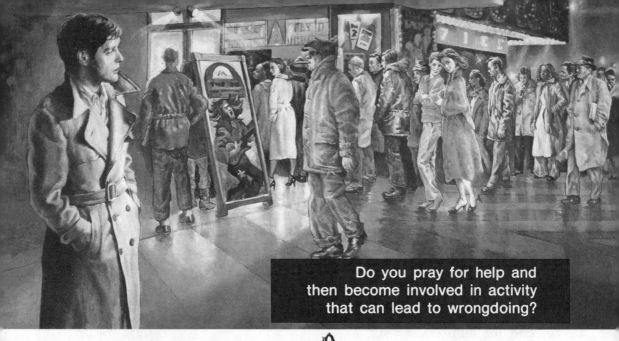

Do you pray for help and then become involved in activity that can lead to wrongdoing?

our prayers to Jehovah? Actually, anything that will affect our relationship with God is a proper subject for prayer, including our physical health, as well as the rearing of children. (2 Kings 20:1-3; Judges 13:8) The apostle John wrote: *"No matter what it is that we ask according to his will, he hears us."* (1 John 5:14) So the important thing is that our requests be in harmony with God's will. This means that we first need to learn what his will is. (Proverbs 3:5, 6) Then if we take into consideration God's will and purpose when we pray, rather than simply being concerned with our own personal interests, our prayers will be acceptable to Jehovah. It is proper that we thank Jehovah every day for the good things he provides.—John 6:11, 23; Acts 14:16, 17.

Jesus gave his followers a model prayer to guide them as to the kind of prayer God accepts. (Matthew 6:9-13) This prayer shows that God's name, his kingdom and the doing of his will on earth come first. Next, we may ask for our personal needs, such as our daily food, the forgiveness of sins, and the deliverance from temptation and from the wicked one, Satan the Devil.

PRAYERS TO HELP OTHERS

¹⁴ Jesus showed by his example the importance of praying in

---

13. (a) How did Jesus show what should be the matters of first concern in our prayers? (b) What are things of secondary importance that we should pray about?
14. How does the Bible show the importance of praying in behalf of others?

behalf of others. (Luke 22:32; 23:34; John 17:20) The apostle Paul knew the value of such prayers and often asked others to pray for him. (1 Thessalonians 5:25; 2 Thessalonians 3:1; Romans 15:30) While in prison he wrote: "I am hoping that through the prayers of you people I shall be set at liberty." (Philemon 22; Ephesians 6:18-20) That Paul was soon afterward released from prison indicates the benefit of the prayers that were said for him.

15 Paul also said helpful prayers in behalf of others. "We always pray for you, *that our God may count you worthy of his calling*," he wrote. (2 Thessalonians 1:11) And to another congregation he explained: "We pray to God *that you may do nothing wrong . . . but that you may be doing what is fine*." (2 Corinthians 13:7) Surely it is good to follow Paul's example and to make specific requests in behalf of persons whom we love. Indeed, "a righteous man's supplication [sincere pleading], when it is at work, has much force."—James 5:13-16.

16 When conducting a Bible study, one minister often asks: "Do you pray at other times in addition to the occasion of your weekly Bible study?" To gain the help that we need, we must speak to God often in prayer. (1 Thessalonians 5:17; Luke 18:1-8) Learn to talk humbly to him as you would to a beloved and trusted friend. Truly, what a wonderful privilege it is to be able to address prayer to the glorious Ruler of all the universe, the Hearer of prayer, and know that he hears you!—Psalm 65:2.

15. What kind of requests can we make with regard to persons whom we love?
16. (a) To gain needed help, when should we pray? (b) Why is prayer such a great privilege?

Chapter 28

Getting Along with
One Another in Love

AS YOU grow in knowledge and appreciation of Jehovah God and his purposes, you will want to associate regularly with persons who share this same faith and hope. By doing so, you will become part of God's visible organization, a true Christian brotherhood. *"Have love for the whole association of brothers"* will then be a command you must obey.—1 Peter 2:17; 5:8, 9.

2 Jesus Christ emphasized how important it is that his followers love one another. He said to them: "I am giving you a new commandment, that you love *one another* . . . By this all will know that you are my disciples, if you have love *among yourselves.*" (John 13:34, 35) The expressions "one another" and "among yourselves" clearly show that all true Christians would be together in one group or organization. (Romans 12:5; Ephesians 4:25) And this organization would be identified by the love its members have for one another. If a person does not have love, everything else is useless.—1 Corinthians 13:1-3.

3 Therefore, early Christians were often given such reminders as these: "Have tender affection for one another." "Welcome one another." "Slave for one another." "Become kind to one another, tenderly compassionate." "Continue putting up with one another and forgiving one another freely if anyone has a cause for complaint against another." "Keep comforting one another and building one another up." "Be peaceable with one another."

---

1. (a) How may you become a part of God's organization? (b) What command must you then obey?

2. (a) What new commandment did Jesus give his followers? (b) What do the expressions "one another" and "among yourselves" clearly show? (c) How important is it to have love?

3. How does the Bible emphasize the importance of loving and caring for fellow Christians?

"Have intense love for one another."—Romans 12:10; 15:7; Galatians 5:13; Ephesians 4:32; Colossians 3:13, 14; 1 Thessalonians 5:11, 13; 1 Peter 4:8; 1 John 3:23; 4:7, 11.

[4] However, this does not mean that true Christians are to love only fellow members of God's organization. They are to love others as well. The Bible, in fact, urges them to increase "in love to one another *and to all.*" (1 Thessalonians 3:12; 5:15) Giving the proper balanced viewpoint, the apostle Paul wrote: "Let us work what is good toward all, *but especially toward those related to us in the faith.*" (Galatians 6:10) So while Christians must love all, including their enemies, they especially must love fellow members of God's organization, their spiritual brothers and sisters.—Matthew 5:44.

[5] Early Christians were well known for this love that they had for one another. According to the second-century writer Tertullian, people would say of them: 'Look how they love one another, and how they are ready to die for one another!' Such love is also seen among true Christians today. But does this mean that there are never problems or difficulties among true Christians?

THE RESULTS OF IMPERFECTION

[6] From your study of the Bible you realize that all of us have inherited imperfection from our original parents, Adam and Eve. (Romans 5:12) So we are inclined to do wrong. "We all stumble many times," the Bible says. (James 3:2; Romans 3:23) And you should know that members of God's organization are also imperfect and sometimes do things that are not right. This can result in problems and difficulties even among true Christians.

[7] Consider the situation with two women named Euodia and Syntyche in the early Philippian congregation. The apostle Paul wrote: "Euodia I exhort and Syntyche I exhort to be of the same

---

4. (a) What shows that Christians must love others besides "one another"? (b) Whom especially are Christians to love?
5. What shows that true Christians, in early times and today, have been noted for their love?
6. Why do even true Christians at times sin against one another?
7. (a) Why did Euodia and Syntyche need to be told "to be of the same mind"? (b) What shows that, basically, these were fine Christian women?

What can we learn from the incident involving Euodia and Syntyche?

mind in the Lord." Why did Paul encourage these two women "to be of the same mind"? Clearly, there was some trouble between them. The Bible does not tell what it was. Perhaps they were in some way jealous of each other. Yet, basically, these were fine women. They had been Christians for some time, years before having shared with Paul in the preaching work. So he wrote to the congregation: "Keep assisting these women who have striven side by side with me in the good news."—Philippians 4:1-3.

8 At one time trouble also developed between the apostle Paul and his traveling companion Barnabas. When they were about to leave on their second missionary journey, Barnabas wanted to take along his cousin Mark. However, Paul did not want Mark along, since Mark had left them and gone home during their first missionary journey. (Acts 13:13) The Bible says: "At this there occurred *a sharp burst of anger,* so that they separated from each other." (Acts 15:37-40) Can you imagine that! If you had been there and had seen this "sharp burst of anger," would you have concluded that Paul and Barnabas were not part of God's organization because of the way they behaved?

9 On another occasion the apostle Peter did wrong. He stopped associating closely with Gentile Christians because of fear of being viewed with disfavor by some of the Jewish Christians who

8. (a) What trouble developed between Paul and Barnabas? (b) If you had been present and had seen this trouble, what might you have concluded?
9. (a) What sin did Peter commit, and what caused him to act this way? (b) What did Paul do when he saw what was happening?

were wrongly looking down on their Gentile brothers. (Galatians 2:11-14) When the apostle Paul saw what Peter was doing, he condemned Peter's improper conduct before all those present. How would you have felt if you had been Peter?—Hebrews 12:11.

SOLVING DIFFICULTIES WITH LOVE

[10] Peter could have become angry at Paul. He could have taken offense at the way Paul had corrected him in front of others. But he did not. (Ecclesiastes 7:9) Peter was humble. He accepted the correction, and he did not allow it to cause his love for Paul to cool off. (1 Peter 3:8, 9) Note how Peter later referred to Paul in a letter of encouragement to fellow Christians: "Consider the patience of our Lord as salvation, just as *our beloved brother Paul* according to the wisdom given him also wrote you." (2 Peter 3:15) Yes, Peter allowed love to cover over the difficulty, which in this case had resulted from his own wrong conduct.—Proverbs 10:12.

[11] What about the problem between Paul and Barnabas? This also was solved with love. For later, when Paul wrote to the Corinthian congregation, he spoke of Barnabas as a close fellow worker. (1 Corinthians 9:5, 6) And though Paul appears to have had good reason for doubting Mark's value as a traveling companion, this young man later matured to the point that Paul could write to Timothy: "Take Mark and bring him with you, for he is useful to me for ministering." (2 Timothy 4:11) We can benefit from this example of settling differences.

[12] Well, what about Euodia and Syntyche? Did they settle their differences, allowing love to cover whatever sins they may have committed against each other? The Bible does not tell us what finally happened to them. But, their being good women who had worked side by side with Paul in his Christian min-

---

10. (a) How did Peter react when he was corrected? (b) What can we learn from Peter's example?
11. (a) Despite their angry outburst, how did Paul and Barnabas show that they were true Christians? (b) How can we benefit from their example?
12. (a) Why might we assume that Euodia and Syntyche settled their differences? (b) According to Galatians 5:13-15, why is it vital that Christians work out their differences in love?

istry, we might reasonably assume that they humbly accepted the counsel given. When Paul's letter was received, we can just imagine their going to each other and straightening out their problem in a spirit of love.—Galatians 5:13-15.

¹³ You, too, may find it hard to get along with a certain person, or persons, in the congregation. Although they may have a long way to go in developing true Christian qualities, think about this: Does Jehovah God wait until people get rid of all their bad ways before he loves them? No; the Bible says: "God recommends his own love to us in that, *while we were yet sinners,* Christ died for us." (Romans 5:8) We need to follow that example of God and show love to those who do bad and foolish things.—Ephesians 5:1, 2; 1 John 4:9-11; Psalm 103:10.

¹⁴ Since all of us are so imperfect, Jesus taught that we should not be critical of others. True, others have faults, but we also have them. "Why, then, do you look at the straw in your brother's eye, but do not consider the rafter in your own eye?" Jesus asked. (Matthew 7:1-5) By keeping in mind such wise counsel, we will be helped to get along with our brothers and sisters.

¹⁵ It is absolutely necessary that we be merciful and forgiving.

---

13. What example in showing love does Jehovah God set?
14. What counsel did Jesus give on not being critical of others?
15. (a) Why is it important that we forgive others even when we have a cause for complaint against them? (b) In his illustration in Matthew chapter 18, how did Jesus teach the need to be forgiving?

Did the argument between Paul and Barnabas mean that they were not members of God's organization?

True Christians let love
cover over causes for complaint

True, you may have a real cause for complaint against a brother or a sister. But remember the Bible counsel: "Continue putting up with one another and forgiving one another freely *if anyone has a cause for complaint* against another." But why should you forgive others when you have a genuine cause for complaint against them? Because "Jehovah freely forgave you," the Bible answers. (Colossians 3:13) And if we are to receive his forgiveness, Jesus said, we *must* forgive others. (Matthew 6:9-12, 14, 15) Jehovah, like the king in one of Jesus' illustrations, has forgiven us thousands of times, so cannot we forgive our brothers a few times?—Matthew 18:21-35; Proverbs 19:11.

[16] We simply cannot be practicing the truth and at the same time be treating our brothers and sisters in an unloving, unforgiving way. (1 John 4:20, 21; 3:14-16) So, then, if you ever have some trouble with a fellow Christian, do not stop talking with him. Do not hold resentment, but straighten out the matter in the spirit of love. If you have offended your brother, be ready to apologize and to ask forgiveness.—Matthew 5:23, 24.

[17] But what if someone insults you, or wrongs you in some other way? The Bible counsels: "Do not say: 'Just as he did to me, so I am going to do to him.'" (Proverbs 24:29; Romans 12:17, 18) Jesus Christ advised: "Whoever slaps you on your

16. (a) According to 1 John 4:20, 21, how is love of God related to love of fellow Christians? (b) What action is necessary if your brother has something against you?

17. What is the proper course to take if someone wrongs you?

right cheek, turn the other also to him." (Matthew 5:39) A slap is not intended to injure physically, but only to insult or provoke. Jesus was thus teaching his followers to avoid being drawn into a fight or an argument. Rather than "paying back injury for injury or reviling for reviling," you should "seek peace and pursue it."—1 Peter 3:9, 11; Romans 12:14.

¹⁸ Recall that we must *have love for the whole association of brothers.*" (1 Peter 2:17) Jehovah God sets the example. He is not partial. All races are equal in his sight. (Acts 10:34, 35; 17:26) Those who will be protected through the coming "great tribulation" are taken from "all nations and tribes and peoples and tongues." (Revelation 7:9, 14-17) So, in imitation of God, we should not love others less because they are of a different race, nationality or social position, or have a different skin color.

¹⁹ Get to know well *all* of those in the Christian congregation, and you will come to love and appreciate them. Treat older ones as fathers and mothers, younger ones as brothers and sisters. (1 Timothy 5:1, 2) It is truly a privilege to be a part of God's familylike visible organization, whose members get along so well together in love. How fine it will be to live forever in paradise on earth with such a loving family!—1 Corinthians 13:4-8.

18. What should we learn from God's example of loving all peoples?
19. (a) How should we regard and treat fellow Christians? (b) What great privilege can be ours?

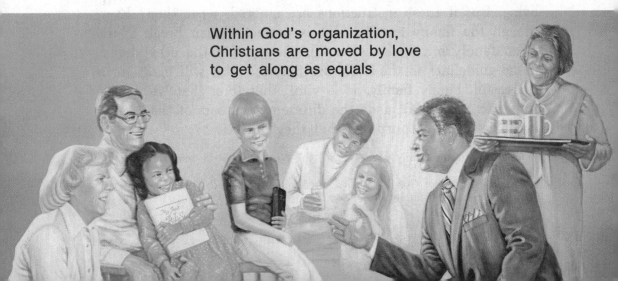

Within God's organization, Christians are moved by love to get along as equals

Chapter 29

Making a Success of Family Life

WHEN Jehovah God created the first man and woman, he joined them together to produce a family. (Genesis 2:21-24; Matthew 19:4-6) It was God's purpose for this married couple to increase by producing children. Then, when the children grew up, they were to marry and form families of their own. It was God's purpose that, in time, happy families would live in every part of the earth. They would make the earth into a beautiful paradise everywhere.—Genesis 1:28.

2 Yet, today, families are breaking apart, and many that are still together are not happy. So a person may ask: 'If the family was really created by God, should we not expect better results?' However, God cannot be blamed for family failures. A manufacturer may make a product and supply instructions on how to use it. But is it the manufacturer's fault if the product fails because the buyer does not follow the instructions? Not at all. The product, even if it is of perfect quality, will fail because it is not used properly. It is like that with the family.

3 Jehovah God has provided instructions in the Bible on family living. But if these instructions are ignored, what then? Even though the family arrangement is perfect, it can break apart. Then family members will not be happy. On the other hand, if the guidelines in the Bible are followed, this will make for a successful, happy family. It is vital, therefore, that we understand just how God made the different members of the family, and what roles he purposed that they fill.

1. (a) How did the family get its start? (b) What was God's purpose regarding the family?
2, 3. (a) Why cannot God be blamed for family failures? (b) What is necessary to enjoy a successful family life?

HOW GOD CREATED THE MAN AND THE WOMAN

[4] Anyone can see that Jehovah did not make men and women the same. It is true that in many ways they are alike. But there are obvious differences in their physical appearance and sexual makeup. Also, they have different emotional qualities. Why the differences? God made them that way to help each to fulfill a different role. After God created the man, God said: "It is not good for the man to continue by himself. I am going to make a helper for him, as a complement of him."—Genesis 2:18.

[5] A complement is something that matches or goes well with some other thing, making it complete. God made woman as a satisfying match for man to assist him in carrying out the God-given instructions to populate and care for the earth. So after creating the woman from a part of the man, God performed the first marriage there in the garden of Eden by 'bringing her to the man.' (Genesis 2:22; 1 Corinthians 11:8, 9) Marriage can be a happy arrangement because the man and the woman were each made with a need that the other has the ability to fulfill. Their different qualities balance one another. When a husband and a wife understand and appreciate each other and cooperate in accord with their assigned roles, they each contribute their part in building a happy home.

THE ROLE OF THE HUSBAND

[6] A marriage or a family needs leadership. The man was created with a greater measure of the qualities and strengths required to provide such leadership. For this reason the Bible says: "A husband is head of his wife as the Christ also is head of the congregation." (Ephesians 5:23) This is practical, for when there is no leadership there is trouble and confusion. For a family to be without headship would be like trying to drive an automobile without a steering wheel. Or, if the wife were to compete with

4. (a) What differences are there between men and women? (b) Why did God create such differences?
5. (a) How was woman made a "complement" to man? (b) Where did the first marriage take place? (c) Why can marriage be a really happy arrangement?
6. (a) Who was made the head of the family? (b) Why is this proper and practical?

such headship, it would be like having two drivers in the car, each with a steering wheel controlling a separate front wheel.

[7] However, many women do not like the idea that a man should be head of the family. One main reason for this is that many husbands have not followed God's instructions on how to exercise proper headship. Nevertheless, it is a recognized fact that for any organization to operate well someone needs to provide direction and to make final decisions. Thus the Bible wisely says: "The head of every man is the Christ; in turn the head of a woman is the man; in turn the head of the Christ is God." (1 Corinthians 11:3) In God's arrangement, God is the only one who does not have a head. Everyone else, including Jesus Christ, as well as husbands and wives, need to accept direction and to submit to decisions of others.

[8] This means that to fulfill their role as husbands, men must accept the headship of Christ. Also, they must follow his example by exercising headship over their wives just as he does over his congregation of followers. How did Christ deal with his earthly followers? It was always in a kind and considerate way. Never was he harsh or short-tempered, even when they were slow to accept his direction. (Mark 9:33-37; 10:35-45; Luke 22:24-27; John 13:4-15) In fact, he willingly gave his life for them. (1 John 3:16) A Christian husband should carefully study Christ's example, and do the best he can to follow it when dealing with his family. As a result, he will not be a domineering, selfish or inconsiderate family head.

[9] On the other hand, however, husbands should consider this: Does your wife complain that you really do not act as head of the family? Does she say that you do not take the lead in the home, planning family activities and exercising the responsibility to make final decisions? But this is what God requires you, as a husband, to do. Of course, it would be wise for you to

---

7. (a) Why do some women not like the idea of man's headship? (b) Does everybody have a head, and why is God's arrangement of headship a wise one?

8. (a) Whose example are husbands supposed to follow in exercising headship? (b) What lessons should husbands learn from that example?

9. (a) What complaint do many wives have? (b) What should husbands wisely keep in mind while exercising headship?

be open to the suggestions and preferences of other members of the family and take these suggestions into consideration as you exercise headship. As husband, you clearly have the more difficult role in the family. But if you make a sincere effort to fulfill it, your wife most likely will feel inclined to give you help and support.—Proverbs 13:10; 15:22.

FULFILLING THE WIFE'S ROLE

[10] As the Bible says, the woman was made as a helper to her husband. (Genesis 2:18) In keeping with that role, the Bible urges: "Let wives be in subjection to their husbands." (Ephesians 5:22) Today female aggressiveness and competition with men have become common. But when wives push ahead, trying to take over headship, their action is almost sure to cause trouble. Many husbands, in effect, say: 'If she wants to run the household, let her go ahead and do it.'

[11] However, you may feel that you are forced to take the lead, since your husband does not do so. But could you do more to help him to carry out his responsibilities as head of the family? Do you show that you look to him for leadership? Do you ask for his suggestions and guidance? Do you avoid in any way belittling what he does? If you really work on fulfilling your God-assigned role in the family, your husband will likely start to assume his.—Colossians 3:18, 19.

[12] This is not to say that a wife should not express her opinions if they differ from those of her husband. She may have a correct viewpoint, and the family would benefit if her husband listened to her. Abraham's wife Sarah is given as an example for Christian wives because of her subjection to her husband. (1 Peter 3:1, 5, 6) Yet she recommended a solution to a household problem, and when Abraham did not agree with her God told him: "Listen to her." (Genesis 21:9-12) Of course,

---

10. (a) What course does the Bible urge for wives? (b) What happens when wives fail to heed the Bible counsel?
11. (a) How can a wife help her husband to take the lead? (b) If a wife fulfills her God-assigned role, what effect is this likely to have on her husband?
12. What shows that wives can properly express their opinions, even if these disagree with their husband's?

when the husband makes a final decision on a matter, the wife should support it if doing so will not cause her to break God's law.—Acts 5:29.

[13] In properly fulfilling her role, there is much that a wife can do in caring for the family. For example, she can prepare nutritious meals, keep the home clean and neat and share in instructing the children. The Bible urges married women "to love their husbands, to love their children, to be sound in mind, chaste, workers at home, good, subjecting themselves to their own husbands, so that the word of God may not be spoken of abusively." (Titus 2:4, 5) The wife and mother who fulfills these duties will win the lasting love and respect of her family. —Proverbs 31:10, 11, 26-28.

THE PLACE OF CHILDREN IN THE FAMILY

[14] Jehovah instructed the first human couple: "Be fruitful and become many." (Genesis 1:28) Yes, God told them to have children. The children were meant to be a blessing to the family. (Psalm 127:3-5) Since they come under the law and command-ment of their parents, the Bible compares the position of a child to that of a slave. (Proverbs 1:8; 6:20-23; Galatians 4:1) Even Jesus continued subject to his parents when he was a child. (Luke 2:51) This means that he obeyed them, doing what they directed. If all children did the same, it would truly contribute to family happiness.

[15] Yet, rather than being a blessing to a family, children today are often a source of heartache to parents. Why? It is due to the failure of the children, as well as the parents, to apply in their lives the Bible's instructions on family living. What are some of these laws and principles of God? Let us examine a few of them on the following pages. As we do, see if you do not agree that, by applying them, you can contribute to the happiness in your family.

13. What will a good wife be doing, and what will be the effect on her family?
14. (a) What is the proper position of children in the family? (b) What can children learn from the example of Jesus?
15. Why are children often a heartache to their parents?

Love and Honor Your Wife

¹⁶ With divine wisdom, the Bible says: "Husbands ought to be loving their wives as their own bodies." (Ephesians 5:28-30) Time and again, experience has proved that for wives to be happy they need to feel that they are loved. This means that a husband should give his wife special attention, including tenderness, understanding and reassurance. He needs to 'assign her honor,' as the Bible says. He does this by taking her into consideration in all that he does. In this way he will earn her respect.—1 Peter 3:7.

16. What are husbands commanded to do, and how are these commands properly carried out?

Respect Your Husband

¹⁷ And what about wives? "The wife should have deep respect for her husband," the Bible declares. (Ephesians 5:33) The failure to heed this counsel is a chief reason why some husbands resent their wives. A wife shows respect by supporting her husband's decisions, and by cooperating wholesouled with him to achieve family goals. By fulfilling her Bible-assigned role as 'helper and complement' to her husband, she makes it easy for her husband to love her.—Genesis 2:18.

17. What are wives commanded to do, and how do they do this?

Be Faithful to Each Other

18 The Bible says: "Husbands and wives must be faithful to each other." To the husband it says: "Be happy with your wife and find your joy with the girl you married . . . why should you give your love to another woman? Why should you prefer the charms of another man's wife?" (Hebrews 13:4; Proverbs 5:18-20, *Today's English Version*) Yes, adultery is against God's law; it leads to trouble in a marriage. "Lots of people think an adulterous affair might spice up a marriage," noted one marriage researcher, but she added that an affair always leads to "real problems."—Proverbs 6:27-29, 32.

18. Why should marriage mates be faithful to each other?

Seek Your Mate's Pleasure

19 Happiness does not come when one seeks sexual pleasure primarily for oneself. Rather, it is obtained by seeking also to please one's mate. The Bible says: "Let the husband render to his wife her due; but let the wife also do likewise to her husband." (1 Corinthians 7:3) The emphasis is on *rendering, giving*. And by giving, the giver also receives genuine pleasure. It is as Jesus Christ said: "There is more happiness in giving than there is in receiving."—Acts 20:35.

19. How can marriage mates obtain the greatest enjoyment from sexual relations?

Give of Yourself to Your Children

20 A child of about eight years of age said: "My dad works all the time. He is never home. He gives me money and lots of toys, but I hardly ever see him. I love him and wish he would not work all the time so I could see him more." How much better homelife is when parents follow the Bible's command to teach their children 'when they sit in their house and when they walk on the road and when they lie down and when they get up'! Giving of yourself to your children, spending quality time with them, is certain to contribute to family happiness.—Deuteronomy 11:19; Proverbs 22:6.

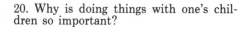

20. Why is doing things with one's children so important?

Provide Needed Discipline

21 Our heavenly Father sets parents a proper example by providing his people corrective instruction, or discipline. Children need discipline. (Hebrews 12:6; Proverbs 29:15) Recognizing this, the Bible urges: "You, fathers, . . . go on bringing [your children] up in the discipline and mental-regulating of Jehovah." The giving of discipline, even if it may include a spanking or a taking away of privileges, is an evidence that parents love their children. The Bible says: "The one loving [his son] is he that does look for him with discipline."—Ephesians 6:4; Proverbs 13:24; 23:13, 14.

21. What does the Bible say about giving discipline to children?

Youths—Resist Worldly Ways

22 The world makes an effort to get youths to break God's laws. Also, as the Bible states, "foolishness is tied up with the heart of a boy." (Proverbs 22:15) So it is a fight to do what is right. Yet the Bible says: "Children it is your Christian duty to obey your parents, for this is the right thing to do." It will bring rich rewards. So, children, be wise. Heed the counsel: "Remember your Creator while you are still young." Resist the temptations to take drugs, get drunk, commit fornication and do other things that are against God's laws.—Ephesians 6:1-4; Ecclesiastes 12:1; Proverbs 1:10-19, *Today's English Version.*

22. What duty do youths have, and what is involved in fulfilling it?

Study the Bible Together

23 If one member of the family studies and applies Bible teachings, it will contribute to family happiness. But if all do—husband, wife and children—what a blessed family that will be! There will be a warm, close relationship, with open communication, as each family member tries to help the others to serve Jehovah God. So make it a family habit to study the Bible together!—Deuteronomy 6:4-9; John 17:3.

23. What benefits will families enjoy by studying the Bible together?

SUCCESSFULLY HANDLING FAMILY PROBLEMS

[24] Even in families that are normally happy, from time to time there will be problems. This is because all of us are imperfect and do wrong things. "We all stumble many times," says the Bible. (James 3:2) So marriage mates should not demand perfection from each other. Instead, each should allow for the other's mistakes. Therefore, neither mate should expect a perfectly happy marriage, since this is not possible for imperfect people to achieve.

[25] Of course, a husband and a wife will want to work at avoiding what irritates the other mate. Yet no matter how hard they try, they will at times do things that upset the other. How, then, should difficulties be handled? The Bible's counsel is: "Love covers a multitude of sins." (1 Peter 4:8) This means that mates who show love will not keep bringing up the mistakes the other has made. Love says, in effect, 'Yes, you made a mistake. But so do I at times. So I'll overlook yours, and you may do the same for me.'—Proverbs 10:12; 19:11.

[26] When couples are willing to admit mistakes and try to correct them, many arguments and heartaches can be avoided. Their goal should be to solve problems, not to win arguments. Even if your mate is in the wrong, make it easier to solve the problem by being kind. If you are at fault, humbly ask forgiveness. Do not postpone it; handle the problem without delay. "Let the sun not set with you in a provoked state."—Ephesians 4:26.

[27] Especially if you are a married person, you need to follow the rule of "keeping an eye, not in personal interest upon just your own matters, but also in personal interest upon those of the others." (Philippians 2:4) You need to obey the Bible command: "Clothe yourselves with the tender affections of compassion, kindness, lowliness of mind, mildness, and long-suffering. Continue putting up with one another and forgiving one another

---

24. Why should marriage mates make allowances for each other's mistakes?
25. How should marriage difficulties be solved in love?
26. When some difficulty arises, what will help in settling the matter?
27. The following of what Bible counsel will help marriage mates to solve their problems?

freely if anyone has a cause for complaint against another. Even as Jehovah freely forgave you, so do you also. But, besides all these things, clothe yourselves with love, for it is a perfect bond of union."—Colossians 3:12-14.

[28] Today many couples do not allow the counsel from God's Word to help them work out their problems, and they seek a divorce. Does God approve of divorce as a way to settle problems? No, he does not. (Malachi 2:15, 16) He meant marriage to be a lifelong arrangement. (Romans 7:2) The Bible allows only one reason for getting a divorce that frees a person to remarry, and that is adultery. If adultery is committed, then the innocent mate may decide whether to get a divorce or not. —Matthew 5:32.

[29] What if your marriage mate has refused to study God's Word with you, or even opposes your Christian activity? The Bible still encourages you to stay with your mate and not to view separation as the easy way out of your problems. Do what you personally can to improve the situation in your home by applying what the Bible says in regard to your own conduct. In time, because of your Christian conduct, you may win over your mate. (1 Corinthians 7:10-16; 1 Peter 3:1, 2) And what a blessing will be yours if your loving patience is rewarded in this way!

[30] Many family problems today involve the children. What can be done if this is the case in your family? First of all, as parents you need to set a good example. This is because children are more inclined to follow what you do than what you say. And when your actions differ from your words, young ones are quick to see it. So, if you want your children to live fine, Christian lives, you yourself must set the example.—Romans 2:21, 22.

[31] Also, you need to reason with children. It is not enough

28. (a) Is divorce the way to settle marriage problems? (b) What does the Bible say is the only reason for divorce that frees one for remarriage?
29. (a) If your marriage mate does not join you in Christian worship, what should you do? (b) What will be a possible result?
30. Why is it so important for parents to set a good example for their children?
31. (a) What more important reason do children need for obeying their parent's counsel? (b) How might you show your youngster the wisdom of obeying God's law that forbids fornication?

simply to tell youngsters: 'I don't want you to commit fornication, because it is wrong.' They need to be shown that it is their Creator, Jehovah God, who says that such things as fornication are wrong. (Ephesians 5:3-5; 1 Thessalonians 4:3-7) But even this is not enough. Children also need to be helped to see why they should obey God's laws, and how this will benefit them. For example, you might draw your youngster's attention to the wonderful way a human baby is formed by the union of a man's sperm and a woman's egg, and ask: 'Don't you think that the One who made possible this miracle of birth knows best how humans should use their God-given powers of reproduction?' (Psalm 139:13-17) Or you could ask: 'Do you think that our Grand Creator would make a law to rob us of enjoyment in life? Rather, should we not be happier if we obeyed his laws?'

[32] Such questions can start your child reasoning on God's law governing the use of the reproductive organs. Welcome his views. If they are not what you desire them to be, do not get angry. Try to understand that your child's generation has drifted a long way from the righteous teachings in the Bible, and then try to show him why his generation's immoral practices are unwise. Perhaps you can draw your child's attention to specific examples of where sexual immorality has led to illegitimate births, venereal diseases or other troubles. In this way he is helped to see the reasonableness and correctness of what the Bible says.

[33] Especially can the Bible-based hope of living forever in Paradise on earth help us to make a success of family life. Why so? Because if we really want to live in God's new system, we will try hard to live now as we hope to live then. This means we will follow closely the instructions and guidance of Jehovah God. As a result, God will crown our present happiness with the enjoyment of everlasting life and abundant happiness throughout the eternity that lies ahead.—Proverbs 3:11-18.

32. (a) What should be your attitude if your child's views do not agree with God's? (b) How can your child be helped to see the wisdom of what the Bible says?
33. Why can the Bible-based hope of living forever in Paradise on earth help us to make a success of family life?

Chapter 30

What You Must Do to Live Forever

JEHOVAH GOD offers you something wonderful—everlasting life in his righteous new system of things. (2 Peter 3:13) But living then depends upon your doing God's will now. The present wicked world, including all who remain a part of it, is about to pass away, "but he that does the will of God remains forever." (1 John 2:17) So you must choose between two courses. One leads to death and the other to eternal life. (Deuteronomy 30:19, 20) Which one will you take?

2 How do you show that you are choosing life? First of all, you must have faith in Jehovah and in his promises. Are you firmly convinced that God exists "and that he becomes *the rewarder of those earnestly seeking him"*? (Hebrews 11:6) You need to trust God as a son or a daughter trusts a loving and merciful father. (Psalm 103:13, 14; Proverbs 3:11, 12) Having such faith, you will not doubt that his counsel is wise or that his ways are right, even if at times you do not understand matters fully.

3 However, more than faith is needed. There must also be works to demonstrate what your true feelings are about Jehovah. (James 2:20, 26) Have you done things to show that you are sorry for any failing in the past to do what is right? Have you been moved to repent or make changes to bring your life course into harmony with Jehovah's will? Have you turned around, that is, rejected any wrong course that you may have been following, and have you begun doing the things God requires?

1. (a) What two courses are open to you? (b) How may you choose the right course?
2. (a) If you have true faith, of what will you be convinced? (b) How will trusting God as a child trusts a loving father help you to serve him?
3. (a) In addition to faith, what else is necessary? (b) What works are needed to show that you are choosing life?

Dedicate yourself to Jehovah . . .

and get baptized

(Acts 3:19; 17:30) Such works will show that you are choosing life.

DEDICATION AND BAPTISM

⁴ What should move you to choose life by doing God's will? Appreciation should. Just think: Jehovah has made possible for you relief from all sickness, suffering, and even death! By the precious gift of his Son he has opened up to you the way to endless life in a paradise earth. (1 Corinthians 6:19, 20; 7:23; John 3:16) When Jehovah's love moves you to love him in return, what should you do? (1 John 4:9, 10; 5:2, 3) You should approach God in Jesus' name and tell him in prayer that you want to be his servant, that you want to belong to him. In this way you dedicate yourself to God. This is a personal, private matter. No one else can do it for you.

⁵ After you have made your dedication to God, he will expect you to live up to it. So prove that you are a person of your word by sticking to this decision, or dedication, as long as you live. (Psalm 50:14) If you keep close to God's visible organization, you can be helped by fellow Christians who will gladly give you loving encouragement and support.—1 Thessalonians 5:11.

⁶ However, you must do more than privately tell Jehovah that you want to belong to him. You need to show before others that

4. (a) What should move you to do God's will? (b) When you decide you want to serve God, what is it proper to do?
5. (a) After you make your dedication to God, what does he expect you to do? (b) What help is available to you in living up to your dedication?
6. (a) When you dedicate your life to God, what step then is necessary? (b) What is the meaning of baptism?

you have made a dedication to serve God. How do you do this? By getting baptized in water. Such water baptism is a public demonstration that a person has dedicated his life to Jehovah and is presenting himself to do His will.

7 That water baptism is an important requirement is shown by the example of Jesus Christ. Jesus did not simply tell his Father that he had come to do His will. (Hebrews 10:7) When he was about to begin his service as a preacher of God's kingdom, Jesus presented himself to Jehovah and was baptized in water. (Matthew 3:13-17) Since Jesus set the pattern, those today who dedicate themselves to Jehovah to do his will should be baptized. (1 Peter 2:21; 3:21) In fact, Jesus commanded his followers to make disciples of people of all nations and then to baptize these new disciples. This is no baptizing of infants. It is a baptism of persons who have become *believers,* having made up their minds to serve Jehovah.—Matthew 28:19; Acts 8:12.

8 If you have made up your mind to serve Jehovah and want to be baptized, what should you do? You should make your desire known to the presiding overseer of the congregation of Jehovah's Witnesses with which you are associating. He, along with other elders in the congregation, will gladly review with you information that you need to know in order to serve God in an acceptable way. Then it can be arranged for you to be baptized.

GOD'S WILL FOR YOU TODAY

9 Before the flood, Jehovah used Noah, "a preacher of righteousness," to warn of the coming destruction and to point to the only place of safety, the ark. (Matthew 24:37-39; 2 Peter 2:5; Hebrews 11:7) God's will is that you now do a similar preaching work. Jesus foretold regarding our time: "This good news of the kingdom will be preached in all the inhabited earth for a witness to all the nations; and then the end will come." (Matthew 24:14) Others must know the things you have learned

---

7. (a) What example did Jesus provide for Christians? (b) Why is the baptism commanded by Jesus not for infants?
8. If you want to be baptized, to whom in the congregation should you make this known, and why?
9. What did Noah do before the flood that it is God's will for you to do now?

about God's purposes if they are to survive this system's end and live forever. (John 17:3) Is your heart not moved to have a part in sharing this life-giving knowledge with others?

[10] Follow Christ's example. He did not wait for people to come to him, but he went looking for those who would listen to the Kingdom message. And he instructed his followers—*all of them* —to do the same. (Matthew 28:19; Acts 4:13; Romans 10:10-15) Following Christ's instruction and example, early Christians called on people in their homes. They went "from house to house" with the Kingdom message. (Luke 10:1-6; Acts 20:20) This is still the main way that true Christians carry on their ministry in our day.

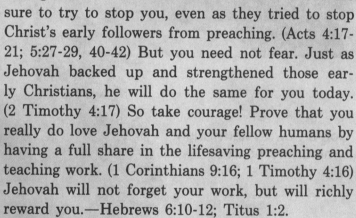

"Remember the wife of Lot"

[11] It takes courage to do this work. Satan and his world are sure to try to stop you, even as they tried to stop Christ's early followers from preaching. (Acts 4:17-21; 5:27-29, 40-42) But you need not fear. Just as Jehovah backed up and strengthened those early Christians, he will do the same for you today. (2 Timothy 4:17) So take courage! Prove that you really do love Jehovah and your fellow humans by having a full share in the lifesaving preaching and teaching work. (1 Corinthians 9:16; 1 Timothy 4:16) Jehovah will not forget your work, but will richly reward you.—Hebrews 6:10-12; Titus 1:2.

[12] There is nothing of real value that this old system has to offer, so never think you are missing out by turning your back on it. "Remember the wife of Lot," Jesus said. (Luke 17:32) After she and her family escaped from Sodom, she looked in a longing way at the things they had left behind. God saw where her heart was, and she became a

10. (a) What example of Jesus should love of people move us to follow? (b) How is much of the preaching work done?

11. (a) Why does it take courage to preach about God's kingdom, but why do we not need to fear? (b) How does Jehovah view the work we do?

12. What can we learn from the example of the wife of Lot?

Keep God's new system bright in your mind and heart

pillar of salt. (Genesis 19:26) Do not be like Lot's wife! Keep your eyes on what is ahead, on "the real life" in God's righteous new order.—1 Timothy 6:19.

CHOOSE ETERNAL LIFE IN PARADISE ON EARTH

[13] Really, there are but two choices. Christ compared it to the choice of either one of two roads. One road, he said, is "broad and spacious." On it travelers are permitted freedom to please themselves. The other road, however, is "cramped." Yes, those on that road are required to obey the instructions and laws of God. The majority, Jesus noted, are taking the broad road, only a few the narrow one. Which road will you choose? In making your choice, keep this in mind: The broad road will suddenly come to a dead end—destruction! On the other hand, the narrow road will lead you right through into God's new system. There you can share in making the earth a glorious paradise, where you can live forever in happiness.—Matthew 7:13, 14.

[14] Do not conclude that there are different roads, or ways, that you can follow to gain life in God's new system. There is only one. There was just the one ark that survived the Flood, not a number of boats. And there will be only one organization—God's visible organization—that will survive the fast-approaching "great tribulation." It is simply not true that all religions lead to the same goal. (Matthew 7:21-23; 24:21) You must be part of Jehovah's organization, doing God's will, in order to receive his blessing of everlasting life.—Psalm 133:1-3.

[15] So keep the picture of God's promised new system of things bright in your mind and heart. Every day think about the grand prize that Jehovah God holds out to you—living forever in Paradise on earth. This is no dream. It is real! For the Bible promise is certain to be fulfilled: "The righteous themselves will possess the earth, and they will reside forever upon it. . . . When the wicked ones are cut off, you will see it."—Psalm 37:29, 34.

---

13. How did Jesus present the choice that all of us have to make?
14. What must you be a part of in order to survive into God's new system?
15. (a) What do we need to do every day? (b) What hope is much more than a dream?

"Continue in the Things That You Learned"

That is what the apostle Paul wrote to young Timothy. (2 Timothy 3:14) After reading this book, you know about the many good things God has in store for those who love him. But you need to continue to progress in a spiritual way. Jehovah's Witnesses will be happy to help you, if you are not already receiving that help. Just write to the address for your country, as listed below, asking that a minister of Jehovah's Witnesses come to your home and regularly study the Bible with you free of charge.

Also, upon your request, additional copies of this book will be sent to you for $2.50 (U.S.) each, postpaid. You can receive, too, the *New World Translation of the Holy Scriptures,* a Bible in modern English, for $3 (U.S.). Send to Watchtower, using one of the addresses below.

ALASKA 99507: 2552 East 48th Ave., Anchorage. **AUSTRALIA:** Box 280, Ingleburn, N.S.W. 2565. **BAHAMAS:** Box N-1247, Nassau, N.P. **BARBADOS:** Fontabelle Rd., Bridgetown. **BELIZE:** Box 257, Belize City. **CANADA L7G 4Y4:** Box 4100, Georgetown, Ontario. **ENGLAND:** Watch Tower House, The Ridgeway, London NW7 1RN. **FIJI:** Box 23, Suva. **GERMANY, FEDERAL REPUBLIC OF:** Postfach 5920, D-6200 Wiesbaden 1. **GHANA:** Box 760, Accra. **GUYANA:** 50 Brickdam, Georgetown 16. **HAWAII 96814:** 1228 Pensacola St., Honolulu. **HONG KONG:** 4 Kent Road, Kowloon Tong. **INDIA:** Post Bag 10, Lonavla, Pune Dis., Mah. 410 401. **IRELAND:** 29A Jamestown Road, Finglas, Dublin 11. **JAMAICA:** Box 180, Kingston 10. **JAPAN:** 1271 Naka-shinden, Ebina, Kanagawa Pref., 243. **KENYA:** Box 47788, Nairobi. **LEEWARD ISLANDS:** Box 119, St. Johns, Antigua. **LIBERIA:** P.O. Box 171, Monrovia. **MALAYSIA:** 20 Scotland Close, Penang. **NEW ZEALAND:** 6-A Western Springs Road, Auckland 3. **NIGERIA:** P.O. Box 194, Yaba, Lagos State. **PAKISTAN:** 197-A Ahmad Block, New Garden Town, Lahore 16. **PANAMA:** Apartado 1835, Panama 9A. **PAPUA NEW GUINEA:** Box 113, Port Moresby. **PHILIPPINES, REPUBLIC OF:** P.O. Box 2044, Manila 2800; 186 Roosevelt Ave., San Francisco del Monte, Quezon City 3010. **SIERRA LEONE:** Box 136, Freetown. **SOUTH AFRICA:** Private Bag 2, Elandsfontein, 1406. **SWEDEN:** Box 5, S-732 00 Arboga. **SWITZERLAND:** Ulmenweg 45; P.O. Box 477, CH-3601 Thun. **TRINIDAD:** 2 La Seiva Road, Maraval, Port of Spain. **UNITED STATES OF AMERICA:** 25 Columbia Heights, Brooklyn, N.Y. 11201. **ZAMBIA, REP. OF:** Box 21598, Kitwe. **ZIMBABWE:** 35 Fife Avenue, Salisbury.